What people are s

T0302949

Famous for Fifteen People

Everything goes in cycles: during the 2010s I contributed regularly to Chris O'Leary's *Bowiesongs* blog, and expressed a vague wish that one day somebody might make a similar study of Momus. Well, that's what John Robinson is doing, with an extraordinary vigour and thoroughness, in his blog *Fifteen People*. So far he's only halfway through the prolific Momus discography, but I'm amazed at the quality of his work: it's teaching me things even I didn't know, or had forgotten! It's also surprisingly funny. 2020 is a bit of a milestone year for Momus: my record about COVID-19, *Vivid,* is released in July, on the same day as Farrar, Straus and Giroux publish *Niche: A Memoir in Pastiche,* my autobiography. All this is kindling interest in my work as it's developed through 4 decades. It would be great to think there was something following, a solid, comprehensive and entertaining account of my songs by someone other than me. Called – oh, I don't know – *Famous for Fifteen People: The Songs of Momus,* by John Robinson.

Nicholas Currie (Momus) is a singer/songwriter with over 30 studio albums, and author of numerous novels and cultural writings, including his recent memoir *Niche* (Farrar, Straus and Giroux, 2020)

Momus is a unique and important artist. *Fifteen People* puts his body of work into context in time and related to the surrounding culture. It is insightful, provokes re-listening and conversation about the work.

Douglas T. Stewart, Singer, songwriter, producer, scriptwriter and leader of the band BMX Bandits

I have spent basically my entire life listening to Momus records and thought I knew everything, but reading John Robinson's *Fifteen People* has made me realise just how much more there is to know and how fascinating and delightful it is to learn it. This is a deep dive into a seemingly never-ending series of brilliant works, written about through astonishing research and heartfelt panache. Not only for Momus fans.
Jacob Wren creates exhibitions, literature and performances as co-artistic director of Montreal-based interdisciplinary group PME-ART. His books include *Polyamorous Love Song* (Book*hug, 2014)

Fifteen People is a mandatory guide to the ludic world of Momus. Here be an encyclopaedia of entertaining explications, decodings of manic referentiality, the hard evidence of the Scottish artist's continued pertinence after more than 40 years of creation…
Dr John Quin, author of *Dr Quin, Medicine Man* (Biteback, 2020). Writing about art, books and music for more than 20 years for publications including ArtReview, frieze, The Quietus, Tagesspiegel, The Wire)

Fifteen People puts a microscope to a titanic talent.
Anthony Reynolds, Musician, journalist and writer, leader of the bands Jack and Jacques

Famous for Fifteen People

The Songs of Momus 1982–1995

John William Daniel Robinson

Famous for Fifteen People

The Songs of Momus 1982–1995

John William Daniel Robinson

zer0 books

Winchester, UK
Washington, USA

JOHN HUNT PUBLISHING

First published by Zero Books, 2021
Zero Books is an imprint of John Hunt Publishing Ltd., No. 3 East St., Alresford,
Hampshire SO24 9EE, UK
office@jhpbooks.com
www.johnhuntpublishing.com
www.zero-books.net

For distributor details and how to order please visit the 'Ordering' section on our website.

Text copyright: John William Daniel Robinson 2020

ISBN: 978 1 78904 727 1
978 1 78904 728 8 (ebook)
Library of Congress Control Number: 2020942465

All rights reserved. Except for brief quotations in critical articles or reviews, no part of this book may be reproduced in any manner without prior written permission from the publishers.

The rights of John William Daniel Robinson as author have been asserted in accordance with the Copyright, Designs and Patents Act 1988.

A CIP catalogue record for this book is available from the British Library.

Design: Stuart Davies

UK: Printed and bound by CPI Group (UK) Ltd, Croydon, CR0 4YY
Printed in North America by CPI GPS partners

We operate a distinctive and ethical publishing philosophy in all areas of our business, from our global network of authors to production and worldwide distribution.

Contents

As soon as we renounce fiction and illusion, we lose reality itself; the moment we subtract fictions from reality, reality itself loses its discursive-logical consistency.
Slavoj Zizek

Right or wrong, it's very pleasant to break something from time to time.
Fyodor Dostoevsky

Acknowledgements

Thanks go to everyone who has supported this book especially Nicholas Currie, who initially suggested the idea, Rob Thomas, Douglas Lain and all the staff at Zero Publishing.

Introduction

Around 1990 I started listening to Radio 1: specifically, Annie Nightingale and John Peel, and one Sunday night in 1991 on Annie's show she played a couple of songs back to back which stood out to me. They were covers of the Jacques Brel song *Jacky*, one by Marc Almond, which was in the charts at that point, and the other by what Annie called a "friend of the show": Momus – whose real name is Nicholas Currie. His cover version, *Nicky*, was arresting. Listening to the bizarre, funny lyrics, representing the singer as a louche womaniser who at the same time regretted and celebrated his lot while looking forward to the nostalgia he would one day have for the times he was singing about, I realised I needed to hear more by him. It was a combination of the humour of the lyrics and the wit inherent in the musical organisation, but more than that there was a clear ambition there, an ambition to hit the charts in some way, that was also, clearly and totally, doomed to failure in the form it took.

I did not own a copy of the song for some time, in fact it was a couple of years before I happened on a vinyl copy of a Momus compilation called *Monsters of Love* which began my real journey into his world and an interest in the artist that has sustained to the present day. In 2019 I started a blog called *Fifteen People*, named after a quotation of Momus updating Warhol's statement regarding fame: "In the future, everyone will be famous for fifteen people." In the blog I am listening to every album he recorded as Momus and writing reactions to them, with the resulting book versions spread out over a number of volumes.

The album reviews themselves are not hagiographic, the story to be told has certain ups and downs and these are acknowledged. The personal story of Nicholas Currie, the man behind Momus, runs through these reviews, and is fascinating in itself. Controversy and setback have followed and dogged his career, but always informed the work of Momus accordingly. I hoped that the blog might allow me to proselytise about Momus to others as the reviews should be comprehensible to new listeners. Momus' work is highly literate, full of complex allusions and philosophical concepts, and I explain these along with the lyrics, the cultural history of the time, musicological issues and his life story.

Once Momus himself became aware of the blog and his fanbase became engaged, he and others were keen that the work should be published as a book. In this volume I cover his career up to the end of his time with Creation, and his first post-Creation album, ending with the revisionist album *Slender Sherbet*. It is concerned with the context and content of those albums and songs, and is not intended as a biography as such, with Momus' own *Niche: A Memoir in Pastiche* published in 2020 providing detail up to the year I begin, 1982.

I think the story of Momus is fascinating and on a par with artistic tales such as those of Georges Bataille, De Sade, Dali, Captain Beefheart, Mishima or David Bowie himself. The tension between what we are allowed to reveal and forced to conceal, or the reverse, is the thread that runs through his work, the battle against self- and imposed censorship and sometimes against the musical establishment.

As you read about each recording, it may be helpful to listen along, and to find images of the covers, as I discuss these as well.

We Set To Wondering…#1 Puritans

1981: Nicholas John Currie was born in Paisley in February 1960, the eldest of three siblings: Nicholas, Mark and Emma. His first 20 years were spent in Paisley, Athens and Montreal where his father worked for the British Council, and he attended Edinburgh Academy as a boarder, which the British Council flew him to and from. Nicholas did not enjoy his time at the school, describing its effect as scarring for life. Although respected there to some extent as a writer and intellectual, he said of the school in an interview for Quietus magazine:

> The other boys were like extras from Lord of The Flies. It's put me off Britain, bourgeois people, males, conservatives, anybody in authority, Western culture in general.

Having started university studies in Edinburgh and Aberdeen, Nicholas Currie dropped out having been persuaded to join a band. Not just any band: formed by the ex-guitarist of post-punk band Josef K, Malcolm Ross, it also featured bassist Dave Weddell, as well as Paul Mason. The Happy Family signed to 4AD after sending an EP to co-founder Ivo Watts-Russell and released this EP in 1982. The band has a jerky, angular sound you would associate with the period and it is fair to say that the presence of half of Josef K is probably what drew 4AD to sign them. The three songs included were the world's first introduction to Currie's lyrical ventures.

Puritans seems to be about a relationship that is falling apart, with the two lovers looking at others for the "secret they possess that's barred from you and me". It is wistful and yearning and has the bass driven post-punk sound you would expect of a band following Josef K. *Innermost Thoughts* is portentous, its title taken from the journals of Cesare Pavese, seeming to describe a one-sided affair in which the male narrator's lover is determined to run away to Australia, possibly to avoid the endless "talking like entries in diaries", a telling line given the genesis of the title. Finally, we have *The Mistake*, a young person's lament about being shorn of money and prospects, which nevertheless ends with something approaching optimism: "Together we can build a home from hope."

The lyrics here are naive, clearly those of someone yet to find a voice, yet to have a clear purpose in music and in thrall to recent artists in post-punk such as Josef K and The Birthday Party. It is a world full of earnest young men who write copious journals and read philosophy on the train to impress the ladies. Nothing wrong with that, but not enough to gather any cultural momentum at the time. The band would continue to work on demos for an album, which appeared later that year.

Now's Our Chance…#2 The Man on Your Street

Following line-up changes, adding drummer Ronnie Torrance from Josef K and keyboard player Neill Martin, The Happy Family album *The Man on Your Street* was released in 1982, with evidence of a deliberate move away from both the sound and the lyrical style of the initial EP. Rather than gloomy and wistful, the album showed more spite towards the modern world and proposed blowing it up to some extent. Instrumentation on the album included saxophone and a clavinet apparently once owned by Midge Ure, and keyboards were a departure from the original Josef K sound. Furthermore, a blog indicates that 1981 was the year Nicholas' parents divorced, with his mother running away with "an unrepentant thatcherite", in his words. Now, I am no psychiatrist, but this event may have some bearing on both this album and many songs to follow.

The first thing to note is the cover, which is awful. My understanding is that the band discounted ideas from the label's regular designer and worked alone instead. There are several different fonts and colours, none of which allow the lettering to stand out against an image of the Earth seen from space, the same world the album rails against. Listing the tracks at the bottom is presumably an attempt to make the album appear like a classic from the 60s or 70s, but in that case why then have the bizarre emaciated shadow figures which we see dancing on the left-hand side? There is something tribal about that image, which is a concept well used at the time, but it hardly matches the album cover or concept which seems to be a pastiche of 60s design, with the concept indicated by the top strip: *Songs from the Career of Dictator Hall. (In Stereo).* The story is broadly as follows. An unnamed salesman (we'll call him Mr S), struggling to make ends meet for his wife, Maria, and their son, Samuel, receives a letter from a man named Hall who has won the lottery and gone into right-wing politics. Hall invites the family to his house in Lake Geneva. He must have previously seduced Maria because she promptly abandons Mr S and runs away. (Yes, this is the point where a psychiatrist would nod and make notes). This event sends Mr S into decline but before he dies, he entreats his Samuel to avenge him.

Meanwhile Hall has become president, married Maria and when their relationship goes a bit awry, rapes her and fathers a daughter with her. Eighteen years later, Samuel has joined the Red Brigade and meets Hall's daughter – who has also been sexually abused by Hall. The two of them start an affair (the psychiatrist would be considering a conference and book deal by this point) and then set out to Turin to assassinate Hall.

The Salesman

A nursery song style riff and whistling, no less, introduces a description of the working life of the Salesman. We get the chiming guitars we would expect from this era but listen to the plinky plonk keyboards…this slice of life is almost reminiscent of the Kinks, a definite sixties throwback. Apparently, a salesman must be bad to succeed, could this be a sideways comment on the record industry? The vocals are rather strained, and a very middle-class attempt to enter the milieu of the working class. It is a kind of music-hall sound and a very irritating chorus.

Letter from Hall

The opening has a parping sound that has me singing Madness' *Driving in My Car* over the next bit. Slow verse, faster chorus describing the man called Hall who apparently met and groomed this couple before he sent the letter. Again, the chorus has a circus vibe to it. This is all very expository in terms of lyrics, we learn that Hall is bored on his yacht, and has been bad-mouthed in the press. There is a cool bridge after the second chorus and a sweeping synth sound which enlivens the third verse. The chorus is again very irritating, though. Mr S begs his wife to stop so they can "work on the family they planned", but they already have a son, don't they?

The Luckiest Citizen

This is much better, a great melody and bouncy bass line in the verse. A genuinely pretty pop song. Which is appropriate, of course, given he is tempting her in. A switch to minor tones from time to time indicates his rotten interior. There is a very interesting middle eight where Hall describes a need for "revolution, not domestic bliss", or more disturbingly, he wants Maria to fight back. The second half has the lyrics descend into misogyny, which fits the character fully, as he describes his need for a "Mata Hari meritocracy": a society where treachery is a virtue.

Revenge!

This one kind of drifts over me. It is stylistically very similar to *Letter from Hall* and you get the point very quickly: Mr S wants Samuel to take revenge. Mr S also speaks very poetically for someone we were told was a working-class salesman. There is saxophone on this that fits in surprisingly well. And handclaps! I can imagine Samuel sitting there holding Mr S' hand and privately wishing he'd just hurry up and die, though.

The Courier

This has a great chorus sung by the dead, apparently, regretting their mistakes in life and needing a courier to carry their messages and do dirty deeds. It is not clear who is employing Samuel – is it literally the forces of Hell?

The Man on Your Street

Musically we are back to the style of *Letter from Hall*, and this song is also from his perspective. There is a melancholy to Hall's musings here that almost makes you sympathise with him, as he tries to justify his way of life and his achievements. That will not last, though.

The opening line, "Now at last I've mastered this business of living", has always stuck with me, I was disappointed to learn that "this business of living" was not an original phrase but came from the writings of Cesare Pavese.

One of the great strengths of this track is the variety of sections it has, there is a progressive feel to it, and each style genuinely fits the mood of the lyrics. This is also the track that most reminds me of the Associates – the quintessential post-punk Scottish band – just listen to the bass after "then again I've bred respect for virtue..."

This track also includes what would become a Momus staple, the calmly spoken monologue, often detailing some horrific sexual incident. Here Hall describes how he assaults his own daughter:

I arrange for my ivy green limousine to break down amongst holly trees
And seize a command performance from my beautiful daughter
And as I commit this unnatural act by the shores of Lake Geneva
I contemplate the fact that blood is much sexier than water.

Which is where any sympathy ebbs away. The song ends with him calling the Citizen's Advice Bureau. Frankly, I think he is long past professional help.

A Night Underground

A bouncy, ridiculously cheerful pop song with a squelchy synth line plays while we hear how Samuel has joined the Red Brigade. This is my favourite song on the album. I am a sucker for a squelchy synth line. Samuel meets Hall's daughter here, and she really is not happy. The cheerfulness of the song juxtaposed with the squelch – I mean squick – of relations between the two just about allows you to accept it in narrative terms. Currie namechecks Hegel here: Samuel is reading philosophy and tons of books "as safe as a sprig of deadly nightshade", which is a nice line. Momus throwing in the names of, and references to, philosophers and books you may not always be totally familiar with is a recurring theme: there is an assumption that the listener is part of the same intellectual cadre as the writer. Why, for instance, does the lyricist assume we know who Hegel is and who the Red Brigade were but does not trust us to know that nightshade is deadly?

Two of a Kind

The lovers go on a romantic excursion (albeit with murderous intent) through the Simplon Tunnel. The music is rather similar to Haircut 100 at this point. The naive, perhaps deliberately simplistic, nature of the lyric writing is demonstrated in this couplet:

We're still in Switzerland
We're climbing fast
I whisper, "Simplon"
You shout, "At last!"

They joke about being terrorists to the border guard – which would get you shot now – and go off through the tunnel. The last minute-and-a-half of the song consists of the following:

Da da da da da Da da da da Da da da da da Da da da da Da da da da da Da da da da Da da da da da Da da da da Da da da da da
Da da da da Da da da da da
Two of a kind
Do do do do do do do do do Do do do do do do do do Do do do

do do do do do do do
Do do do do do do do do Do do do do do do do Do do do
do do do do do do do
Do do do do do do do do Do do do do do do do Do do do
do do do do do do do
Do do do do do do do do Do do do do do do do Do do do
do do do do do do do
Do do do do do do do do Do do do do do do do Do do do
do do do do do do do

Which is written in full on the CD lyric sheet. Never let anyone accuse Mr Currie of pretentiousness.

March in Turin

A slower song, the guitar accompaniment on the acoustic is very similar to work that will emerge in early Momus tracks. The vocal delivery is more like what would follow as well. The lovers wait in Turin to meet and shoot their target. We never find out what happens, but we know they are about to execute their plan as the album ends. Running out into the bright sunlit courtyard all Butch Cassidy and the Sundance Kid. The end has a descending run of church bells and we can only assume absolute carnage follows.

The album's story, of a financially successful man invading a political space and unleashing chaos, is topical today, but at the time this album was largely disregarded. An unsuccessful audition for a BBC show combined with a lack of any definable audience spelled the end of the group.

And that was it for The Happy Family. A set of demos for the EP and album was released later in the decade as *This Business of Living* by James Nice's label, Les Temps Modernes, on cassette but no further new material followed. Currie had decided by now that bands had to operate as democracies, and ironically given the subject matter of this album, he wanted to be a dictator.

He split the band up, returned to university to gain a first and moved to London to start again.

Next Thing You Know…#3 The Beast with 3 Backs

One of the songs recorded as a demo for The Happy Family was called *The Poison Boyfriend,* which represented a departure into new territory. The songs Currie started writing after The Happy Family moved into new areas of psycho-sexual dynamics and explored concepts of promiscuity and perversion. He wanted to explore love, romance and relationships in a more explicit way than pop music would allow. This new approach called for a new persona and having considered several possible names, including Chanticleer, Nicky January and Sam Hall, he settled on Momus; the classical god of mockery and satire, a character from Kafka and an appropriate mask for one who would unflatteringly depict our grossest desire and mistakes. Momus the god wanted to install a window in the chest of each human in order to see their desires; Momus the musician wanted to illuminate in a similar way. Nicholas' friendship with Mike Alway, the founder of él Records, led to the promise of a deal, and a possible future move to WEA. Mike sent Momus to Belgium, where the first Momus EP was recorded in a jazz studio on Rue aux Fleurs, where Jacques Brel also started.

So 1985 and the first true Momus release: *The Beast with 3 Backs*. The EP consisted of three songs each detailing a love triangle. The music here is based around the acoustic guitar with calm but clear singing and plaintive melodies, a synthesiser providing sonic effects, and the use of prepared piano and recorder. Momus aimed to find the chord that would melt hearts and make people cry with a sound and image very much that of the classic folk singer/songwriter and was much influenced by Brel. Which is not to say that the music did not still contain elements of post-punk, as we shall see. The EP cover was designed by Mike Alway and depicted the 3 of the title as a green snake, an emblem of voyeurism and jealousy, with a photograph of the German painter Ernst Kirchner watching peasants dance, another emblem for Momus of his own isolation as an artist and human.

Ballad of the Barrel Organist

The title itself has strong and immediate connotations of Brel, of cabaret and music hall. The harshly strummed guitar is alternately pretty and sinister, the lyrics outline the tale of a couple running in from the rain to an assignation which seems to involve a voyeur, or possibly a partner not present. It is important to note how clear and precise the detail of the encounter is, there is no overt pretension or poetry to these lyrics now. The lovers look at the stains and marks on the bed that record their time together, and nervously hear the sounds of their relationship straining to break apart:

Don't stop the night, we peel back the sheets
And glimpse the life history lying underneath in stark relief
Stop the night, of the creak in the boards
The creak that forebodes the voyeur and the Christmas thief

They wish the night they first made love could come again, but:

Stop the night of this pain in my neck
That wrecks any chance of a semi-acceptable sexual technique.

Their love making days fall away as the voyeur, or some other third party, becomes not an intrusion into their relationship, but rather some kind of spark to return to:

For this uninvited, unrequited, undelighted, uninspired
Missionary, visionary, mercenary, "stick it up or I fire!"
Little boy lost down memory lane – ex-lover

There is an old lady who owns a spare key, presumably the landlady, who they hope will arrive and end the embarrassment of this unsuccessful coupling. Or join in. Who knows. We get – again – a nursery rhyme being used, here it is the old lady who swallowed a fly, as a metaphor for the problems which are building up and the memories they share.

We swallow our pride and catch our breath
We swallow our breath and catch a sigh
We swallow a spy to watch our death
Out of the corner of your eye
Little boy lost down memory lane
Your coppertone, scatterbrain, crack shot crank
Exasperated, lacerated, copy-cat clerk from Barclay's Bank
Little boy lost down memory lane

There is an exasperated rant at a "copy-cat clerk" from Barclay's Bank. Maybe they were refused a mortgage. At any rate, in the end "perhaps we'll die" is the sinister refrain as they lie in desperation considering the end of their lives: as orgasm is "le petit mort" so the end of their love is actual death, in a semiotic sense, living their lives as symbols of their feelings.

Third Party, Fire and Theft

No acoustic this time, we get a prepared piano and some evidence of the remaining post-punk influence in a staccato guitar backing and snare drum. This is the tale of (what may be) an insurance salesman who cannot perform for his wife, who is mocking him for it, and his fears of an adulterer coming to take his place. This seems to be confirmed by finding cigarette ash in the bed. Good job he has insurance.

His impotence is described in this witty pair of lines regarding his wife, Virginia:

Lately Ginny can't raise me ready
For the country roads inside her dressing gown

The cigarette ash is from Black Cat cigarettes, and he relates this in a filthy verse to the adulterer not only leaving ash in the bed, but "sweeping the ash from his sack": a part of his anatomy, in pleasuring Virginia. This also suggests that he is renewing the bed's use, removing the ash that has built up from lack of use.

Any day now the adulterer will arrive in my suburb
Knock at the door with a pretext to enter my Habitat house
There are black cats in the sheets, I've been anticipating trouble
Next thing you know he'll be sweeping the ash from the sack
Next thing you know he'll be giving her
A piece of his mind on her back
Sweeping the ash from the sack
Isn't it good to know
You've got third party, fire and theft?

There is guitar feedback – a rarity with Momus – in the middle and it really works to represent the possible violence when the two men meet. Which does not come to much as the narrator "can't afford to sprain his wrist", which of course a guitar player cannot risk. Instead he acquiesces to the adulterer, and even welcomes his "services":

So limp and pale from the wear and tear
Of high-powered, hard-nosed lives
Me and my ilk write him fat blank cheques
On our naked, waiting wives

The last verse throws in references to Laura Ashley, Durex and Marlboro. This shows a desire to ground the story in the real world but as Momus would find later, it also proves to be a risky strategy to use real brand names in such a twisted narrative. All of this is related to the concept of insurance, of protection from Third Party, Fire and Theft, each of these concepts being then symbolically identified with some aspect of sexuality and adultery.

Hotel Marquis de Sade

The story of two middle-class English boys and a middle-class English girl having a threesome in a Mediterranean hotel. Calling it the Hotel Marquis de Sade is a little obvious but makes the point as well as anything. The dangerous, potentially violent psychological games that are being played is evidenced in the lyric:

The thrill of the bullring
Was our thrill as well
There was blood on the bell-pull
In the hot hotel
Mediterranean

Given that Nicholas Currie lived in Greece for a while, it is easy to muse if this is autobiographical. In *Niche,* his memoirs, passages suggest it relates to a threesome which did take place, but from which he was excluded, and with two girls and one boy instead. It is played on an acoustic guitar with some form of woodwind and backing vocals, as well as atmospheric effects, and very pretty, although the actual chorus of "beast with three backs" and associated "ba's" is rather grating. There is simple physical innuendo in the description of each activity they indulge in:

And after siesta
The table is set
With a leg and a breast and a drumstick
And we eat and forget

As he describes the slightly tawdry encounter, including watching the stains on the ceiling, the claustrophobia which is apparent from the arrangement and melodic lines takes hold. The highlight is the last minute where Momus whispers lines from T.S. Eliot's *The Wasteland*, which is about imagining a third person being present: in the poem this is Jesus, of course. It is spooky and by far the most memorable part of the EP for me, and describes the eeriness of the threesome in better clarity than any other lyric could:

> *Who is the third who walks always beside you?*
> *When I count, there are only you and I together*
> *But when I look ahead up the white road*
> *There is always another one walking beside you*
> *Gliding wrapt in a brown mantle, hooded*
> *I don't know whether a man or a woman*
> *But who is that on the other side of you?*

To a discordant and eerie woodwind sound, this ends abruptly and is disturbing in the way that its relationship to the three characters is rather difficult to pin down. This song ends the EP. The EP included the tag line: "First in a series of Immoral Tales and Imaginary Lives. Next: Momus sings the Old Testament to the new instruments." The first full Momus album, Circus Maximus, was released 3 months later, along similar lines musically and was indeed a concept album based on the Old Testament.

Preferring the Ache…#4 Circus Maximus

Again on Cherry Red imprint él, the first full album by Momus appeared in early 1986. As promised, it was a concept album based around the Old Testament. The musical style was retained from the previous EP, mainly based around acoustic guitar, synth and piano, and still very much in the mode of Brel and cabaret. The biblical stories concerned are, of course, about perversion and generally awful things happening. Where the album strays from the biblical theme, i.e. the second half, problems of pacing and style emerge but there is a lot of interest here. The CD album and newer releases include an EP of Brel covers released shortly after, which will be discussed in the next chapter.

Lucky Like St Sebastian

That is Sebastian there, on the cover, only it is Momus of course, in the role of the Christian martyr. Sebastian was tied to a tree and shot with arrows on the orders of the Roman emperor Diocletian but survived this according to legend. He was eventually beaten to death, again on the orders of the emperor. As a saint he was believed to offer protection from plague, and therefore from the time of the Black Death he was represented as the epitome of the opposite of this, a beautiful youth. Artwork has generally shown his attempted execution with arrows, a moment shown in sadistic detail and normally showing him in a somewhat sadomasochistic light. The story of St Sebastian gave artists from medieval times onwards the opportunity to openly paint images of a nude young man, giving the images a queer subtext that persisted into the twentieth century. The 1976 film *Sebastian*, directed by Derek Jarman, controversially put this into stark relief. In his second novel, *Confessions of a Mask*, Yukio Mishima, the celebrated Japanese writer, wrote in a thinly disguised autobiography about a young man's isolation, slow acceptance of his sexuality and obsession with sadomasochistic aspects of sex and death. His first sexual experience involves masturbating over an image of St Sebastian. The image is used here as Momus is singing about that sadomasochistic element, the desire to be a martyr, the religious ecstasy that would come from a death freely given.

This is a key track, the first on the first album, and it lays out the iconoclasm which will characterise this phase. The song is about Paul (actually from the New Testament). Paul feels guilty about the Christians he has killed as Saul, so requests a martyr's death like St Sebastian:

And he wrote important chapters in the Bible
But the blood on his writing hand reeked to high heaven
And Paul resolved to die

But despite having a friend who is a Roman Senator, he is told:

Should you be so lucky like St Sebastian
Preferring the ache to the aspirin
Swooning as they shoot the arrows
Through your narrow chest
Stripping naked in the Circus Maximus
With a martyr-eating lioness
Bartering with flesh for a little pain
Scenes like this give sadomasochism a bad name

Momus is talking here about the strange sexuality in images of the Christian martyrs, and the belief that such deaths were a blessing to the victims. Momus then talks instead about his own sufferings in love, comparing his rejection by a girl as a similar martyrdom and to the sufferings of Dante's Inferno: but acknowledging that this suffering is hyperbole, because, unfortunately, no-one is really suffering:

But Alighieri if you'll listen there's a difference
Between your Beatrice and my Paula
She's anonymous and now a waitress
It's comic but not divine
The tragedy is no-one's dying!

Beatrice Portinari is a guide to heaven in the Divine Comedy and a real woman who Dante was obsessed by, despite only meeting her on two occasions. Like Paul, Momus wants to suffer in an appropriate way:

Should I be so lucky like St Sebastian
Going out with a bang, just hear me
Whimpering with joy as Mr Death receives his blue-eyed boy

The line about "whimpering with joy as Mr Death receives his blue-eyed-boy" confirms the masochism and is a reference to the poem *Buffalo Bill's* by e e cummings, a line Momus will return to in later songs. This second half of the song has Momus comparing himself to a Christian martyr because a waitress he likes will not go out with him. His tortures in this regard are like being in Dante's Inferno, and the tragedy in this case is that "no-one's dying". It is utterly ridiculous, pompous and hugely over-reaches with its literary and religious allusions but is quite a charming song. Frankly, we've all been this version of Momus at some point when young, feeling that our romantic disasters are on a par with the tortures of Hell, and many have written pretentious poetry to that effect, while in some strange way enjoying the feelings of desperation that accompany it. The song ends with a line which similarly invokes martyrdom, and links the idea of performance to actual suffering:

There's just one thing the martyr wants to say:
He says "Tell me, Mrs Lincoln, did you enjoy the play?"

The Lesson of Sodom (according to Lot)

The Old Testament story of what happened after the destruction of Sodom and Gomorrah. Lot having been spared with his daughters (but not his wife, if you remember she was turned to a pillar of salt having looked back), they live in a cave. For some reason believing there are no other men remaining, the daughters "lay" with their father to repopulate the world. In the Bible they do this without his full consent having made him drunk, whereas the song describes him as drunk but fully knowing what he is doing:

Is it my drunkenness or my first-born's kiss
That makes my second-born's hips sway like there is no tomorrow?

And the next verse confirms that he is quite aware, and using drunkenness as an alibi:

With these alibis, a pair of closed eyes & a bottle of wine
There's no need to die for your pleasure
I'm getting the best of both worlds in incest
The daughters of Salt – they insist

There is a lot of word play here involving the "salt in your wounds" and how you spoil the child if you spare them the "rod"…

The lesson of Sodom according to God:
You spoil the child if you spare the rod
But we had a problem, me & my girls
I was the only man in the world

By the end of the song Lot is no longer sure what the lesson of Sodom is, his head filled instead with inanities, and the whole thing points out the ridiculous nature of some of these old Bible stories. It is sung and played gently with synth washes and percussion – including cowbell.

The lesson of Sodom according to Lot:
If a bottle of wine is all you've got
Between the salt in your wounds & Lot, girls
The lesson of Sodom is...
I forgot

The disjunction between the morality preached by the Bible and the morality exercised by many of its major characters – with God's blessing – and by many Christians – is the target of this attack, and of much of the album.

John the Baptist Jones

With similar instrumentation, this tells the – again – New Testament story of the man who baptised Jesus, then enraged Herod's wife and ended up beheaded and presented on a dinner platter. "I was ahead," it starts, and that is by no means the last beheading-based pun here.

John the Baptist is presented almost as if he is a conman "neck and neck with the kings of crime", who comes to grief when he meets Salome. When she dances the dance of the seven veils, we get the wonderful line, "Salome, there was only the crockery below me".

In history, Herodias was the wife of Herod, and she had previously been married to his half-brother. John the Baptist criticised this marriage as immoral, and Herodias wanted him dead. Herod enjoyed John's preaching and did not want to enrage his followers, so imprisoned but did not kill him. Herodias' daughter danced for Herod – the dance of the Seven Veils – and pleased him to the extent that he promised to do whatever she wanted. Under the influence of her mother, and annoyed by John's rejection of her, she asked for John's head on a platter, and Herod had to keep his promise.

This song uses comic sounding woodwind to tell the tale, highlighting the black humour of the puns. The ending moves into a more eerie melody, where he begs for a reprieve. This ending is so serious you wonder if the rest of it is supposed to be funny or not.

My sweet Salome, can you reprieve me? For just one night, dear
You put yourself below me
Heavens above Salome, put yourself below me
...For just one night

John begs Salome to put herself below him, sexually potentially, but also in status, in order to save himself. This did not end well for him.

King Solomon's Song and Mine

The story of slaves working in King Solomon's Mine. The narrator complains about the poverty he and his girlfriend, Alison, are living in while in the mine, which is understandable. Alison is Ali Smith in reality; a girl Momus was smitten with at university and who went on to become an important novelist.

Musically, it is influenced by the band The Passage, founded by members of the Manchester musician's collective in 1979, including Tony Friel (of The Fall) and Dick Witts.

After being press-ganged into working for Solomon: the verse plays with the idea of working for a "song": which means to work for very little or no pay, while contributing to an artistic endeavour: a "song", literally an anthem which King Solomon uses to reassert control.

Solomon wants a palace and a temple for his god Yahweh
But you and me sweet Alison we get sweet FA
And now, King Solomon, I'm working for a song in your mine

This song could easily be a discussion of low pay and working conditions in general, aimed at greedy modern business and the way in which the social contract is ripped up for those considered – in this case literally – beneath us:

You trade our daylight for Turkish Delight
You trade our fear for euphoria
But we trade the real for your underground rail
And your foreman's rules
O my love, let's start a trade union for fools

Solomon and his queen take cocaine and have wild parties while his slaves argue unsuccessfully with the foreman. The narrator describes how his children, while going to school with the foreman's sons, will also end up working down the mine. This makes the song a distant, distant, distant cousin of the Manic Street Preacher's *If you tolerate this*.

Now we're living happily, Alison and I
We can't stop singing Solomon's song, we were singing it on the night
We conceived our healthy children, who thanks to the union line
Are at school with the sons of the foreman
With a future down the mine
And soon, King Solomon, they'll be working for your song and mine

The song concludes with a warning: the narrator and his girlfriend have traded everything for a song they are singing: a song to the union and a song to the king. We are being told not to place faith in kings, nor in unions who demand we sing for them as well. The perhaps simplistic message is spelled out: "the rich get richer and the poor get…": Sweet FA, seems to be the conclusion.

Little Lord Obedience

One of my favourite of all Momus' songs, this plaintive song seems to talk about our ultimate obedience to the rules of existence, we must all procreate, grow old and die. At the start of life there are "fingernails and hair to spare", but this changes as time goes on:

Faceless when he docks, faceless when he's lost at sea
The ocean is green, admission is free
Only here, here at the source
There are fingernails and hair to spare
But when the order comes to go and the sirens blow
And the hair goes grey,
He obeys, He obeys

It mingles this with the story of Jesus, who also obeyed God's commands to sacrifice himself. There is a sailor – who represents all men – who must obey when the gangplank lowers and the order comes to go, i.e. to die. He also obeys when in the "port in every girl" where he must procreate. It's all a bit gloomy and fatalistic really, the inevitability of life and death, but whereas "Christ found the source of the Bible" and "Livingstone the source of the Nile", so the sailor and his partner find "the source of the child", crediting humanity with a greater creativity than God in the ability to make new life: "No one comes without leaving someone else".

Away in a manger, no crib for a bed
Little Lord Obedience
Lays down his sweet, entirely sexless head
Christ found the source of the Bible
And Livingstone the source of the Nile
But the sailor and his amazon
Find the source of the child

In the dock of the baby
The resort where strangers liaise
The port in every girl where the sailor obeys

Naked when we are born, naked when we have sex, the vulnerability of our state at birth, procreation and death is not only noted but celebrated for our humanity: but at the end, we must obey and leave the place we came to, the woman we came to, the world we came to:

Naked when he docks, naked when he's lost at sea
There he loses his stripes, there he loses his body
Only here, here at the source
The fashionable dress is flesh
But when the order comes to go and the sirens blow
And the flesh decays
He obeys, he obeys

The chorus is sung to the tune of *Away in a Manger*, with backing singers joining as the song progresses, and is quite lovely. You may agree or disagree with the philosophy on show here, or his description of all women as Amazons, but it is undeniably moving.

The Day the Circus Came to Town

It was inevitable that a circus-based song would appear at some point, by which I mean a song with oompahs and cabaret sounds. Momus describes a circus in Leith, where things go disastrously wrong. The town described is uptight, Calvinist, repressed sexually and poised to explode. There are some specifically Scottish references, with Deacon Brodie sawing a corpse in two. Deacon Brodie was a cabinet maker, deacon and councillor. He was also a thief who used his day trade to gain access to victims' houses. After he was caught and sentenced to death in 1788 a rumour persisted that he saved himself from hanging with a metal tube and collar, bribing the hangman to remove his body quickly enough that he could recover and escape.

The circus that arrives brings scandal and mayhem to a buttoned-up town: which spreads as a virus to the animals of the town first:

And everybody laughed or did not laugh
When a couple of mongrels coupled on the path
The day the circus came to town

The collapse of normal morals is in the comparison between the normal: ten years in a decade, and the abnormal: an orchestra in drag:

The day the circus came to town
There were ten years in a decade
A hundred pennies in a pound
And everybody clapped or did not clap
When an orchestra swept past in drag
The day the circus came to town

The narrator is torn between two instincts, the Calvinist, Puritan impulse of their upbringing and the upheaval and sway of the circus: maybe this represents Momus' being torn between his roots and the hectic madness of the industry he finds himself in. Either is fine, though, because he describes it as a crime to "be of one mind": it is wrong to only see things in one way, we need to be cubist in the way we perceive the world.

Because being of one mind is a capital crime
I will pack & unpack at the drop of a hat
And I will join or leave that circus
At any given point

At any given point
At any given point in time

The idea of "oddness" is conveyed by a boy with long hair, and the consequence to air traffic control if God really was in his heaven:

And everybody cheered or did not cheer
When a boy took off his hat & his hair appeared
The day the circus came to town
The day the circus came to town
God was in his heaven like a goldfish in a bowl
To the visible dismay of air traffic control

There is also a dreadful incident at a wake:

Last night's party met the day's first hearse
And, spilling vodka on the wake made a fatal mistake
With a match and flabbergasted watched them all
Fall flambeed six feet underground

Which now makes me shout "You let Dougal do a funeral!?" This does not seem to be a story from the Old Testament, dealing as it now does with "the ghost of Deacon Brodie": the housebreaker, who is seen to saw a corpse in two. It must be important, though, because towards the end of the song Momus switches into a big band mode on the synthesiser and we hear cymbals and arpeggiating strings building up to a considerable climax, singing about the need to pack and unpack: to join and leave groups as you see fit and to fit into whatever culture you are at that moment in: perhaps also to pack and unpack meaning, to find semantic connection and richness in all our experiences, even the puritanical.

The Rape of Lucretia

A story of the Roman Empire, and the overthrow of the monarchy in favour of an emperor. The last King of Rome was Lucius Tarquinius Superbus, known as "the proud". He was a tyrant, and this incited the rebellion which led to the founding of the Roman Empire. He had three sons, one of whom, Sextus, raped his cousin's wife, Lucretia Collatinus, threatening to expose her (untruthfully) as an adulteress if she did not acquiesce. Lucretia told her husband all this, and took her own life out of shame. Collatinus and others then formed an alliance to remove Tarquinius from power. Eventually the king was deposed and died in exile. Faust is a hero of folklore and literature, a magician who sells his soul to the Devil in exchange for power.

This song is a call and response between Dr Faust and Tarquinius, initially characters from the modern day, but merging with their ancestors as the tale is told. At first, Mr Tarquinius has a sexual problem:

(TARQUINIUS) – O Dr Faust I've got a pain
Where I sit on the throne
Where an Englishman's home is his kingdom
(FAUST) – Mr Tarquinius of Romford
You've got blue blood on the brain
But I know a Roman sanatorium
Where they'll cure you with a story
From 2500 years ago

A female chorus sings "the rape of Lucretia", giving a classic/musical feel to the piece. Despite the man's protestations, Faust continues the story of when a woman was "done by the son of the King". In this verse he mentions the founders of Rome, Romulus and Remus, and mocks the idea of merely "throwing up" your hands in horror as a gesture when more meaningful action is required. He also quotes the gladiator's phrase issued before combat to the death.

Romulus and Remus
Orphans of the forest
Grow to their majority
Throw up their hands in horror
The democratic gesture
When Sextus puts his Sextus where no king should he
Singing "We who are about to die salute thee!"

The modern day Tarquinius, sensing that he is being told not to put it about so much, replies negatively: the song uses a harpsichord very prominently to give a classical feel to the music and on the line "where the beast sucks" a baroque trill plays, a harbinger of the style that Momus would one day pursue, and possibly this album influenced lounge and chamber pop artists yet to emerge.

(TARQUINIUS) – O Dr Faust
I should've guessed
That a doctor named after the self-confessed lover
Of Mephistopheles would say "Take two of these after meals"
And mean leeches – for all your fine speeches
Your anthem is "Where the beast sucks there suck I"

The doctor retorts that he is not that Faust: although he does not want to help the man, he will. Since Tarquinius is clearly a royalist, he probably believes that the Roman slogan SPQR has a certain meaning, in fact it is an abbreviation for a Latin phrase simply meaning "The People and Senate of Rome".

My soul's not with the devil but the NHS
And although I am loathe to
I've taken an oath to

Cure people like you who think SPQR stands for
"Sense Prevents the Queen's Removal"

The singer returns to the idea that for a monarchy to stand, it must only involve itself sexually. Many monarchies have been noted to mainly interbreed, and catastrophe has followed when they have attempted to have sex with those outside the wider family. Perhaps an example might come to mind?

You ushered in democracy, you understood that monarchy
Stands by incest, falls by sexual intercourse

The song ends with a slower singing of the title, and the chorus girls end the piece.

Paper Wraps Rock

My reaction to this song is generally: oh dear. Yes, feeling lovelorn and melancholy can be a source of comfort in some way. But that sensation is not the fault of the one you are lovelorn over. This song talks about Platonic love, and how never giving yourself to someone is the best way to remain desirable. Which comes across, no matter what the intent or how accurate some of the observations are, as a petulant incel (as we would call them today) moaning about being in the friend zone. The song also uses metaphors for revolution, media and sexual politics, none of which comes through clearly to the listener.

Greta Garbo and Marilyn Monroe were of course stars, icons, sex symbols whose very attraction was partly that they were completely unattainable. As Momus' lyric points out, to be desired forever, you must never actually be caught. His lyric also playfully paints a picture of Plato running away from an over-affectionate Socrates. The song title itself comes from the game "Rock, Scissors, Paper", which has many variations worldwide. Each of two players hides their fist behind their back, then simultaneously they reveal a shape, either a flat palm to represent paper, opened fingers to represent scissors or a fist to represent a rock. The winner is decided by: scissors cut paper, paper 'wraps' rock, rock blunts scissors. In this song, the rock and scissors represent revolution and social transformation. The paper represents a cover: image and media distorting and undermining the revolution.

You can never overestimate Garbo
You can never undress Monroe
They may not have heard of Plato
But there's one thing they did know
If you want to be desired for a thousand years
Keeping it Platonic is a good idea
"Cut it out Socrates can't we just talk"
Scissors cut paper, but paper wraps rock

Keeping to the biblical theme, Momus addresses Mary, perhaps an ultimate example of media manipulation, the young woman, the maiden who became a virgin through word play and sophistry: the verse seems to accuse Mary of adultery, effectively:

Never underestimate Mary
The original virginal bride
Interpretations may vary but I say
God was her piece on the side

The next verse contains lyrics you might hear from those incels I mentioned, the misogynistic concept that women are somehow both doxies – prostitutes – and unattainable at the same time:

Prudence is the proper doxy's friend
The paradox is heaven sent
The wickedest words are in the Good Book

Scissors cut paper, but paper wraps rock

Momus sees the images of women in this song, and in the media, as masks for the opinions and views of men. Which is why they can never give themselves to anyone, because under the appearance they have, they are in fact men. He relates this to the story of Helen of Troy, who was in many ways just a vehicle for politics and war. He also has in mind the way she is used by Mephistopheles to tempt Faust, where she is just an image and not a reality. This being the key point of the song, it is the chorus, and has a beautiful backing, mandolin and melody ascending to represent the surface and descending to represent the reality.

Never underestimate the face of Helen of Troy
The face of a woman who never agrees to please
She's Paris in a drag of plaster and papyrus
That's why they never undress, they never undress
They never undress in this non-stop striptease

This still comes across in a difficult and misogynistic way regardless of the intent: there is no way a casual listener can know the symbolism intended by the rock, paper and scissors or the meaning behind the "Paris in a drag of plaster" content. There is what seems to be an adolescent anger at women in this verse:

Never underestimate "Never"
And you'll live to love another day
A woman never made a living
By giving anything away

The verses describe various ways in which women distance themselves from the ones who desire them, including this unfortunate stanza:

Never underestimate the huntress
The protected species of whore
The chariot of Diana Regina's an enormous
Limousine with bulletproof doors

Which I will immediately draw a veil over. The song goes on to describe further ways of creating a division from the real world:

It's rule number one for the wise coquette
Stick a long filter on your cigarette
Shimmer through a window that's twice locked
Scissors cut paper, oh, but paper wraps rock

The next verse suggests celibacy as a way of avoiding conflict with desire. To keep away from this female deception you should keep out of the "kitchens" and "sweatshops"...where presumably all women reside in this rather warped view.

If you want to be more major than a majorette
Stay as rigid and as frigid as a statuette
Stay out of the kitchens and the sweatshops
Scissors cut paper, but paper wraps rock

The whole thing draws to an execrable conclusion with a piano lesson underlining the petulance I mentioned: there is no way around the fact these lines sound like a teenage boy complaining that no-one will sleep with him. "Every Green Bus Drives Fast" and "Every Good Boy Deserves Favour" are ways to remember EGBDF which are the notes on the lines of a music stave.

Undress your best behaviour Helen of Troy
Every Green Bus Drives Fast and so does time
Brush off the plaster of Paris
Every Good Boy, Every Good Boy

Every Good Boy Deserves Favour, where's mine?

The last verse, sung slowly and with drama over acoustic guitar only, and ending with harsh chords on the final words, suggests the singer's real anger is over being forgotten, rather than never having "had" the object of his affection. This implies that it would have been better never to have been there to be forgotten. The idea that to desire, but never to possess is preferable is one that Momus restates in several forms over his career, the purest expression probably being *A White Oriental Flower* on the album *Little Red Songbook*. This verse also admits that the narrator themselves is guilty of some dissimulation.

She will forget you in all except your name
In all except the face you wore
And the empty words you were good at saying
Or else all except the pretentious knots
That covered the paper
That wrapped up rock

"Paper Wraps Rock" is intended as an analogy representing the triumph of media imagery over reality, how the women on screens are not real at all, but representations, often created by men. The song just does not seem to follow that thought through or explain it clearly. It comes across as bitter, misogynistic and quite unpleasant. Momus admits this himself on the next album, as we shall see.

Rules of the Game of Quoits

This is the story of a sexual liaison in a gymnasium where a boy and girl are supposed to be playing quoits, throwing hoops – quoits – over pegs, but end up doing something else instead. The rules of the game are sexual, psychological and practical. You must thrust the quoit. Or not: that may be a euphemism.

The song is accompanied mainly on guitar, with backing vocals breathy in the background and percussion made to sound like the impact of sticks on hoops.

The girl in the rubber shoes has run away from home
To the gymnasium
The sun in the blinds is blue and the girl moves through the room
Like an aquarium

Outlining the rules means describing the sexual turmoil caused by the girl: the chorus tries to represent the confusion that is felt when trying to negotiate sexual relationships when young. The rules, at the end of the day, can be ignored anyway.

Rules of the game of quoits
Use the dimmest light or the brightest light
When the hoops start melting and the sticks catch fire
Rules of the game of quoits
Use the softest matting or the hardest floor
When the hoops start melting and the sticks catch fire
Tunics may be worn or torn away
And the rules of the game may be ignored

The following verse describes the boy, ruddy, a worker, who "enters like a tent" to follow the girl:

The boy with the ruddy face has left his place of work
For the gymnasium
He enters like a tent where the girl has left her scent
Like a geranium

Following the second chorus the liaison between the two begins, the girl is on top and here, again, a fear of female sexuality and empowerment seems to be apparent. As she is on top of the boy, she literally "erases him".

The girl in the rubber shoes pins the ruddy-faced boy to the floor
Of the gymnasium
She's crawling on the spot, she's the ink-rubber, he's the blot
And she erases him

After another chorus, the album ends with a wash of synths and sound effects, a piano playing "There was an old lady..." presumably as a reference to the previous EP, and both Momus and a backing singer intoning: "For love will endure or not endure, regardless of where we are" (From *The Threepenny Opera*). The last note of which is clearly too low for Momus as you can hear his voice breaking.

So that is the first album over. At the time, and even listening to it now, it is extremely unusual in its approach to the singer-songwriter dynamic and has brave lyrical themes. In my opinion, there are two great songs on here in *Lucky Like St Sebastian* and *Little Lord Obedience,* the rest perhaps not so much. There are occasional attempts at a bigger, more widescreen sound as on *The Day the Circus Came to Town* and *Rules of the Game of Quoits,* which do not fully work owing to what I assume are budgetary limitations. The album garnered critical plaudits and was relatively successful for él. It also brought him to the attention of Creation Records, which he would soon sign to, following an EP of Brel covers.

Waiting for 1999…#5 "Nicky"

There could be no doubt in the mind of anyone hearing the output of Momus to this point, that Jacques Brel was a considerable influence. This was fully acknowledged in his interviews and discussions at the time and led to the release of this EP of covers. The three songs are not based on the "traditional" translations of the original songs and have been revised to match Momus' own concerns. It would also be the last release on él records before a much-heralded move to Creation.

Nicky

The original of this was a parodic and satirical song about the industry of fame and celebrity, and Jacques mocked himself mercilessly in it. In this update Momus sings about his own image, in the past and future. There's a real humour and even warmth to *Nicky* matched by Momus' production and use of synthesiser. The character in the lyrics is arrogant, but also mocks his own arrogance, in a knowing, intelligent and well-paced song. It is funny as well, with little musical jabs at David Bowie and Cliff Richard.

Don't Leave

Which is a re-translation of what is more commonly known as *If You Go Away*, but is now much more devastating. It more closely follows the original lyrics and ends with Momus wishing to be no more than a shadow, under the bed of his lover, watching her happy with others, being a "shadow of a shadow, the shadow of your man". The subtle electronics behind this unsettle the listener into experiencing the void of despair projected.

See a Friend in Tears

Momus intended the re-translation of this to reflect the fact that

Brel was dying of cancer when he wrote it, and to include his musings of mortality when approaching death. The lyrics are accordingly heart-breaking, and while they describe hopeless and immutable facts of existence, there is some hope spread within. The song is also quite depressing when one considers how little has changed since this was written, and as I write this how relevant it all still is:

So men are still at war in Ireland
For certain songs and certain dates
The tender gave way to the firebrand
And Europe gave way to the States

This is not just one of my favourite Momus songs or one of my favourite Brel songs: it is one of my favourite songs full stop. Yes, there are two lines in the song that – should you sing it now – would definitely need changing… "without the elegance of negroes, we lack the courage to be Jews"… but how can you deny the impact of:

It's true our cities are exhausted
Made by and for the middle aged
Our weakness gave them more than force did
We thought that love could cure a toothache.

Both the album and this EP brought Momus to the attention of Alan McGee at Creation, and he signed up with them. This brought a bigger budget and the option of a full band, which were implemented on the next album. Before that, though, a final EP was released on Creation, called *Murderers, The Hope of Women*.

Proper Little Madams…#6 Murderers, the Hope of Women

When Momus started writing music, chiefly using acoustic guitar, he wanted to find the chord that would melt people's hearts. Now on Creation Records, this ambition slowly changed, the music would move away from acoustic sounds to electronic. A final EP in the acoustic style was released in October 1986 for Blue Mountain Music, produced by Julian Standen. Momus sings and plays acoustic on the tracks, with electric guitar added by Paul Inder Kilminster: the son of Lemmy Kilminster, from Motorhead. Whereas *Beast with 3 Backs* had been three songs about threesomes, and sex, this EP consists of three songs about death: "The last pornographic frontier of the bourgeoisie," as it was described by Peter Greenaway. The three tracks were named for an expressionist play *Murderer, the Hope of Women* by Oskar Kokoschka. These tracks were also included as the opening three tracks of the second album, *The Poison Boyfriend,* when released on CD. The cover of *Murderers*…features photography by Thomi Wroblewski, a Canadian who had previously worked with Siouxsie and the Banshees and Talking Heads, and showed Momus and friend Zoe Pascale acting out some kind of ritualised murder, the death of the human spirit.

Murderers, the Hope of Women

A song which outlines the theory of male/female marriage as a prison, and slow murder, for women, with the title taken from the symbolist play by Oskar Kokoschka and also influenced by the writer Paul Wedekind. Of the song Momus said:

> This song is a feminist anthem: heteronormative marriage is a long drawn out knife crime, a capitulation to inadequate normality, a murder of human potentiality

Momus is the killer who marries "Sweet Fanny Adams", a reference to a nineteenth-century murder victim, an 8-year-old girl who was killed by Frederick Baker, a clerk. In the song, Momus smothers her with "domestic bliss". Marriage and "normal" life are described as a series of roles, masks that we wear:

With this knife I cut the cake
Who will be my bride today
Sweet Fanny Adams
Watch her climb the step ladder
A present from her step father
Sweet Fanny Adams
See her reaching out and stripping down the muslin drapes
A cover for her nakedness, a veil for her face
With curtains for your wedding dress
You must take your place amongst
The Proper Little Madams
And now because I love you
I must take my place too

Momus' place as a husband is as a murderer, of his partner's lifeforce:

Murderers, The Hope of Women
Death in every new beginning
I must take this woman for my sentence of life
And she must take my knife

He is extremely scathing about the tedium of marriage and talks about the way women are forced to alter and control their bodies through birth control. As the sexual passion leaves their marriage, they "rent a television" to replace what they used to do together.

Like a puppet upon a throne
Of oestrogen and progesterone
Sweet Fanny Adams
This is where your misery starts
This is where your mystery stops
We'll rent a television
To replace Pandora's Box
And I will wear a business face
And you will learn your proper place

Finally his wife, from boredom, frustration and a lack of attention, takes her own life:

Underneath the suntan
from the sun lamp that we bought
Your face is paler than
the pale face of a corpse
And from the seventh floor of our bungalow
You flung yourself down to where they stood below
those proper little madams.

It could almost be a feminist riposte to the more adolescent aspects of *Paper Wraps Rock*; it is a beautiful sounding song, again contrasting imagery against sound, and even features a bit of an electric guitar solo from Paul Inder. Marriage as a prison, heteronormative behaviour, like neurotypical behaviour, is marked out as uninspired, uncreative and unfulfilling in all of Momus' work.

Eleven Executioners

The first cabaret in Munich, established in the 1920s, was called *Die Elf Scharfrichter*, or *Eleven Executioners*. The Executioners were a group of performers who overcame censorship issues by making the cabaret club a private party. Coming on stage to a grotesque song: "Whoever is a friend of death, Adorn with song and sound will we", the group performed songs, drama and parodic interpretations which were bloody, sexual and grotesque. The performers included Marya Delvard and playwright Frank Wedekind.

In this song, the various executioners in the cabaret bar and their audience are described and they end up fighting each other violently. Momus plays with historical anachronism and parody just as Wedekind would in his own satirical ballads, collectively called the *Moritaten*. The song also pays a debt to Friedrich Hollaender, the writer of songs for Marlene Dietrich.

Eleven top hats
In the club vestibule
Eleven gentlemen's cloaks
Hanging up by the black swimming pool
Eleven gentlemen dancing
Each in a style of his own
One is discreetly conversing
On a cordless telephone

Momus describes each executioner's target, and this is a critique of the modern age: each executioner representing some media lie or image we are presented with, newspaper and television propaganda:

And the first he kills only the wicked
And the second kills only the good
And the third he kills people more handsome than him
And the fourth kills the misunderstood
And the fifth kills the women who've loved him
And the sixth kills the couldn't-care-less
The seventh kills people who fill questionnaires in
The eighth kills the deeply depressed

And the ninth kills the twentieth century
And the tenth waits to kill you and me
The eleventh kills only our fear of the tenth
The best executioner he

Momus does not actually think the eleventh executioner is a good thing: life only seems to have purpose because it ends, and we should in fact be afraid of death. The executioners fight among themselves, one reads a military catalogue, the one sent to kill us has lost his scythe: The way in which each argues and fights matches his intended victim. It is appropriate that the executioner for the twentieth century is obsessed with military equipment, for instance. The third says the fourth is too ugly: which means he cannot kill him, etc.

At some ungodly hour in the morning
The predictable quarrels begin
The first gentleman without warning
Slugs the second one square on the chin
And the third says the fourth is too ugly
And the fifth warns the sixth not to start
And the seventh stops dead in his telephone call
A stiletto has punctured his heart
And the eighth is sick in the cistern
And the floodwaters fuse all the lights
And the ninth drops his copy of "Jane's Defence Systems" on the floor
In an act of sheer spite
And the tenth drums his fingers and swings his feet
Because somebody's stolen his scythe
Till an expert in brinksmanship brings him complete
A medium range nuclear device

All of this is set to a manic waltz, the guitar strumming in a staccato attack on our ears, keyboard chords stabbing along with it. There is a glimpse of self-awareness:

And now lights will be trained on the bar
And a puppet will sing a morality
While an idiot strums a guitar.

A depressing lap-dance is described, which Momus is watching along with the executioners. It ends with a call and answer of "rattle tum a gypsum", which is a reference to an Appalachian folk song of the early twentieth century, alternated with what are calls from a Scottish children's ball game. "Plainy!" for example, means to simply bounce a ball against a wall; "Clappy!" means that having thrown the ball you must clap before it returns to you, etc.

Rattle tum a gypsum gypsum...Plainy
Rattle tum a gypsum gypsum...Clappy
Rattle tum a gypsum gypsum...Rolly
Rattle tum a gypsum gypsum...Backy

This collocation of thoughts and images with pop cultural and artistic references marks out the nature of music hall and cabaret, a deliberate fusing of the low- and high-brow, highly artistic statements presented as a spectacle anyone can appreciate: in short, this is a love song to cabaret of the period, and a love song to the fear of death that sustains all our activity.

What Will Death be Like?

Played solely on acoustic guitar, with atmospheric effects, this is a deliberately repetitive list of things that death will emphatically NOT be like, with the actual question answered by just cutting the song off abruptly. Indebted to Brel's *La Mort*, the song focuses our minds on the act of dying and the fears that we have of that process. Momus wanted to provide transgression, to address issues pop music is not supposed to address. It is another very reference laden song, if you understand everything in here you must be very erudite indeed, and to prove this I shall provide an example.

The song says that death will not be like the Tractatus of Wittgenstein. The Austrian philosopher Ludwig Wittgenstein (1889–1951) published only one book in his lifetime: *The Tractatus Logico-Philosophicus* (1921).

The Tractatus is seen as a crystallisation of Wittgenstein's early work, in which he discusses the relationship between propositions (statements about the world which may or may not be true) and the world as experienced. The work contains seven main propositions and subordinate statements which follow from each proposition. It is an ambitious work seeking to define the limits of what philosophy has to say about science and make explicit the difference between what can be said and what can be shown. For instance, if we know that p causes q, then we can infer from q to the existence of p. If R also exists, we can only show it and not SAY/infer/deduce anything from it because we have not stated any relationship between R and (for instance) p or q.

In seeking to codify the possible uses of inference and deduction, Wittgenstein used and popularised logical truth tables, in which the chain of deduction from premises to conclusions is ratified step by step and eliminates the need to have a "law of inference". (If p causes q and q causes r there is no need for a specific further "rule" inferring from r to p).

The Tractatus does also talk about silence linked to these ideas, the final proposition says only, "Whereof one cannot speak, thereof one must be silent". Perhaps, therefore, of death itself, Momus has nothing to say in the end. The song contains many references of this nature.

It is a very beautiful song as well, which builds carefully

towards the climax where Momus just throws you into the pit. Incidentally, there is at least one cover of this song: by Jens Friebe on his album *Nackte Angst zieh dich an wir gehen aus* – translated to German.

So ends the last Momus work consciously produced in the mode of folk singer or singer-songwriter. The next album would take in a more eclectic set of styles, with a more luscious, fuller sound and atmosphere than was hitherto possible.

Closer to the Heart…#7 The Poison Boyfriend

Armed with the finance of Creation Records and the blessing of Alan McGee, Momus embarked on a second album. He was provided with producer Julian Standen and an assembled team of session musicians, and recorded in the Chocolate Factory studio in New Cross, London. There were various possible titles for this album. At one point Momus planned a concept album about the BBC, to be called BBC1. In the end, it was named after, but did not include, a demo track from 1982. *The Poison Boyfriend* is the beginning of a full-on assault on stardom of some form. Just look at the cover: look into the eyes, not around the eyes, look into the eyes…a blue-filtered image, cold in tone but also rendered emotional by the proximity of the face. It is reminiscent of Robert Fripps's 1979 album cover for *Exposure*. The photo for this album was taken by Nick Weslowski of the Monochrome Set, the sleeve was designed by Vici MacDonald, then of *Smash Hits*.

Did this assault succeed in a commercial sense? Well, this is the second Momus album I bought, and it was 50p from a discount shop in Canterbury in 1992, 5 years later.

The Gatecrasher

It is immediately evident that the sound has shifted. The track fades in with atmospherics, looped flute and guitar samples from Leonard Cohen's *I Kept a Woman Waiting* which call to mind a hazy London night, and a strange teenager crashing a party. The story is told laconically, a spoken voice bringing to mind Tom Waits or Nick Cave. The song describes him as struggling to fit in, sporting antique dark glasses and snatching vodka from those who arrive after him. He cannot relate to or connect with the girls at the party and finds himself daydreaming about a waitress in Italy. Is this strange young man Momus? Brecht's

Baal, invading the party with ruminations of evil? It could be. It could certainly be me, or many lonely and academic young men, especially this verse:

He takes in the faces, never quite placing them
Squinting his short-sighted eyes
And each one reminds him of someone he's known
Or someone he faintly dislikes
And he can't understand the naive curiosity
Forcing two strangers to talk
When language is always and everywhere language
And people are like cheese and chalk.

These lyrics are perfect, exactly describing the horror of parties where you do not want to socialise, but do not want to be alone, and drink to oblivion. While the music is still based around an acoustic guitar, the keyboards, bass and backing vocals are clearly sending the song to a different place, more cinematic in sound and approach. The Gatecrasher is disconnected from the others at the party, not even knowing how or why to approach them.

And he doesn't make passes at the girls in the corner
In their Bolshevik glasses and black
When they giggle a little and look at him funny
The gatecrasher only looks back

Momus does not hint at events or feelings in his songs of this period, he describes in detail and precisely how things are and what is happening, which makes it more unusual that critics saw his work as oblique and difficult to parse. It is likely that they did not listen closely or did not understand some references. This verse, where he explains what the young man looks like, requires some knowledge of cinema, as *Les Quatre Cent Coups* was Francois Truffaut's first film. There is a reference to an infected eye, you may note.

And he looks so appealing with eyes like a bloodhound
And hair like the "Quatre Cent Coups"
With the holes in his trousers designed to arouse us
He looks like he'd know what to do
On the rims of his eyes there's a trace of infection
Or maybe the mark of a tear
And is it mascara or is it bacteria, there where the white, where the white disappears?

Momus is interested in recollection and memory, and in this song a Proustian flashback is triggered by an unlikely taste:

Absentmindedly licking the tip of a finger
He's just used for scratching his ear
He wrinkles his nose at the taste of the wax
Which, like him, is acidic and sour
And just for a second something comes back to him
Something so real and remote
That he tips back his vodka to blank out the thought
And he grins as it scorches his throat

The Gatecrasher recalls his mother, and a girl he met in Italy, and then thinks of his current loneliness, his inability to belong in the time and place he finds himself in now and will find himself trapped in for the future. The bitterness he has tasted is not only a reminder of the past but a shade of his future failures:

Or he wonders why Hitler liked lemon verbena
And whether he loved Eva Braun
Or maybe he thinks of his cheap bed and breakfast
On the far side of town

The song ends as it began, exotic sounds and mental images fading out to leave us in the Great Britain that Momus has little time for, parochial and arrogant.

Violets

Momus was inspired by a cabaret movement in London at the time, which included acts such as The Tiger Lillies and The Band of Holy Joy, Preacher Harry Powell and Kevin Wright. A Weillesque cabaret song, but now with improved instrumentation and accordions, this song is an exploration of the Troubles in Ireland and terrorism in Italy, using military and religious imagery accordingly. The threat of terrorism both in Ireland and across the world is represented by the proliferation of literal worms and snakes which "twist and turn" in the Irish Sea. A "generous American" representing the US involvement with the IRA is satirically included, with the Proustian line "savouring his childhood in an after-dinner mint".

The Reverend Ian Paisley grabs his god and shouts
The Pope sits in the Vatican and doubts
The generous American is loosening his belt
Savouring his childhood in an after-dinner mint

Some sections of the song refer to a relationship Momus had at the time with Zoe Pascale, a French girl he knew. In the lyrics book *Lusts of a Moron* the initial letters of some lines are emboldened to spell IRA TV, there being a subtext that given a TV show, terrorists might calm down a bit. I am not sure that giving everyone the ability to broadcast on YouTube and Twitter has calmed things down at all. It may have made things a tiny bit worse.

While the violets are sinking in the rain
Videos drown the sound of a distant train

The blind old man has smashed his violin
In the Irish Sea the vipers return
Could've been your conscience but I guess that never works
So treat me like an equal 'til it hurts

The final stanza is in Italian, and sings of violets overwhelming us, the canals becoming a Tower of Babel, a lack of communication causing the troubles we experience and being abandoned in a hotel, dying of boredom and loneliness. Given this sort of imagery, the song is extremely poppy and upbeat, perhaps burying the meaning a little too much.

Islington John

The story of a trip to Islington in a reggae style, with Momus as the predatory invader of territory, there to steal "your poppy flower". It is a nightmarish trip in some respects, with romance underlying the disorder. The lyrics were composed by cut-up techniques borrowed from Bowie and William Burroughs. Momus despairs of the fate of beautiful women – to become mothers, trapped in the domesticity he bemoaned on *Murderers, the Hope of Women* and he would return to this theme on *His Majesty the Baby* much later. He sees himself as stealing these girls from others, in some way to save them.

Sweetheart Stout is a real brand of stout made by Tennent's, a Scottish brewery. Would a line like "hey lonely, you with the negro face" be written now? Brel could get away with it in the 70s, (see the Brel EP *Nicky*) but now?

This part of town is all flatfish tramps
Beautiful women becoming mothers
All night long the piano grins
I sit drinking sweetheart stout
Hey lonely you with the negro face
Say lonely what time does the music start?

Suddenly the actress belly laughs
And I put my hand on hers

The song is set to a reggae beat with a chorus which climbs the scale like a burglar swarming up a ladder. The woman who is being pursued is an actress, not for the last time in a Momus song. She "goes up to the ugly man and they kiss": is this a self-deprecating reference? They meet a crowd, who are football fans. Momus does not like football fans, as will be made clear in a later interview. They form part of the brutalism he does not enjoy in British culture. He is attacked by one of them and ends up on the floor.

I get a nosebleed under the blue lamp
The actress goes up to the ugly man and they kiss
The wind ruffles the polythene
On a woman drunk on powdered milk and gas
Me and the actress meet a crowd walking backwards
Football fans attacking gypsy caravans
Someone hits my head from the back
As I'm peeping at cookery down an extractor stack

By writing a description of the trip and then recombining the lyrics, the trip is rendered nightmarish, with dead dogs, tramps and women drunk on "powdered milk and gas", a phrase borrowed from Burroughs. It ends with the titular character drunk and making little sense:

Islington John lifted the nylon
Lay amongst the broken antiques and smiled
Reeking of coffee and piss
Sober enough just to say this:
"I will pay for the fire extinguisher
The sand bucket and case

If you will let me pay for this man's face"

The song ends with a held and suspended chord played repeatedly, a bass recorder warbling over the end, with extra percussion provided by a bhangra drummer, bringing tension and a lack of true resolution to the piece, which concludes the description of the brutalism encountered.

Three Wars

A song which harks back to the acoustic guitar driven sound of the earlier EP on Creation, *Murderers, the Hope of Women.* We have a character's life story in three acts: puberty, middle age and old age, each presented as a war against one or more enemies: the First and Second World Wars, and a proposed Third War. Puberty is a battle against the maths teacher (based on boarding school reality) who wants to subtract your innocence (divide your legs, add his proclivities and multiply your mental issues), the girl who rejects you, the parents who are now your enemies, and above all your own body: the thyroid and pituitary glands being responsible for male development, hormones and aggression.

The first war, the war of 14 to 18
Begins with an uprising of adrenalin
The first war begins with the testicles descending
And desire assassinating the child that you once were
The war begins at school when you rebel against the maths teacher
Who touched you up behind his desk
And ends when you've failed your final maths exam
And had your first success with sex
The war brings new discoveries
How to make dog fights with your thyroid and pituitary glands
How the Zeppelin can fly at your command

Your enemies at this point are the parents who you previously got on with, and the girls who reject you. The song makes reference to the famous Christmas Truce of World War I, and to the quavering voice of an adolescent boy:

And from the trenches of your newly found opinions
Quickly dug, quickly abandoned
The white flag waves for an armistice on Christmas Day
Then your voice rings round the family front room
Like a drill sergeant's in front of his platoon
Broken too soon
But you survive

Middle age is a battle against the younger men who want to replace you, the women who reject you, your own children who rebel against you in their turn, and above all your own body. It considers the sense of pointlessness that the middle-aged man feels for his workplace, when comparing his work to his health it seems much less important:

The second war, the war of 39 to 45
Begins when you identify your own inner Third Reich
The second war begins with a sudden hypochondria
A visit to a doctor who waves a piece of paper and says
"This time it's just a false alarm"

The man gives up his ambitions when younger men have more fire than him: he has found some kind of faith beyond a belief in industry.

The war begins at work with some intoxicating news
When the letter comes that offers you promotion
And ends when you decide to let them offer it
To younger men with more ambition
The war brings new perspectives when you suddenly see through

The politics of power which possessed you
Through all your working hours

In the Second War the "whizz kids of the industry" become your enemy, along with the one woman who accepted you. The character also has a son, who he meets at weekends, but who is already suffering his own First War:

Already adolescent and unreconciled
Who laughs at you, you and your new-found piety
And his laugh rings round your faint desire for god
Like an order from an inner firing squad
Breaking the ties of blood

Importantly the character survives these wars, but not the third war against death. The final verse lifts the song tremendously, the chord shift at 4'33" very effective in representing the escalation in hostilities. The lyric for this verse is very powerful, borrowing from Samuel Beckett in the last line:

But the third war is the war that never comes
The war that never comes to everyone
Begins the second after next by accident
Ends everything except itself
The war brings nothing, the unimaginable
That the old imagine all the time
Imagine imagination dying

Momus then lays the blame for death at all our doors for "refusing the creation of new ways to live", not so subtly referencing his new label. The Third War begins when "the great invention falls apart", and our bodies decay: a war which no-one survives.

This is one of the last songs which consciously searches for that magic chord, and it is almost successful, but it is hard to imagine the writer is truly as cynical about life as the character presented. Especially given the optimism of the next song.

Flame into Being

The concept of "flame into being" was borrowed from D.H. Lawrence, with a production from Julian Standen aiming at a rousing and melodramatic pop. This is a very literary sounding track opening with a reference to Paganini, the violinist and composer. Of course, Momus was never trying to be any kind of "Paganini".

Now the weight of the books has crushed my delicate fingers
I'm not trying to be Paganini any more
All I dream about these days is sex with strangers
Rats in spats and bowler hats on the dance floor
Some days my head is the turret for a machine gun
And the world is torn apart by a hail of words
In tongues of fire the rookie priest reads the lesson
And I would like to quote him chapter and verse

Julian Standen is American, and intended this song to be in an American pop style, which perhaps explains some of the Americanisms which creep into the lyrics. This is a song absolutely of its time, to the extent that Martin Amis practically peeps out from under the chorus, and "All I dream about these days is sex with strangers", which with the AIDS crisis of the time would indeed be only a dream. The uplifting chorus is about generating new life and ideas: bringing a flame into being.

I'm in love with everyone who knows it's hard
To build a way of seeing
Who knows that nevertheless that's the only way
To flame into being

Momus describes his life as if it were a sentimental American film: referencing The Pogues' *Rainy Night in Soho* as a cliché of romantic life:

I was always the sucker that got led into temptation
When I didn't have a job and couldn't pay the bills
But stretch me out on your tasteless warehouse sofa
And there or somewhere else I'll do your will
Maybe I'll come out clubbing on a rainy night in Soho
So many clichés have sentimental truth, don't you find?

He then compares himself to the biblical character Holofernes, killed by Judith: and undercuts this with a more prosaic reference, lines which seem to reflect the Dr Hook hit *When you're in love with a beautiful woman*:

You be Judith and I'll be Holofernes
Living with a beautiful woman
I'm jealous all the time

There is genuine wit and warmth in the lyrics that describe his apparent rival, it is odd to hear a reference to something as "normal" as Levis 501s in a Momus song, but we also have a reference to Caesar and the Ides of March:

So take me to the people who'll gratify my ego
Because under the swagger I don't know who I am
Caesar beware the ides of adolescence
Here comes some new Brutus in black 501s
From the pores of his skin you can smell the cappuccino
And his avaricious eyes are shining like the sun
Black bat night come down from your roost now
And cover me with your wings
Under my eyes I shall wear your engagement ring

The following section references the song *Windmills of my mind* in its pattern of fifths, and uses clichéd romantic imagery which is far displaced from the reality of Momus, he was nowhere near having a baby at the time, was always sober and talks about some kind of writers block which he gets when with her.

But as soon as I decide that this is not the place for me to stay
I feel currents that buoy me up and bear me away
And burglars or writers will carry this love away too
Don't regret this, just forget me, let me release you
And as soon as I decide I'm more fertile or just more sober
Maybe I'll think of you like a touching American film
How I left you washing the face of our baby
How whenever I live alone
My hands and eyes work again

This is a very pretty song, with a catchy chorus and which could have made for a reasonable single release, but perhaps more sentimental than a Momus song would normally be at this time.

Situation Comedy Blues

Momus planned his second album to be a concept album about the BBC. Several demos were recorded for this and can be found on his LiveJournal account. The album never happened but several of the tracks were released in one form or another over the next few albums. This is one of them.

It is about a comedy writer who must choose between his career and his woman, and we hear plot details of the sitcom he is writing. The constant question of what was more important, women or art, ran through his work at this point. The sound of this song is very much like a cheesy sitcom theme, fast paced, electronic and with backing vocals singing the main tune. The narrator sees himself as light relief for the workers of the world: but his own situation is not so rosy:

Call me the barman standing waiting for the workers
To drink their work away
I'm the man who serves the laughter
To the drunkards of disaster
After they've got plastered on the news
And I've got the situation comedy blues

He describes the problem he has: his own relationship with his girlfriend is falling apart because he has "lost his sense of humour":

This man is sober
And so he's gone to bed with another writer's scripts
And his wife has had to move in with her mother

He then describes the situation comedy he has been writing. In the UK during the 70s there was a comedy series called *Love Thy Neighbour*, which dealt with the culture clash when a black family moved in next door to a white family, the head of which was an old fashioned and somewhat prejudiced man. The series is very uncomfortable to watch now, as the bigotry of the main character is the main focus of the show's humour, and it is not clear where the audience's loyalties are supposed to be. The series that the narrator of this song is writing is something similar but involving a gay family moving next door to a Pakistani family: Love thy Gay-Bour perhaps? Momus is deliberately using slightly off language here to describe the characters, who are clichés, to illustrate how terrible the sitcom concept is.

He's been devising a new series
Where the first man to appear is
Pakistani and the second is a queer
Who rings the bell in tights and biker's gear
And he tells them that he's sorry to disturb them

But the sari that the wife had on today was out of sight
And could he maybe borrow it tonight?

The inherent racism and homophobia of the sitcom writer is clear from the next verse as well, which describes exactly the kind of unfunny nonsense that would appear in *Love Thy Neighbour*. These are sitcom ideas some years out of date, even in 1987:

So the Paki asks the queen in to his brilliantly-lit kitchen
Where he demonstrates his do-it-yourself tools
He's the type who doesn't gladly suffer fools
But he electrocutes his finger in his biggest Black and Decker
When his wife appears in towel and rubber hat
And the bath she's running floods the neighbours' flat

The song has a breakdown for the middle eight, the narrator sings quietly as he describes the illusion that his woman has come back to him:

I've been sitting here unhappily
Trying to write this comedy
When I hear a sudden laugh in the next room
And thinking it's my woman who's come home
I call her name expectantly and, glad that she's come back to me
I throw away my trivialising pen .
And then the television laughs again

He is deceived by his own medium, and ends the song crying for Marie to return to him. The chorus repeats and fades, the cheesy pop securing some laughs but the inappropriate descriptions of the characters leaving a bad taste. The song never really fits in with the otherwise literary feel of the album, and it is clear it is from a different project.

Sex for the Disabled

Up to now, Momus had steered clear of actual politics, but this was a direct and personal attack on Thatcher and Thatcherism. The attack starts from the premise that things "went wrong" sometime after Altamont, the 1969 music festival at which a death occurred, and to many it seemed that the "hippy dream" also died. The Age of Aquarius became a darker and less sensitive age, an age of economists and capital.

Both "Sex for the Disabled" and "Get fit for life", slogans used in the song, were slogans in the real world used by the left and right wing, respectively. This is a narrative song about a man who crashes his motorbike into a gym, crashing into a female bodybuilder. The crash represents the events at Altamont and the death of that dream. This is another song about a gymnasium in which a woman takes control, as was *Rules of the Game of Quoits*.

Before the accident you were just a square
And I was a Hell's Angel in leathers and long hair
Before the accident you were a fanatic
And I was a motorbike mechanic
And which of us was stronger then
And which of us was stranger
A woman pumping iron or a liberal Hell's Angel?
Before the accident when my somersaulting Triumph
Entered the gymnasium of the female Goliath

Momus sings about the way in which the political right prepared to take power. The puritanism of the right is compared to the liberal behaviour of the left wing:

Before the accident you kept out of sight
Working behind curtains till your body shape was right
The only man you touched was your tutor in karate
I fucked every eligible party

He represents the liberal left, she IS Thatcher. It is not a subtle song in this sense, referring to cuts, and privatisation:

As I lay in agony from a thousand savage cuts,
you privatised the hospital and you wished me luck.

Although Altamont happened in 1969, the Conservatives and Thatcher came to power in 1979, and this change is further discussed in this lyric, which references a popular new-age book of the 70s:

Before the accident before '79
Before the wheelchair that was such a difficult time
Every man an anarchist, we were all into "Zen
And the Art of Motorcycle Maintenance" then

The accident and subsequent confinement to a wheelchair also represent the change from hippy ideology to capitalism. The main character is a Hell's Angel, as it was the Hell's Angels causing chaos at Altamont that is often depicted as the death of 60s idealism. This is an idea I fully concur with; you need only look at how the technological hell we currently live in was generated by individuals like Bill Gates and Richard Branson who were originally hippies, and the computer revolution was also a product of the peace movement. This is backed up by the following lyrics:

Before the accident when you came to power
And the poor got on their bikes and we got off ours
And the Age of Aquarius changed overnight
To an Age of Economists serving the right
Yeah, our Triumphs turned to wheelchairs, oh don't times change?

Conservative minister Norman Tebbit was infamous for the

phrase "get on your bike" referring to the efforts of people to find work. The fact that there are no jobs to be found anywhere you bike to being irrelevant, of course. The song also refers to the Triumphs of the hippy movement – Triumph is of course a brand of motorbike – turning to wheelchairs, representing drawbacks or failure. Finally, the failure of the left to capitalise (so to speak) on its popularity in the 60s and the movement it spawned is summed up as castration, and the complaints of what is now a minority:

So now you're the angels, the thugs in authority
And we're just another castrated minority
And across our leather jackets it says "No Sex for the Disabled"
And across your macho breasts "Unfit for life"

The song has a powerful progressive structure, adding instrumentation as it builds and using effective backing vocals to stress the actual and genuine anger which you can hear in the delivery. It ends dramatically, with a backing choir described by Momus as a football stadium chorus, with power chords and instruments tailing away just as the hopes and dreams of the 60s peace movement did. The venom in the lyrics, the stately pace of the song and the guitars remind me in fact of bands like Carter USM from the late 80s/early 90s period: I can genuinely imagine this being a song on 101 Damnations for instance, or the Love Album. This is not the sort of comparison that will be made very often of Momus' work, so you can understand how unusual this song is in the canon.

Interestingly, the F word is bleeped out on this album, on the CD version I have and on the streaming version of the Album on Amazon Music. I do not know if this was intentional, or insisted on by Creation, or required for airplay (not that this track would be on radio much).

Closer to You

An incredibly important track, I do not think even Momus realises how much this track clearly shapes his output over subsequent years. It is a spoken word monologue, with a sung chorus, over a slow, sensual beat. He is inspired by the production team behind the band Imagination, Jolley and Swain. He also namechecks Cameo and Isaac Hayes *By the Time I get to Phoenix* as inspiration. The track drifts sensually in a way nothing by Momus has achieved up to this point, as he transfers his main influence from Brel to Gainsbourg. The drum beat was programmed on a Roland 606 belonging to Douglas Benford, and includes slowly building backing vocals provided by singer Louis Phillipe. It is Barry White if Barry White had read a great deal of French literature and stared at girls on the Tube. Momus describes it as a realisation of the sound suggested by Paddy McAloon of Prefab Sprout when he said, "I don't know how to describe the modern rose, if I can't refer to her shape against her clothes with the fever of purple prose": a modern, post-feminist man struggling to be erotic without resorting to sexualised images of the feminine. It is a sound full of contradiction and contrast, unusual for pop music and unique for Creation.

Momus' next several albums would be indebted to the sound created here, and the character he is portraying would pretty much be set as Momus well into the 90s. The opening line, "And maybe you're the circle girl", is immediately arresting. Rather than the cinematic, widescreen sound of the rest of the album, this is a personal booty call intended to be heard in your headphones. The character (an exaggerated version of Momus) describes several girls he lusts after, speaking directly to them. It is so intimate it is almost uncomfortable, and occasionally falls over the edge of ridiculous:

> *I'm looking at the way your toes poke out of your sandals,*
> *at funny angles to your feet, and how you know it turns me on.*

The verses are erotic, charged with a perverse, stalker-like intensity. There is no doubt at all that Jarvis Cocker heard this song and transferred the style to Pulp's work, just listen to *My Legendary Girlfriend, I Spy* and even *Common People*, and you can clearly hear the influence from:

> *Or maybe you're the foundation painter at the Central School, looking so fine-boned I could carry you home in your portfolio case.*

In fact, Jarvis Cocker wrote to Momus and asked him to produce Pulp as a consequence of listening to his work. Momus declined.

The song having described the girls goes on to discuss Momus himself and his music. Here he even namechecks actual Momus songs including *Paper Wraps Rock* and admits:

> *some of those are bitter records, records which accuse women, girls like you, of using your attractiveness wantonly and wilfully to trap and to paralyse men who want them and can never have them, men who sometimes feel the perverse urge to trash the women they desire the most, who imagine they despise all those immaculate visions...what adolescent crap, what kind of idiot would sing that? Oh, not me...*

The guitars shimmer and circle more prominently as the song progresses to its (what can only be described as) climax, as the song discusses creativity and how it is a substitute in men for the real creativity of reproduction, an activity which men are barred from. Finally, we get the statement of Paul Klee's epitaph:

> *Here lies the painter Paul Klee,*
> *somewhat closer to the heart of creation than usual,*
> *but far from close enough.*

It is erotic. It really is. Of all the tracks on this album which attempt different things, this is an absolute bullseye in terms of intent vs. outcome. Momus clearly recognised this to some extent, as the style and character were transferred to the next album.

The next album would come with a much more focused sound and considerable advances in lyric writing, in fact the second album for Creation would cement Momus' critical reputation.

It was also around this time that a legendary tour with Primal Scream took place. Alan McGee and Momus have both written about this, with Momus claiming that he enjoyed the experience more than was reported.

In his book *Riots, Raves and Running a Label,* Alan McGee writes about an incident in Berlin, in the no-man's land between East and West. Primal Scream were out looking for vodka while Momus was left on the bus. Bobby Gillespie (lead singer of Primal Scream) rang Alan and asked, "Alan, can we leave Momus in No Man's land?" Alan says in his book, "He'd been driving them nuts on the bus. They couldn't stand him." Supportive of his new signing, Alan replied, "Please don't do that," and despite Bobby's repeated requests, Momus remained on the tour. Alan says he regrets that decision, as if Momus had been found in no-man's land, "It could have been amazing, he could have been locked up for a couple of years..." However accurate all that is, to have been a fly on the wall of that tour bus would have been fascinating, and no doubt literally intoxicating.

Twitching the Lace…#8 Tender Pervert

The Poison Boyfriend was successful enough, critically at least, to give Momus considerable autonomy over his next album, which he was to produce himself. Having moved sonically and spiritually away from cabaret, from folk and from Brel to Serge Gainsbourg and a more erotic mode of expression, it was inevitable that sex, or at least sexuality, would feature prominently on the album. Margaret Thatcher had recently declared an intention to ban content that promoted homosexuality as a "lifestyle", and anger at this partially fuelled the content of the new songs. The album was going to be called *The Homosexual* until Alan McGee called Momus in to point out that Polygram would not release the album under that name. I should say that if "Momus at Creation Records" was a drinking game, then Alan McGee calling Momus in for a chat about some issue with album content or titles should probably be worth a double shot of vodka, if you don't need your liver as such.

Momus felt that straight people should support the Gay Pride movement against the Conservative backlash, and this informed the content of the album. The album, released in April 1988, is therefore packed with references to, for instance, Mishima, Ovid, Joe Orton and Bataille. Not for the last time you may feel you need a pile of reference books in order to make sense of it all.

The album sleeve includes a quote from gay playwright Joe Orton: "Give me the ability to rage corectly" (sic): an exhortation to rebel against orthodoxy in a controlled and sustainable manner."

There is also a quote from Deuteronomy (a link to the debut album *Circus Maximus*): "Circumcise the foreskin of your heart," which means, do not only be a true follower in your physical appearance, but make yourself divine in your heart.

Momus himself describes this album as his "statement":

looking at the cover, with Momus in front of a Hyde Park tree with blossom at night, related to the lyrics of "Bishonen", he is certainly trying to strike a classic and timeless pose. Indicating a devil's horns, inspired by a photograph of Picasso with bull's horns by Gjon Mili, he is truly saying that he is a demon, and yet is depicted as angelic within the album itself. This mass of contradiction is fully in tune with the lyrical and conceptual nature of the album itself.

The Angels are Voyeurs

A very synthesised track, with a warm cabaret feel and a catchy keyboard riff during the introduction and rhythm programming by Dean Klevatt. Not as dark or as "rock" as you might expect from the cover and the song titles. We are very much in the territory that – for instance – The Pet Shop Boys or even Depeche Mode could have inhabited at this point.

Wim Wenders had recently released the film *Wings of Desire*: which showed angels coming down from heaven to observe human behaviour. This film informs the general theme of the track, except that it is God who is "intoxicated" by our sexual behaviour and our tendency to "tamper with the things we most depend on", which gives him a "hard-on". For an extraordinary being, the ordinary concerns of his creation are sexually interesting to him.

God is a tender pervert and the angels are voyeurs
Watching us forever, their vision never blurs
They make us then forget us for a hundred million years
And then by chance they glance at us and something in them stirs
They find us so provocative, so weak, so full of pride
Our cleverness, our nakedness, fills them with delight
The way we hold our coffee cups, the way we pick our words
God is a tender pervert and his angels
His angels are voyeurs

When God is too busy masturbating, he sends the angels to view us instead. They find their own amusement in the ways we try to destroy ourselves, an interest in self-destruction and sado-masochism that mirrors that of *Lucky Like St Sebastian*.

It intoxicates the Spaceman, watching how we thrill ourselves
Not by sex but by devising new ways to kill ourselves
He sees the way we tamper with the things we most depend on
The danger stands his hair on end and gives him a hard-on
He calls his angels down to watch that slut the world get hers
God is a tender pervert and his angels
His angels are voyeurs

Of course, the rest of the tracks on the album are stories the angels see as they visit Earth. Which makes this a concept album and maybe even progressive pop…

Love on Ice

I remember very early after first listening to Momus, I was in Edinburgh at the festival, and saw the book *Lusts of a Moron: The Lyrics of Momus* on sale in a bookshop, presumably Waterstones. The young guy behind the counter enthusiastically discussed Momus with me, saying how *Love on Ice* was probably the funniest of his songs and how clever they were and it was great to meet someone else who listened to him and how long was I up in Edinburgh? It was a couple of years, though, before I acquired a CD copy of the relevant album, so the songs on *Tender Pervert* were just poems to me, to which I imagined bizarre music and arrangements. It is also highly indicative of my character and possible spectrum disorder that I have only just realised while typing the above that the guy behind the counter was probably chatting me up. Which highlights, I guess, that the tactic employed on this album – singing about queer issues – was gaining a new audience in that demographic.

What caught my aspiring beau's attention in this song was the deliberate reversal of orientation in the main characters. The song is about an ice-skating couple who win the Olympic gold medal for their routine, but are afraid to come out of the closet about their sexuality, specifically that he is "only doing it for Christopher" and she is "only doing it for Jane". Christopher and Jane are their manager and PR assistant/cocaine provider. It is made very clear that the characters being sung about are NOT Christopher Dean and Jayne Torvill who famously won the Olympics for Great Britain with a routine set to Ravel's *Bolero* in 1984.

The music is a crazed waltz – time structure with annoying Casio barps and farts over the top. It is pointedly Weillesque and was originally intended for the BBC album project. The lyrics outline the situation clearly. The couple put on a show for the cameras and the press but are not really what they portray at all. This was a time when a gay guy and girl could not perform together and be openly gay, when to be gay was not "ordinary".

We're all cuddles and smiles
At the press photocall
Though you hate to touch me
And I couldn't love you at all
Because I'm not an ordinary guy
And you're not an ordinary girl
But that's how we have to appear now we're
The best in the world

The lyrics are playful, firing numbers at us and then the truth, that the skaters are in love with "Christopher" and "Jane". After this verse they are trapped in a cycle of public appearances, advertising a diet and other products.

One perfect couple on four perfect blades
We execute two perfect figures of eight

We accept the bouquets but we'd just like to say
Before these flowers wither like all accolades
I'm only doing this for Christopher
And you're only doing it for Jane

The pair eventually lose to a Russian couple who "skated like robots" and rumours about their sexuality lead to their being forced out of the closet. Their collapse continues and in the end they are doing PR and cocaine for Christopher and Jane. Overall the song is a cynical look at fame and the inherent homophobia of the British press of the time, and a comment on how sporting heroes are viewed as "acceptable" only if they conform to certain standards of morality and behaviour.

One perfect couple on four perfect blades
We execute two perfect figures of eight
But the ice is a mirror in which people see
Their nation and their sexuality
And now we've come out of the closet
No-one remembers our names
And Christopher isn't our manager
And we need the PR more than Jane needs our cocaine

At the same time, it's another time capsule song, in that it would be hard to see anyone having to conceal their sexuality in the same way now, and the clichés of the press reports (he has died of AIDS, she is on Greenham Common) date it like carbon-14.

I Was a Maoist Intellectual

A faux-Brechtian song in which Momus satirises both himself and the music industry in his role as a "Maoist Intellectual" in the plague-pit that is the "Business". It could almost be autobiographical, and he demonstrates a sense of humour at the pompousness and "pretentiousness" that Momus was often criticised for. The song could also be a parody of left-wing musicians of the time, such as Billy Bragg. This noble aim is accompanied by some of the most 80s Casio keyboard samples you could hope to hear, and clown whistles. The specific source material included Brecht's song *Of Poor BB*, itself a shadow of a self-epitaph by the French poet Francois Villon. He also references the Brecht song *To Those Born Later* which includes the phrase "that is how I made use of the time on Earth allotted me".

The character in the song is sincere and committed to cultural revolution inspired by Chairman Mao but fails to take account of the role fashion plays in the popularity he enjoys, and ends up being a marginalised footnote in musical history. In a call-back to *Flame into Being* we hear how he burned the midnight oil to "build (a) way of seeing", in order to tell the public how the way they are living is wrong: a sure way to irritate the public into a hatred of you. Initially though he is successful:

Whenever I played my protest songs the press applauded me
Rolled out the red carpet, parted the Red Sea
But the petit bourgeois philistines stayed away
They preferred their artists to have nothing to say

Momus goes on to explore the way in which the narrator presented his world view to others: unsurprisingly, people do not like to be told that the way they live is "bad".

I showed the people how they lived and told them it was bad
Showed them the insanity inside the bureaucrat
And the archetypes and stereotypes that were my stock in trade
Toppled all the ivory towers that privilege had made
Though I tried to change your mind I never tried your patience
All I tried to do was to point out your exploitation
But the powers that be took this to be a personal insult
And refused to help me build my personality cult

A line which sounds very like a description of Momus' own pop career describes his downfall from being "three things the working classes hated: agitated, organised and over-educated". This "agitate, organise, educate" is the description given by George Bernard Shaw of the aims of the Fabian Society – a socialist organisation in the UK which seeks to advance socialism gradually, rather than in a revolutionary manner.

I left the normal world behind and started living in
A hinterland between dissolution and self discipline
I burned the midnight oil to build my way of seeing
A miner at the coal face of meaning
The rich despised the songs I wrote which told the poor their worth
Told the shy to speak and told the meek to take the earth
But my downfall came from being three things the working classes hated:
Agitated, organised and over-educated

There is a bitter ending, as the singer ends up working as a doorman, trying to give out his music in its "forgotten format" and having "given up ideology the day I lost my looks". In the end, "the energy released by my frustration was nearly enough for reincarnation". Momus points out the irony of this himself in his sleeve notes for the compilation *Pubic Intellectual*: he ends up a "hotel doorman" himself, letting others into the hotel that represents the industry.

> This song sees me making a tragedy into a farce: the intellectual becomes a hotel doorman, trying to hand out his records to the stars who pass him. It was all to come true in the 90s, as Brett Anderson, Damon Albarn and Jarvis Cocker tipped me discreetly on their way to the upstairs suites. Admittedly, though, much worse things happened to the

intellectuals under Mao.

Another line states that he never found "a publisher for my Little Red Book". The Little Red Book was a book of sayings by Chairman Mao. It eventually became an album title for Momus as well. Essentially the song describes the pointlessness of trying to be a sincere force for intellectual or political change while inside a system run by the upper classes for capitalist gain. It is a brash and cynical statement, but the self-referential nature of it may be a bit self-defeating and even hypocritical. I mean, clearly the person singing this song on this album is trying for fame of some form.

The Homosexual

The putative title track of the album and its conceptual heart. The song describes a war, essentially, between different forms of masculinity: the pre- and post-modern male, the alpha and beta, the macho and the feminine. A sneering "macho" male derides a more effeminate man for his perceived homosexuality, but behind his back his wife is having an affair with the "queer". The singer is the effeminate male who is bedding many women "behind their husband's backs" and making them sing "notes of pleasure their husbands will never hear... no fucking fear". It is a story that many men could identify with; I myself have been told many times over 30 years that I am gay, which is news to me, to the extent that you end up questioning yourself. The song is also about that perceived war between the intelligent and the anti-intellectual, the War Against Intelligence that The Fall described and that Pulp hinted at.

I love women but I'm thinking of giving in
I love women but what's the point of arguing
With the men from boarding schools and building sites
Who've told me I'm a homosexual all my life

One stop past Embankment and the coughs begin
Hell hath no fury like an insecure Englishman
You don't need psychoanalysts to translate this
There is an open homosexual in our midst"

Momus takes revenge on these hyper masculine homophobes by pretending outwardly to be the homosexual they perceive him to be, while privately pleasuring their women, more accurately and effectively than they could manage themselves, a sexual revenge.

The homosexual they call me it's all the same to me
That spectre they projected I will now pretend to be
Since their neurosis is what passes for normality
It's okay with me if I'm queer
Since their tone-deafness is called the love of music
I won't disabuse them
I'll make love with their women
I'll make them sing notes of pleasure
Their husbands will never hear

Indeed, it is very clear that both Jarvis Cocker and Brett Anderson (Suede), who were friends of Momus, listened closely to this album, and this song in particular. It is snarling, revenge driven and seductive. The beeped out/censored "fucked" on *Poison Boyfriend* is a thing of the past: this, like many songs to come, is very much NSFW and includes moans of pleasure from an unknown German lady (much like my gap year). The song was based on a true story involving Mike Alway (Founder of él Records) as the perceived "homosexual". This song has been covered by the Australian singer/songwriter Kirin J. Callinan among others.

Bishonen

This is Momus' most critically acclaimed song: *Bishonen* is the quintessential Momus song, the point at which the "Tender Pervert" really comes into focus. The unreliable narrator is now fully in place and we begin to have the real life of Momus/ Nicholas Currie dovetailing with the story of the character singing these songs, meaning we cannot know if anything is true or not.

The music of *Bishonen* is a gentle arpeggiating sequence on synthesiser and guitar which builds and falls away as the narrative demands. There are atmospheric effects to connote the eastern atmosphere, to emphasise the alien nature of the narrative's locations and to highlight the lack of moral normalcy on display. The musical structure, repetitive but adaptive, was based on Michael Nyman's formal works and on a pop song written by Douglas Benford called *The Landed Gentry*. The Peter Greenaway film *The Draughtsman's Contract*, which features Nyman's work, seems to have been an influence, as do the manoeuvres of the vicious courtiers in films like *Les Liaisons Dangereuses*.

Momus has also stated the song to be influenced by *L'Andropause* by George Brassens, a song about male impotence and ageing, and by both Mishima and by a chapter in Ian Buruma's book *A Japanese Mirror* which discussed him.

The main character describes his life in a spoken, seductive monologue which again sets a template for the work of Pulp and others a few years hence. He is "born in the town of Paisley in early 1960", so this is Momus himself but describing an alternative world where he was brought up by an "old eternal bachelor" obsessed with Japanese myths and traditions, who trains him to be a Bishonen, a beautiful, sexually ambiguous warrior "doomed to fall like blossom".

The training involves seduction techniques, sword fighting and oratory.

The words were to cut down and to kill the muscle-bound
The swords to fell my intellectual enemies
And women should be hated but first impersonated
Charm, he said, is essential to misogyny
He taught me how to woo the girls in order to outdo the girls
And the fun would come when I'd got them to love me

The old man who raises him clearly has carnal thoughts towards him, but also gives him a retainer (and presumably lover) who goes with him into the world.

How could I disobey that surreptitious gay
Who brought me up according to a fantasy?
For when the old man stared at me
He drowned in evil beauty
Thinking of the early death in store for me

The two young men go into the world fighting "bullies" and are followed by the old man who feels he has been forgotten by the son he has raised to die young. At 28 years old the young man gives up travelling and goes to work in a bank: ashamed that he has not died young as his stepfather planned. He also marries a girl, completely betraying what was planned for him; a shame which leads him to adopt the same perverse course that his father followed:

I stay awake some nights when my wife turns off the lights
And starts breathing regularly next to me
And I think of fallen petals and bodies pierced by metal
And how I'll never now fulfil my destiny
Father spare my shame, let me pass my name
To a boy with greater beauty and more bravery
For if I have a son I'm going to raise him to die young
And lay him in the grave that you prepared for me.

It is a fantastic song and considered Momus' best by many reviewers at the time and since. It perfectly captures the mood and essence of the story that was intended to be told, and while there are several verses, there is no fat to trim, with each couplet perfectly and concisely stating what is needed to both add to the story and convey character development. The music perfectly fits the narrative and theme. It ebbs and flows in perfect conjunction with the narrative. There is no doubt that with this composition Momus had finally arrived and found a form of expression that completely suited the character and his talents. This track is supposed to end side one of the album, but we must address an extra track added onto the CD: *Right Hand Heart*.

Right Hand Heart

An acoustic version of a song which would be re-recorded later for the next album, *Don't Stop the Night*. This version was recorded at Scarf studio, along with the rest of *Tender Pervert*, by Momus and Nigel Palmer. It's a tale of hatred which disguises self-loathing, as a guy meets a girl who has dextrocardia: her heart is on the right-hand side of her body – and it repulses him to the extent that he cannot have sex with her, but another boy comes along who can.

The guy's repulsion turns out to be self-loathing at himself: he also has a right-hand heart. The song centres around acoustic guitar and sounds somewhat out of place on the mainly electronic album. It is very slight compared with the songs it follows and precedes.

Momus considers the later, disco version of this song to be the official one, and it is not supposed to be on the CD version of this album. The song was released as a free 7" disc with early copies of the LP version of Tender Pervert with a B-Side of *Poison Boyfriend*, an early Momus demo recorded with Neill Martin of The Happy Family during *The Man on Your Street* sessions in 1982.

A Complete History of Sexual Jealousy Parts 17–24

A solid and superbly written pop song, with an intro mimicking New Orders' *Blue Monday*, and full of Pet Shop Boys samples and influence. Of all the tracks on this album it was the closest to a single release. Until Alan McGee called Momus into his office (two shots) to explain that the use of the word "sexual" in the title precluded this. It was a very different time.

It is a psycho-sexual tale of a man who is jealous of almost everyone, for different reasons, so insecure that he is jealous even of men his lover will never go to bed with, just for the depth of their desire for her. Equally, he is jealous of the greater hate his enemies hold for him than he does for them.

There is some self-conscious word play here which also hints at greater sexual indiscretion. "I'm jealous of the man the man you broke the heart of broke the heart of" suggests a hideously complicated pansexual love triangle/quadrilateral, as does, "If looks could kill I'd kill the men whose looks would kill you if looks could kill", a line which cleverly highlights the narrator's jealousy while making it clear that he is not physically capable of harming anyone, except with Paddington-esque hard stares.

It is hard to fathom that the Momus who wrote this song is even the same Momus that released *Circus Maximus*. This track sounds contemporary (for the time), very commercial and manages to incorporate the psycho-sexual narrative and self-analysis in candy covered, glossy pop music. In it Momus comes close to achieving the symbiosis of pop/art which Neil Tennant achieved with, for instance, *West End Girls*, but perhaps the lyrics are too arch and still too explicit to fully achieve the airplay and chart success so clearly aimed for.

This song is also the subject of possibly the most unlikely cover version in Momus' history, when included on the 1996 album *Soft Vengeance* by Manfred Mann's Earth Band. This album also includes a cover version of *Nothing Ever Happens* by Del Amitri, whose lead singer and writer is Justin Currie (Nicholas Currie's cousin). *Nothing Ever Happens* got a single release by Manfred Mann's Earth Band, but not *Complete History*!

Ice King

There is a symmetry between this and the previous song. Whereas the narrator of *Complete History* has a surfeit of jealousy and emotion, the character here is concealing his emotions in order to make his partner work harder to engage him. He is desperate to hide the depth of his feelings from his beloved because he sees "how hard you work to turn a cold man on". He believes that because they dislike emotional men, if they saw the depth of his feelings, "How long would you stay with me?"

On first hearing this song, the music is surprisingly un-Momus-esque: the verses have a cold, mechanical line running through them with vocals which are remote, aloof and more or less spoken. However, the chorus and bridge are warm, soulful and emotional, reflecting the duality of the narrator's character. The music and vocal style borrow heavily from Prince, and it is clear that Momus' voice is not really up to the job, with the extended vocal range really requiring someone with a more soulful and warmer tone. It is also a surprisingly un-perverse song: the narrator is basically just playing it cool and being hard to get: tactics that pretty much everyone has engaged in at some time or other with a partner or friend. I cannot help feeling that it is a song he should maybe have just sold to someone else. In fact, given that Momus is able to write pop of the quality and order of *Complete History* and *Ice King*, I wonder why he did not write songs for other people at this time.

This song in particular is reminiscent of *You Have Placed a Chill in My Heart* by the Eurythmics, both thematically and sonically, and from the same year. His own material, as on this album and the next, *Don't Stop the Night*, is excellent and musically commercial but containing themes that render them extremely difficult to market – leading to many more office discussions with Mr McGee. So why did he not write albums for himself and fund them by writing pop songs for others?

Momus would actually follow this course later, writing songs for Japanese pop artists, but it seems not to have been considered as a course of action in the UK market: I think that the team genuinely thought at this point that Momus himself would front these songs into the top ten, and render the Top of the Pops studio into something like the Hospital Church de la Caridad in George Bataille's *Story of the Eye*, destroying all conventions and convents. It was not to be.

In the Sanatorium

Another widescreen, immediately cinematic and atmospheric work, in which sound effects of thunder and rain hang over the tale of a man who is tending his sick girlfriend in a sanatorium. He is using her illness to isolate her, having put cards from other well-wishers "on the fire". The treatment she receives will make her "well, or weaker still", and it is made clear that the narrator would prefer her to become weaker, being "half in love with this disease, that keeps you close to me".

Momus' vocals are very warm and very close to the microphone, making this an uneasy listening experience. He is invading privacy, personal space and the entire soul of the woman he has imprisoned. While she sleeps he reads her *The Immoralist* by André Gide, a text about the abuse of emotional power which fits the narrative situation.

Finally he falls further into perversion as he molests the almost unconscious woman:

I wonder, as I watch you sleep
If this possessive streak
Will make me force my love
Or if the trick is cheap

And if you took your drug
And if you're deep enough asleep.

The song ends with atmospherics from the storm, half-buried eastern singing and a lot of unease. A hanging cadence is used so that there is no resolution to the home key as the sounds fade out, making the sonic layering used more disorienting. You have no doubt that this story is only going to progress, and not improve. As is often the case in Momus' work, the beauty of the music, the lilting guitar, warm synthesiser washes and soft vocals are dissonant with the perverse and evil nature of the narrator's wishes, further fuelling tension and discomfort in the listener, all of which makes this one of my favourite of his songs. The music is based on a Gainsbourg song: *Depression au dessus du jardin*, and quotes again the line from *The Threepenny Opera* which closed *Circus Maximus*.

The Charm of Innocence

A counterpoint to *Bishonen*, this song masterfully relates the life story of a character much like Dorian Gray, who finds that whatever activity he engages in, he remains "innocent", a fact which in some ways he finds a burden. In the opening chorus he describes his immaculate state as both a crown of thorns and an albatross, but also, sometimes, a rabbit's foot or good luck charm. As in *Bishonen*, and the album in general, the chorus is a lush soundscape, with the verse a quietly spoken monologue accompanied by plucked guitar. The character in this song goes to a private school but is aroused by girls he meets at the weekends. However, when able to "corner a stranger with nakedness" – specifically au-pairs paid to look after him, he is ashamed to be naked and considers himself a prude.

These contradictions continue throughout his life, whether photographing women whose veins make them look like "blue cheese", or finding girls who will "let him try anything just to find out how it felt". He describes losing his virginity in a room with garish decoration, where "paisley patterns witnessed an abortion". Momus is of course from Paisley, so this could be a reference to an actual location, this could be autobiographical, but who knows? The narrator joins the army, and thereafter ends up pimping out Algerian prostitutes in the 18th Arrondissement of Paris, which is a distinctly Brel-esque touch.

Following an instrumental break, the character talks of the future, of sitting by a fire and "twitching the lace as the schoolgirls go past", while reading the Georges Bataille novels which have influenced this song, and waiting to die. He bemoans the way in which his actions have escalated, as he engages in more and more lurid activity hoping it will end his innocence:

I thought it would end with the first obscene phone call,
the second professional kill
but somehow detached from my actual behaviour
this innocence burdens me still.

In a direct reference to Oscar Wilde's only novel, he ends the song in his attic, painting out the blush in his self-portrait and painting in the crow's feet which he should have. A great narrative song, influenced by St Augustine, by Mishima once more and potentially by Kierkegaard in its depiction of a seductive and illusory sense of innocence.

The Angels are Voyeurs

We zoom out again, watching the angels, invigorated by our stories and our self-destruction, pleasure themselves, with their ejecta forming new celestial bodies more attractive to behold.

The pervert and his angels hide amongst the stars and watch
And as we blow ourselves to bits the angels pump their cocks
Their semen flows across the sky and forms new milky wheys

And somewhere in some galaxy in less than seven days
They make a planet more curvaceous and much sexier than ours
Full of bigger sinners, More worthy of voyeurs

A quiet end to the album, with a chord sequence very reminiscent of early Genesis in my humble opinion (unintentionally and not a criticism!) and rounding the concept off perfectly. This album gained positive critical reviews and seemed to indicate a turning point for Momus: a critical mass gathered, and a sufficiently commercial release would push the artist into the mainstream. Accordingly, a potential hit single was to follow. This would be *The Hairstyle of the Devil,* Momus' most well-known track at the time.

Inexplicable Charisma...#9 The Hairstyle of the Devil

Released in March 1989, this was the first Creation Records single to reach the top 100; it reached No. 2 in the independent charts and was DJ Steve Wright's Record of the Week on BBC Radio 1 daytime. The cover shows Momus as the Devil of the title, receiving the hairstyle of the title.

The year 1988 saw Momus tour with Felt, Alan McGee's Biff Bang Pow and The Beloved, who were a dance/pop act with an acid-house sound absolutely of the time. When Biff Bang Pow dropped out of a tour, The Shamen took their place, right at the time they were changing from a psychedelic rock band influenced by the 13th Floor Elevators to an acid-house group who would shortly have a massive hit with *Progen* (*Move any Mountain*).

Momus eschewed any direct involvement with the psychedelic movement, did not take drugs and yet was clearly influenced by the musical shift taking place. When he returned home from touring *Tender Pervert*, he returned to Scarf Studio in Mile End with the engineer Nigel Palmer and worked on a new track heavily influenced by house and Detroit techno.

The resultant track required lyrics, and Momus told the very personal story of a love triangle between himself, a promoter working for Factory Records called Nicki Kefalas (who was actually issued the label asset number FAC161) and Martin Heath, the founder of Rhythm King records (who had signed among others The Beatmasters and S-Express). Each male in the triangle hears about the other from the girl, and becomes fascinated with "the inexplicable charisma of the rival".

The music uses samples from Kevin Saunderson and has a propulsive dance beat. The tune was based on a revision of the chord sequence from a Charles Aznavour song *Yesterday when I was Young*, via a cover version by New York singer Little Annie, from her album *Jackomo*. The production is superb and seems clinically designed to be a hit. There are various mixes, including the 7″ version mixed by The Grid (Dave Ball/Richard Norris), the 12″ version and an album version included on the CD release of *Don't Stop the Night*. The song was a turntable hit, played by Radio 1, a success on the independent charts and a notable calling-card for Creation. It even breached the top 100 Official Chart of the time. Momus returned to the studio shortly after to work on a follow up, which would become the song *Lord of the Dance*. This would not be released as a single, however, and thereafter Momus and another recording engineer, Doug Martin, moved into Spike Studio to complete the next album.

Why was *Hairstyle of the Devil* not a bigger hit? Momus himself points out the coldness of the lyrics, the reliance on wordplay and wit without the benefit of warmth and empathy that later artists such as Jarvis Cocker would have. There is an element of misogyny in the lyrics too, the female in the relationship is told "shut up, don't answer back" by at least one man in the triangle. Momus has said since that "…the 'misogyny' in the line 'Shut up, don't answer back' is meant to show that curiosity about the third party in a triangle is held in an unstable balance with pain. The character both does and doesn't want to know about his rival."

Momus as a character is not very relatable to a general audience, not like the East End lads done good of the Pet Shop Boys, nor the working-class heroes of the Human League, Pulp or Suede, and clearly not a Detroit techno wizard. It is also fair to say that the presence of Nicki Kefalas on the cover does not detract enough from the visage of Momus, who may simply not have been conventionally attractive enough for a general pop audience of the time. And in case you are wondering, Beck apparently never heard it. The intention for this song to have greater success seems evidenced for me by the profusion of hooks, by the forcefulness of the chorus and the fact that although utilising a minor key, the melody and chord sequence are inclined to resolve in a pleasing way. Listen to the recording at about 3′ 20″; note how the ascending portamento effect reaches the high tone you would expect it to and contrast this with the unresolved endings of *Islington John* or *In the Sanatorium,* or the teasing swirling of strings in later song *Voyager*: this song aims to please, to have what Momus would later describe as "catnip".

The single version of *Hairstyle of the Devil* was backed with *Amongst Women Only,* which was included on the album and will be discussed there. The 12″ version also included the track *Monsters of Love,* which would be included on the 1990 compilation of the same name.

I've Watched All Your Desire...#10 Don't Stop the Night

Don't Stop the Night was recorded after *Hairstyle of the Devil* and *Lord of the Dance,* at the Spike in London with engineer Doug Martin, and released in November 1989. The album was originally envisaged as a concept album about different forms of (mainly sexual) abuse: abuse of patients by doctors, students by teachers, the working class by the upper class etc. The album was to be called *Sexual Crimes of the Professional Classes,* but in the end *Don't Stop the Night* was taken from one of the song titles. The album became a more generalised meditation on the 80s, a final farewell to the decade's greed, overwhelming capitalism and sexual promiscuity. This is by some degree the most "British" Momus album, and the clearest stab at pop fame and fortune his career would entertain.

The cover features Momus in close-up, using black and white to suggest a cold, clinical and emotionless "1980s" man, with white shirt and wristwatch. The lettering of Momus itself is large, capitalised and colourful, the back and inner sleeves have more colourful versions of Momus' face, with his hands cupped over his ears, less to hear no evil, than to hear it more clearly. The photographer is Michael Daks and the overall sleeve design by Vici MacDonald. No-one else is credited on the CD or album cover that I have. Importantly perhaps, the lyrics are included, along with a disclaimer, "All characters are fictitious and any resemblance to persons living or dead is entirely coincidental", the effect of which is of course to immediately make you wonder who the songs are about. I am sure that will not be an issue. Also, the CD includes the single mix of *Hairstyle of the Devil,* which is certainly about real people, as previously discussed.

Trust Me, I'm a Doctor

The original theme of professional misconduct is immediately apparent. This doctor is jaded, bored, disinterested in life and sexuality and seems to be abusing his position almost out of a perverse sense of duty more than desire. He has "long since lost all interest in feelings of pleasure and pain" but while he will never feel such things again, there is "still hope for you". This is if the actress who is his patient pulls through, and he suggests this may work "if we operate immediately". There seems to be no hope for the doctor himself, although he begs his patient to help him "break this frozen sea within", a reference to Kafka's exhortation to take an axe to our internal ice rinks. Given that "operate" is almost certainly a coded reference to the sexual abuse that is taking place, we are fully in the realm of the 80s psychopath here such as Patrick Bateman or (in many people's opinion) Ferris Bueller.

Musically, this continues the theme apparent on *Hairstyle* of disco/techno. A strident beat is mixed with cold keyboard and piano sounds and a discordant guitar blasts accompanying chords at odds with the calm delivery of the lyrics. There is even a guitar solo, a clean and cold line scything icily through the surgery, influenced by the work of Magazine and post-punk in general, with that Detroit influence throbbing in the bass. The squelchy synth effects and R2D2/*Sooty and Sweep* style clicks, beeps and whistles make the finale of the song sonically very satisfying, perhaps representing as they do the equipment the doctor has switched on for his "operation". The track feels very machine like, as if we are witnessing the very clockwork mechanism of the decade.

Right Hand Heart

A version of this song had already been included in acoustic form on *Tender Pervert* for the CD release, but this is the version Momus considers canon. A story of sexual sickness: a man so debauched in himself that he cannot bring himself to couple with a girl who has dextrocardia. This is of course because he has a right-hand heart himself. Instead he watches her have sex with a boy "with no heart at all"; Momus on his website describes this new character as something like Robert Mapplethorpe's photograph *Man in a Polyester Suit*. It's funky and sample driven (from Gilbert O'Sullivan's *I'm a writer…not a fighter*) and the spoken sections become quite disorienting with the filters that have been applied. It sounds like the description of a million over-privileged parties in London at the time. As in many of the songs on this album, there is probably nothing more sickening on here than happens in upper class shindigs every day. This song is purportedly akin to Prince's songs from his infamous *Black* album, so much a spiritual twin to this album.

Lord of the Dance

The follow up to *Hairstyle of the Devil* was not, in the end, released as a single, perhaps because it is lacking the hooks and the lyrical gravitas of the former. *Lord of the Dance* uses bhangra beats – then a more obscure sub-culture – to bolster lyrics re-inventing all religious deities as a "beautiful woman" or possibly a drag-queen who rules the world as if it were a gay disco. Both Buddhist and Christian quotations are used to illustrate the idea of religion as a nightclub: "In the beautiful fever of the disco diva/She has come to set you free". Interestingly perhaps, we are told that "ecstasy is transitory": possibly a slight dig at rave culture. The lyrics also refer to "the end of the world" and the second coming of the Messiah at Armageddon: apparently a reference to the spoken word piece *The Last Days of Mankind* by Karl Krauss.

Lifestyles of the Rich and Famous

Battle not with monsters…

Stock Aitken and Waterman were three record producers

who, working together, had created a hit factory for the 80s. They churned out hit after hit to a fairly set formula and sound. In 1989 alone they were responsible for six UK number 1 singles, including those by Jason Donovan and Sonia. They also wrote early hits for Kylie Minogue and created the production for Dead or Alive's *You Spin Me Round* among many others. They were, of course, heavily parodied by artists such as the Jamms/KLF (*Kylie said to Jason*) and Morris Minor and the Majors (*This is the Chorus*). In *Lifestyles*…Momus sought to parody and skewer the sound and more importantly the attitude of 80s music and lifestyle, by telling the story of a guy who has lost out to someone more successful, more grasping and greedy, and who can only watch while the girls flock to this horrendous winner. The opening lines immediately capture the empty existence:

Photographs by the paparazzi
Joyrides in his Maserati
Invites from every arty fashion victim
To every warehouse party

The narrator is aware he has lost his girl to the new and more successful (richer) guy, but is happy to watch, perhaps thinking he deserves to lose: this is the 80s after all:

And I've watched all your desire
With fascination
Watched its satisfaction.

He has been reading: Martin Amis, Brett Easton Ellis and other key 80s texts related to sociopathic behaviour. In the chorus Momus namechecks those he believes responsible for the mess: Stock, Aitken, Waterman, Margaret Thatcher and Sigmund Freud.

"I'm wrong the world is right" becomes a key phrase, spoken

contemporaneously with Thatcher's pronouncement that there is "no such thing as society". So you are on your own, you are wrong to dislike the situation, and you had better not rebel. And finally, "when you're up, everybody wants your babies", or rather, legal access to your money. Goodbye to the 80s indeed...

This song succeeds astoundingly well, to the extent that it could be a SAW production. It could have been a hit! Musically it is like a postcard straight from 1989; this is exactly what was in the charts at the time. The choppy keyboards, the firework type effects, the *Rite of Spring* orchestral sample stabbing at your eardrum and the relentless chirpiness...God I hated this type of music at the time. Love this though.

How Do You Find My Sister?

There was a lot of sleaze in late 80s Britain. You could hardly pick up a paper without reading about an auto-erotic asphyxiation, a toe-sucking scandal or accusations of soliciting sex with prostitutes, usually involving arguments about what was in brown paper envelopes handed to sex workers. Members of Parliament and bankers featured prominently in all this, and 1989 was also the year when the film *Scandal* was released, which focused on the Christine Keeler/Profumo affair which contributed to the downfall of a British government of the 60s. The Pet Shop Boys were involved in the soundtrack of *Scandal*. So this song, based on a comic song by Serge Gainsbourg, is a tale of revenge across classes. The working-class narrator has raised – from birth – his sister Lulu to be an escort to the rich and famous. "Lulu" is the name of a similar character in Frank Wedekind's work known as the *Lulu* plays, where she is whipped across the stage by a ringmaster (as in this song), and she also inspired the character played by Louise Brooks in the silent film *Pandora's Box* (1929) as well as the album *Lulu* (2011) by Lou Reed and Metallica.

Lulu's first customer is Johnson – about whom we know nothing further. Her next customer is a Tory whip called

Finlayson from Woking.

Once he has enough dirt on all these disgusting people, the blackmail begins, resulting in sexual depravity: "Kneel before me, kiss it, call me sir." Is he now as bad as those he is punishing? Possibly. One of the victims (of whom he quaintly has a Polaroid picture) is a Mr Henrik Issinger. This, possibly, is the reason for including the carefully printed lyrics and the disclaimer quoted previously.

This is a slower, still "squelchy" sounding song, with an LL Cool J sample, and shouts of "DJ" and "Ringmaster" related to the Wedekind text above. It's clearly arranged as a comic song, with "ba" backing vocals multi-tracked by Momus, but although comic, the character and all of his victims are horrific people, and the true victim poor Lulu, who must be "flushed out once a week by a quack down Harley Street". This ends side one of the vinyl album.

The CD includes *Hairstyle of the Devil* here, the single mix. As discussed in the previous entry, this is a quintessential 80s pop song, which could have been a bigger hit, but understandably was not. It certainly fits in with the coldness of the protagonist of *How do you find my sister* and with the perverse relationships to be found on side two of the album.

Don't Stop the Night

A new version of *Ballad of the Barrel Organist* from the first Momus EP, *The Beast with 3 Backs*. It is telling that this new, commercially-minded Momus feels the need to reinvent such an early song for the new paradigm. Sordid details following…

The song certainly fits with the themes of the album, featuring a threesome somewhat like that depicted in *Hairstyle of the Devil*, and utilising samples from 70s disco and Sylvester to create a danceable solution to the 80s. It is remarkably cheerful sounding given the lyrics about voyeurism and cuckolding, and an intruder stares through wardrobe doors somewhat like the narrator in Pulp's *Babies*. The ending is particularly spritely and eminently enjoyable.

Amongst Women Only

The narrator of this song has been abandoned by his girlfriend for his "clumsy butter fingers" and "brutal masculinity", but as consolation, or revenge, or both, he fantasises about her masturbating by herself or "amongst women only". It is a song of word play with swirling string sounds that mimic the "harem full of eastern promiscuity" that she now lives in in his mind. We have – not for the first time – the sounds of a woman pleasuring herself to accompany this, as she "arouses herself to her crisis herself". Momus describes the song as correcting the misogyny of previous songs, however to me it really just describes the narrator controlling his ex-girlfriend's behaviour in the only way he can – in his fantasies, and in one of the most clichéd scenarios men can muster, in fact it puts me in mind of this. It is a pretty song, though, and the break down in the middle while the imaginary girlfriend "goes on for hours" achieves the erotic atmosphere it aspires to.

The Guitar Lesson

Inspired by Balthus' painting *The Guitar Lesson* of 1934, where the abuser is a female guitar teacher, this tells the story of a paedophile guitar teacher and a 12-year-old female student. The music is a soft arpeggio again, with a sequence borrowed from Léo Ferré's song *Avec Le Temps*, a song of regret at lost loves and opportunities. The music also sounds like a lesson, a practice piece deceptive in its simplicity for the student. The girl is described in terms which are quite worrying…

Distant eyes full of space
In her posture no trace of coquette
No defiance

These lines suggest she has given up resistance, that this has happened before, maybe many times. Her mother comes into the room, feels a chill, perhaps sensing something is wrong, and leaves even as the student "looks forlorn". As the lesson progresses there are hints that this relationship is not quite right, as the teacher "gently corrects the curve of her back" and draws behind her ear "a few strands of hair gone astray".

After the lesson is done, she shows him her bracelet, then they sit together, where the line is crossed with one of the most disturbing lyrics in pop music:

> *And touching the place where her breasts will be I press my hand flat.*

The girl then sits on his lap and her skirt "travels up under my palm"; however, she remains calm "as if listening to the distant sound of a burglar alarm", which is replicated by synth effects at this point, a jarring noise cutting into the beauty of the underlying music and stabbing into our ears the reality of what is happening in the narrative.

The narrator then seems to be unable to describe what happened next, just that:

> *Now, from afar, it seems to resemble*
> *A strange composition in oil*
> *Of a man, a guitar, and an innocent little girl.*

That he is aware of her innocence somehow makes the character more chilling; he is fully aware of the damage he is doing. The music fades out with a martial beat replacing the sound effects and keyboards, finally leaving just the arpeggio playing on a synthesised guitar, which stops abruptly.

For a potentially mainstream pop performer to sing on a topic of this nature, and to moreover place himself in the role of the abuser, is either very brave or very foolish. To connect oneself to this imagery in the mind of the public you would have to have a cavalier attitude, at best, to your potential chart success: or at worst, complete indifference. I am not sure which it is in this case, but perhaps the Faustian pact that would be necessary for fame, and the requirement to write ten more *Lifestyles of the Rich and Famous* every year was no longer Momus' idea of a good time. The greater exposure to the vapidity and hypocrisy of the music industry he had by now surely experienced may have engendered a desire to bite the hand that fed him. This would certainly explain the odder lyrics on this album and (more to the point) the entire next album.

There is a relatively high-profile cover version of *The Guitar Lesson* by Steven Wilson (lead singer of Porcupine Tree). One of a surprising number of links between Momus and progressive rock! The cover version is from his album actually called *Cover Version* released in 2014 which couples various songs to Wilson's own compositions, except with this Momus song, which is linked to another cover version of the Folk song *The Unquiet Grave*.

The Cabriolet

Having removed the future career option of guitar teacher, Momus, in a prescient move, went on to ensure he would never be called upon as an Uber Driver.

The Cabriolet started its life on a demo tape called *Samizdat* as a daft song about Boy George. The drama and tension within the chorus and bridge lent themselves more appropriately, however, to this life and death tale. As Momus drives home from a party with a girl he is not interested in, he accidentally drives off the road and crashes his Cabriolet. The girl is good-looking and he cannot explain why he does not find her as attractive as everyone else seems to. This changes after the crash. As she lies dead and he lies badly injured:

Your face unstained, unharmed but drained pale
Is suddenly more strange and beautiful
than anything I've ever seen or ever will.

Finally, in the extremis of death, he can experience something he has never felt before:

In the sudden shock of silence,
with the morning star above you
Lying bizarre in the wreck of my car …
… I love you.

This statement of love is all the more shocking not only because he is in love with a corpse, but because after all the lies, cheating, abuse and perversion we have encountered on the album, this is finally genuine; he loves her, truly, and this is the most transgressive thing of all.

The music for this is beautiful, a moving chord sequence with a dramatic progression and closing fade that perfectly fits the scene that is being described.

The influences on this lyric seem to include J.G. Ballard's novel *Crash* (characters who are sexually aroused by/in car crashes), *Warm Leatherette* by The Normal, *The Girl with the Patent Leather Face* by Soft Cell, and *Permafrost* by Magazine, all of which are worth exploring.

Shaftesbury Avenue

A burst of traffic noise and synth takes us into the heart of London, where Momus is chatting us up and inviting us to a café round the corner. Of course you would go; the trip we take through London takes us through the West End with its "Tottenham Hotspurs", "Japs and Prunes", and "Tarts with faces like the Phantom of the Opera" and on into Chinatown, onto Gerrard Street where Momus wishes he could speak

Cantonese or Vietnamese in order to seduce those girls as well. More charitably, this song is about the opening-up of London, and the first indication of Momus moving into the wider world. He certainly thinks that this globalisation is a positive thing. In an interview with Miranda Sawyer for Select magazine, a couple of years later in 1994, he said:

> …I get on a tube train and suddenly it fills up with all these ugly people and I think, what are all these ugly people doing and then I realise it's a football crowd. And they all have an IQ of about 80. I hate to point this out, but the bulk of football fans are stupid. They can't help it...they're the spawn of the industrial revolution...I'm going to sound like an awful geneticist, but there's a lot of poor genetic stock around and we have to filter it and we have to interbreed so we get better and higher genetic stock. When you see people of mixed origin they're often more intelligent. They might have to learn two different languages and they have to live in two worlds and understand the cultural relativism that people just don't understand if they've grown up in one culture. People from different backgrounds should mix and their eyes would be opened.

I am pretty sure that to some extent Momus is deliberately setting out to shock here, in a slightly self-destructive way, but in many respects, I think he is generally correct to say that mixing with other cultures does benefit everyone involved, as does living abroad. The East would beckon for Momus later, so the song seems to predict some aspects of his future in this sense.

The song is another slab of 80s pop: the chorus is a real earworm, and that orchestral hit effect is employed wholesale. This could easily be a Pet Shop Boys song, with a similar overblown production and cinematic approach. But even as he sings of Kiss FM, the BBC and British sleaze, you feel that this is a farewell to the 80s and to this style of music.

Following the relative commercial failure of both *Hairstyle of the Devil* and *Don't Stop the Night*, Momus lost some faith with Britain and with Creation Records – a mutual decline certainly. He became in his own words "an internal exile" and moved away from pastiche of current pop trends into a world more inspired by French and European artists, as well as electronic and experimental sounds. In the meantime, a compilation album was released by Creation Records, which included two new tracks.

Why Should They Admire Us?...#11 Monsters of Love

I am 99 per cent certain that the 1990 album *Monsters of Love: Singles 1985–1990* was the first album I obtained by Momus, from an independent music store in Canterbury and on vinyl, in 1992. Having heard *Nicky* on the radio, that makes *Morality is Vanity* the second Momus song I heard, and the one which sealed my fate. The fact that the same store sold cassette albums for £5 and had a reasonable stock of Momus was a bonus; I thus obtained *Don't Stop the Night* and *Voyager*. The other early albums took longer to acquire; I had to order them from the chain store Our Price and they were among my earliest CD purchases.

It feels like Momus was marking time at this point till the next album. He retreated somewhat from the British indie scene and moved into a flat in Cleveland Street, London. Perhaps Creation had lost faith a little following the lack of commercial success from *Don't Stop the Night*, perhaps Momus was disenchanted. At any rate he now wrote and worked in an atmosphere of French and continental pop, equipped with an Atari ST 1040 and Akai S900 Sampler, and worked on, among other things, his new project which would become *Hippopotamomus*.

In the meantime, Creation released a compilation of his work in June 1990. The sleeve design is by Thomi Wroblewski, who also did the *Tender Pervert* cover: It's fairly abstract and the imagery suggests the threesomes sung about on the first EP, a ballerina Thomi knew, revolving around what seems to be a set of compass points in front of an orange planet or sun.

To call it a "Singles" compilation is a little misleading; the album contains two EPs totalling six songs, two new songs and one single with its B-side.

The album opens with a "new" song which I suspect existed in some form for many years: *Morality is Vanity*. This song absolutely hooked me. The form is music hall mixed with burlesque, and the theme is that the moral people of this world parade their morality as a cloak in the same way that the immoral display their vices:

Seven million people died in the great war
A bout of influenza quadrupled that score
Why pimp to posterity?
Why should they admire us?
All the heroes of Valhalla weigh less than a virus.

There is a sample of how concise, well-crafted and laser sharp the lyrics of this song are. That verse was read out by Dr Ben Goldacre on the BBC Radio 4 show *Quote, Unquote* as an example of a positive representation of science in song.

The discussion of crime as a fashion, of morality as a fashion just as vacuous, pricks the self-aggrandising of those who are, apparently, "moral", but are no better than criminals in their parading of the habits they adopt. The message is that all behaviours are equally selfish in intent. The *Cave of the Golden Calf* that is mentioned was a real and infamous cabaret which existed in Heddon Street, London shortly before World War 1.

Purely because of this song I sought out all of Momus' earlier work. Purely because of *Hairstyle* I sought out the latter work. *Morality is Vanity* is followed by the three songs from *Beast with 3 Backs* and the three songs from *Murderers, The Hope of Women*.

The other "new" song is *Gilda*. Although it was written for a French singer called Jil Kaplan, I can find no evidence she recorded it. This is a straightforward song about the character of Gilda who is a femme fatale played by Rita Hayworth in the film of the same name. It uses quotes from the film and is again in a music-hall idiom. Hate can be a very exciting emotion, she says. Your own reaction to the song is purely predicated on your knowledge and interest in the original film.

Gilda is followed by a mix of *Hairstyle of the Devil*. It is a shorter version than that on the album. It suffers from the edit and lacks the breakdown section I discussed in the entry on that song.

The compilation ends with the B-Side to *Hairstyle*: *Monsters of Love*. This is the third song, after *Nicky* and *Morality is Vanity*, which completely sold me to Momus. Or sold Momus to me, whichever way you wish to put it.

I do not even know why the song affects me so much. It starts with a simple bass figure that for some reason is an earworm for me; it suggests something important is happening, I think, something at least that requires attention. It is cinematic, in the same way that Monty Norman's bass intro to Bond films suggests something important is coming. The song is about a client meeting with a prostitute in a Marrakesh hotel room – I think. But the description suggests much more. Firstly, the whole middle eastern scenario brought to mind for me the scenes in *Hellraiser* where the puzzle box which summons Cenobites is sold to unwitting victims…"what's your pleasure?"

Moreover, the lady involved seems to have some kind of preternatural power. Speaking of *Hellraiser*, in Clive Barker's short story *Jacqueline Ess: Her will and testament*, he writes about a bored housewife who gains the power to manipulate matter to her whim. When this power becomes overwhelming, she commits suicide while making love by sharpening her lover's member to a point in order to pierce her heart. The lady in this song is compared to a spider releasing a fly, and I feel she is possessed of power herself. The act of lovemaking with her is described in perverse terms. The result of coupling with her is an insane breed of animal:

From the siesta of Reason come monsters of love
The horse-lizard, the lamb-badger
The thrush-lemur, the wildcat-gazelle

The crow-monkey, the bat-jaguar
The dog-dromedary, the slug-whale.

This lyrical monstrousness is accompanied by washes of synthesiser noise and an effect something like a water-gong being struck to emphasise the drama of the events unfolding. A zither sound is used to further suggest "otherness".

There was no way, on hearing this album, that I was not going to track down and consume whatever Momus albums I could. It was interesting, intellectual, possibly in ways I did not then or now understand, and sometimes felt relevant to my own (lack of) love life.

Writing a song for a French singer was very much the route Momus took at this point. For his next album, whether intentional or not, he would not pursue the commercialism that *Don't Stop the Night* had seemingly worshipped. It could be argued that the next album blocked off any such avenues, in the UK at least; it was to be called *Hippopotamomus*.

The Prosecution Rests its Case…#12 Hippopotamomus

Between *Don't Stop the Night* and the release of *Hippopotamomus* in 1991, a considerable amount changed. The decade was new, the government was new and Thatcher-free (although still Conservative), the Berlin Wall had fallen and the Soviet block was dissolved. Creation Records, while still nominally supporting Momus, was increasingly drug-orientated and Momus' failure to have a commercial hit was probably a factor in the decline of his relationship with the label. Attempts to move to Mute Records fell through, and Momus worked in his flat on the next album with minimal involvement from the label, listening to Gainsbourg, Mylene Farmer and British trip-hop and acid jazz.

Rather than a jaded view of perversion and sexuality, the new album would celebrate sensuality and take a more jocular, even joyful attitude to a liberated world view. This perspective would be European in style and take its philosophical cues from French intellectualism and eroticism. The main musical influence would be *Vu de l'extérieur*, a 1973 album by Serge Gainsbourg (who died in 1991), which is a concept album with childish, sexual and scatological jokes and themes. In particular, the album includes a track called *Hippopodame* about an encounter with a larger lady lyrically compared to a hippo, and another song called *Pamela Popo* which plays with a dual meaning of Popo as faeces. The other decision taken by Momus was to present the whole project as if it were aimed at children – not actual children, of course, but the child within each person listening:

"…the part of us that refuses guilt, that plays with mud pies, that soils its nappy, that loves to suck and be sucked".

This came across, unfortunately, as if the intention were to create an album of nursery rhymes and songs about sex. The use of childish themes, lyrics and tunes helped to foment this misunderstanding and is one of the reasons the album received 0/10 from the NME when reviewed by Betty Page. But by no means the only reason: this is one of the most misunderstood albums in the Momus discography and had a wide range of responses and critiques, from extremely positive to… not. I can only imagine what Alan McGee's response was when first presented with the completed album.

The first problem was possibly the flat it was recorded in, described by Momus as a "bubble", which suggests that outside influence, and critique, was lacking. And by "outside" I mean outside the music industry. Very few people would get the reference to Gainsbourg in the album title, for instance, and without that understanding I can imagine most members of the public, on seeing the album title, rejecting any thought of listening to it. Puns in album titles are not generally harbingers of greatness. There are other creative decisions on the album that, while artistically valid, are, commercially speaking, headscratchers. Firstly, the cover. Designed by Me Company (founded by Paul White) it features the album name (odd decision #1 in itself) in a modern capitalised font, with the artist name not in bold so it doesn't stand out (odd decision #2) over an image of the Michelin Man (odd decision #3) which does have a vaguely hippo like face which is just going to confuse a casual viewer more (odd decision #4), causing them to ask: why the Michelin Man? Why "Hippo"? What is the connection and why is the album just called Hippopotamus? Why have they spelled Hippopotamus incorrectly? Who is it by? I may, of course, be underestimating the general public. They are, after all, well known for making good decisions.

Of course, the Michelin Man – whose "real" name is Bibendum – is used because there is a song of the same name, which we will discuss later. The CD cover includes further information about the album; it was partly completed by Doug Martin at The Spike, like the previous recordings. Douglas Benford (who provided the drum machine on *The Poison Boyfriend*) provides "wiggly electronic noise" under his DJ/remix moniker of Lovecut DB.

"Preacher" Harry Powell provides the baritone on the title track. Since "Reverend" Harry Powell is the killer in Charles Laughton's film *The Night of the Hunter*, this is really the pseudonym of singer Ian Smith, who recorded some material on the label Golden Pathway under the Preacher name in the 80s. Momus provided keyboards for some of his tracks and his appearance here is reciprocal.

Backing vocals are provided by Vicky Cassady, Zoe Pascale and Tammy Yoseloff. The guitar soloing is provided by Noko (Norman Fisher-Jones), who played alongside Howard Devoto in the band Luxuria. The whole album is dedicated to Gainsbourg. We also get a mention of the lyrics book *Lusts of a Moron*.

His new agent, Angie Somerside, is credited, and her address given, and even more interesting, we get the following: "Complaints: 127 Cleveland Street, London W1P 5PL".

Since this is the actual address of the flat, this suggests that 1) Complaints were expected; 2) Complaints were welcome; 3) Any other kind of mail and fan visits (preferably female, no doubt) were welcome. This address was how I got onto some form of fan mailing list, through which I obtained a live compilation video in 1993. (Now, sorrowfully, long gone, lost in an attic somewhere no doubt being rediscovered at Christmas by David Bowie or Mel Smith).

Hippopotamomus

Squelchy noises: mud and muck, oomska, Preacher Harry provides baritone punctuation of the title and the name of the volcano Popocatepetl; Flanders and Swann provide the ghost of music hall past. Momus lustily and in a bass voice full of phlegm and God knows what fluids delivers the story of a hippo, who "loves only disgusting things". As he fucks a fellow hippo the volcano erupts and seals him with the other hippo, just like the bodies at Pompeii. After what is presumably a long time he is found by scientists and along with his fuckee displayed at the Natural History Museum in an exhibition labelled "copulating artiodactyl mammals". So far, a twisted Gary Larson cartoon. This is a silly, but catchy, song, with a great beat and cool synth noises. But what makes it a Momus song, what makes it HippopotaMOMUS, is the last verse:

So press your nose against the glass of the case of the
Hippopotamomus
Lithe, wriggling schoolgirl, blowing kisses, making eyes
So blithely unaware, as you snigger at my lust
You'll be in this position by and by

This discussion of the erosion and eradication of innocence by circumstance marks out the song and the artist as meaningful. Critics – one in particular – lambasted Momus' use of schoolgirls and the underage in these songs, but in order for them to work, innocence has to be deployed as the other, innocence in all these songs is the perversion that cannot be countenanced. Sooner or later, by or by, that schoolgirl will be in that position. That is not a perverse boast on the Hippopotamomus' part. He cannot have anything to do with it, he is just stating a fact. As night follows day, the girl will become a woman, and she will mirror what she has laughed at in the reflection of the glass surrounding the Hippopotamomus and his mate; and find the source of the child.

I Ate a Girl Right Up

In 1991 Jonathan Demme directed *The Silence of the Lambs* based on a novel by Thomas Harris about Clarice Starling, an FBI agent who must enlist the help of a cannibalistic monster named Hannibal Lecter to help her track a serial killer. A huge hit and Oscar winner.

Now imagine in that same year writing a song about a man

eating a girl "right up", and NOT basing it on that film, but instead on a book by Christian Enzensberger called *Smut, An Anatomy of Dirt* (1972). This book has a philosophy of dirt as a marker of history, and moreover, that fascist movements are obsessed with cleanliness, and, therefore, to wallow in, consume and digest dirt is a solution to fascism.

You will not be surprised to learn that pretty much everyone who reviewed this album assumed this song was about cannibalism and compared it to Hannibal Lecter. Surprisingly, few music critics had read Enzensberger's work.

This is a fun song: the opening sound effect could be a hippo burping, then something which could be a fax machine receiving, then a bouncy bass line apparently mixed from a Game Boy, and the song begins. The narrator could be Bibendum, or any god of debauchery, as he asks forgiveness for eating a girl up not "just because I was hungry", and he is not really sorry. This is the sexual being as child, wanting to fill itself up with sweets and gaining psycho-sexual pleasure from consumption. He understands the revulsion that lines such as:

I guzzled down her bowels, all squidgy
I gobbled up her breasts and tummy

will generate, but denies he is a cannibal. He does this because:

Everybody needs from time to time
To remember the fact that they're an animal
To cross the line dividing clean from dirty.

The song only discusses the consumption of the girl, not killing her or the question of consent. It is not about killing; it is about consuming and wallowing in our own filth. How the girl's body became...available...is not relevant.

In the NME review of 6/7/91, Betty Page wrote:

> But then we must suffer *I Ate A Girl Right Up*, Momus' response to American Psycho, a sort of polite sicko, a very English have-a-cuppa cannibal. "I don't know what came over me," he recites tweely. "I'd do it all again, it was yummy". Imagine Neil Tennant as Jack The Ripper and there you have it. Sorry. Not funny, not ironic – violence against women is not a subject for humorous treatment.

As respondents pointed out, as Momus would point out himself, this missed the point entirely. It is not a psycho or killer who is described. It is not about literal cannibalism, and it is not about violence against women. The violence is against civilisation, or against society. The timing, though, as discussed above, was unfortunate.

Never mind, though; if nothing else, this is an experiment with new sounds and an attempt to integrate new technologies into the music.

Michelin Man/a.k.a Made of Rubber

Another jokey, sex-driven song. Influenced by Chuck Berry and his *Ding-A-Ling* style doo-wop innuendo fests. The Michelin Man himself, Bibendum, an inflatable potential sex-doll was ideal for a bouncy and cheesy pop song. Literally "pneumatic" like the sexualised characters in Huxley's *Brave New World,* and champion of consumption himself with his Michelin restaurants, the Michelin Man with his redesigned hippo face was an ideal mascot for Momus' purposes. This song itself starts with a bass line similar to that in Cameo's *Word Up,* and describes a date between the Michelin Man and Josephine Baker, a French dancer, singer, Resistance-era spy and civil rights activist. She must *Pump It Up* (presumably a reference to Technotronic's hit *Pump up the Jam* or the M/A/R/R/S hit *Pump up the Volume*) in order to use the Michelin Man until her bed is "junk".

Momus had used, or mentioned, brand names before in his

songs, but he had never incorporated a company mascot into a sex scene. *The Beast with 3 Backs* did not include a ménage à trois between Snap, Crackle and Pop, for instance. The reason for this is that companies tend to be rather protective of their brands: and in this case, the Michelin Man logo was both used on the cover, and in the name of a song. He may as well have called the album Mickey Momouse and sung about a pair of unnaturally large ears with their enveloping lobes.

So at some point the song came to the attention of Michelin and was discussed at what must have been a very surreal board meeting where they read the lyrics out. Legal action was, not surprisingly, threatened. Alan McGee called Momus in for one of their regular meetings and they agreed to remove the song and alter the cover. In fact as I understand things, all remaining copies were destroyed. Which is why my 50p copy in Peterborough 4 years later is so surprising.

The album was re-released with the offending song removed and a new but no less confusing cover, which featured a hippo's face in cartoonish form, but no Bibendum.

A Dull Documentary

The song which totally sickened Betty Page owing to its narrative, and which is, it must be said, quite irritating to listen to from a sonic viewpoint.

A babysitter invites her boyfriend round and they have sex "by the light of a dull documentary"; apparently this was another song intended for the BBC album. The controversial aspect of the song is that while they are having sex, the little girl they are babysitting walks in and watches:

When you open your thighs to me
I see the little girl stretching her eyes at me.

The narrator recalls when he was five and witnessed something similar. He links this to Freud and his discussion of the "primal scene" – the first time a child witnesses the sex act.

Makes me remember the good things I've seen
And I'll go on providing this spectacle
'Til we come or the little girl goes
Go on providing the rhythm of life

Initially the little girl is playing Chopsticks on the piano and unfortunately this is the tune that accompanies much of the song, thus the irritation. Betty Page said of the song:

> Hero Gainsbourg also had a bit of a "thing" about sex with minors, so Momus starts bringing little girls into his stories. In A Dull Documentary he has sex with a babysitter in front of the telly and carries on when the little girl comes into the room.

This is a gross misrepresentation. The little girl is not involved in the sex; she witnesses it, but the song is about losing innocence through gained knowledge. The first line is about the little girl trying on Mummy's lipstick; entering the adult world, she sees the world she is practicing being a part of. The narrator's own first sexual memory is of people shrieking and laughing, not a negative or abusive experience. Allowing the little girl to see what is happening is part of "the rhythm of life"; a kind of education, twisted, but well-intentioned. Momus has certainly sung about child abuse, but this is not really what is happening here in the way Page is implying.

Nor is it anything new; consider the song *Little Children* sung by Billy J. Kramer in 1964:

Little children, you better not tell what you see
And if you're good I'll give you candy and a quarter

If you're quiet like you ought be
And keep a secret with me

Where was Betty then?

Marquis of Sadness

Enigma had released the single *Sadeness (Part 1)* in 1990, thus the Sadness/De Sade pun was corny already. Nevertheless, De Sade was still terra incognita for most people; his books were still banned in Britain as was *Salo*, Pasolini's version of *120 Days of Sodom*. For Momus, De Sade and French erotic fiction in general was a route to sexual liberation, both personally and for the framework of this album.

Co-sung by then flatmate Vicky, this song is the tale of a new writer in residence at a university who brings all the female poetry students in to read him their "bad but intimate" verses and no doubt to discuss all those erotic French writers such as De Sade, Gide, Paul Verlaine etc. Although a bitter and sad man, the poetry the girls write is evidence "Of our desire to make him desire us". The verses are sung chiefly by Vicky as the girls, the chorus is Momus as the writer in residence:

I'll get along quite nicely in this university
In my little office with its sofa and its key
They'll call on me at all hours for gin and sympathy…

The chorus sung by Momus has that choppy 80s keyboard in the background, otherwise we are in the album's natural territory of video game samples and barping brass synth. The scenario overall is reminiscent of a Malcolm Bradbury novel such as *The History Man*, or the related Radio 3 sitcom *Patterson*.

The girls collapse into giggles at the end, apparently from being tickled; this album seems to employ method acting rather than previous Momus techniques of sonic dissonance or

Brechtian alienation.

Bluestocking

Thematically similar, a song about what we would now term sapiosexuality. A cheeky backing with what sound like spankings coupled with satisfied sighs leads into Momus declaring his love for someone because they are well read and "give head": both physically and intellectually. This type of girl is sometimes called a "Bluestocking" from the eighteenth-century society of the same name. Originally it suggested a frumpy and perhaps sexless person, but that meaning is subverted here and since.

We also get a long list of texts which the girl has read, which could also serve as a primer for Momus' work to date:

> *Ovid, Anais Nin, the Song of Solomon, The Perfumed Garden and Georges Bataille's The Story of the Eye The Petronius Satyricon, the Arabian Nights, the Decameron The Marquis de Sade's 120 Days And Serge Gainsbourg singing songs to Sweet Jane B...... Sacher Masoch and DHL, Portnoy's Complaint and mine as well Frank Harris, The Life and Loves Lusts of a Moron, Wings of a Dove The Latins of the Silver Age The triolets of Paul Verlaine Lautreamont and G. Cabrera Infante Mishima Yukio and Sweet Jane B*

Note the inclusion of Momus' own lyrics book *Lusts of a Moron*. The song ends with a reading of phrases from *The Lover* by Marguerite Duras. This is read by Zoe Pascale (a.k.a Catherine Brouard) of whom Momus said on imomus.livejournal.com:

> it was Catherine who first played me Brassens...and taught me sensual playfulness, and how to explore and share fantasies where anything went. She was my erotic professor and my entrée into French culture, and she had to have a cameo role on this record.

Her reading is certainly erotic, very ASMR if you believe in such things, and brings side one to a satisfactory conclusion following a variable first half.

Ventriloquists and Dolls

This is easily the best song on the album. It essentially throws out the beeping and booping and jokiness and throws down a great bassline, rock drumbeat and atmospheric synth instead. Spooky aerial notes in the background give the impression of a city in the dark and under fog, with the production giving the right sort of flattened/locked-in sound that night-time fog would give. A music-hall performance has finished and a ventriloquist steps out into the night that we can already hear is cold and gets into his Fiesta. A piano steps in to accompany this and establish a sense of drama. Moving into the chorus we get echoing backing vocals and handclaps as well as a machine-gun sound effect punctuating the last line here as the chorus lists pairs that live in symbiosis:

Ventriloquists and dolls
Tailors and their dummies
Moving in parallel worlds
Like wolves and little girls
Gangsters and their molls.

The piano remains for the second verse and a dramatic guitar part by Noko joins in as well, ramping up the tension as we hear about the ventriloquist's flat, filled with unnerving dolls, one in particular:

And dangling from the beams on tangled strings, a marionette
And his carving's been so painstaking it looks for all the world
Like flesh and blood
Realistic to a fault, his dolls are portraits carved in wood Of little girls.

The second chorus is followed by a great, short, angular guitar solo that leads into and merges into the final verse. As the final verse starts the drum beat changes, with the bass drum now on every beat rather than every other, while the bass guitar plays a tight pattern in between each beat. This seems to make the overall song funkier and creates a meter in which the lyric on each bass note is stressed allowing the singer to lay greater emphasis on particular words. We get the unpleasant image of the ventriloquist removing his wooden leg and then:

And though his face is frighteningly ugly
and he takes her by surprise and very fast
The doll he crushes under him immediately agrees
to everything he asks.

Apart from the synth and bass, the instrumentation drops out for the final three words, allowing us to pause and consider the insidious nature of the perversion under discussion, then crashes back in for the final chorus. The music becomes quieter after this, with atmospheric effects taking us back to that city at night, with the fog rolling in, and gunfire in the distance.

A great track, funky, rock orientated, with that manly guitar we were promised and a philosophical discussion hovering: is the ventriloquist doing anything wrong? A painted girl is not a girl, after all (and as we will come back to), but where does that end? With simulated child abuse in virtual reality? Is there a moral line where the play of something becomes the thing itself, or where pretending to commit a crime becomes the crime itself? Is your inner self – your imagination – when imagining a crime, guilty of the crime itself? If so, how would you demonstrate there is intent and mens rea?

That is the chief puzzle of this album and will be headed face on in the final track. I feel it is linked to ontological arguments: where the question arises: is existence a descriptive factor? Is a thing that exists different qualitatively to something identical in every respect except that it does not exist?

The Painter and his Model

A very similar sounding song, lyrically, about another famously dysfunctional type of relationship. Here, the artist is reproducing his model within his artwork, by using pieces of her dress and underwear to represent her dress and her underwear. He then asks how he should represent her "Little pink mouth, with lips but no teeth".

I do not think we are supposed to think for one minute he is going to remove and staple bits of the model to the canvas. It to me sounds as if he is representing the model, and sex with the model, by having sex with the model. The model becomes represented in the artwork by being the artwork. The lyrics name-check *The Theatre and its Double*, a book, or rather a collection of essays, by Antonin Artaud about this topic. Antonin wrote: "I cannot conceive any work of art as having a separate existence from life itself," insisting that life and the imagined life are identical, and: "The mind believes what it sees and does what it believes; that is the secret of fascination."

Both these statements and the evident philosophy of this song seem to put our errant ventriloquist from the previous song back on the hook: his artistic life is also his real life and the "painted girl" he crushes may as well be the real one. His salvation may rest in that additional requirement of guilty intent – "mens rea" – and the potential difference in impact of real and imagined actions. The case – for it is a case – with defence and prosecution, is building. Musically, this sounds very 80s to me. Pleasant, slight, with a piano lead line which could be from any soul/funk band of the period.

A Monkey for Sallie

"Sallie" is Sallie Fellowes, who worked for the Art Department at Rough Trade and who Momus went out with for a while. She went on to marry Bill Drummond of the KLF and then divorce him. This song commemorates her and her brief involvement with Momus. Rough Trade would not last much longer either.

It is hard to philosophise about this song. It's about a monkey that is obsessed with sex (there was no real monkey): it plays with itself all day and night and this song includes one of my favourite lyrical stanzas in all music: if anyone asks why I like the music of Momus…this:

I bought a monkey for Sallie
And let it run amok
It jumps into our bed at night
And fiddles with my cock.

What do the Beatles have? "Blackbird singing in the dead of night…" Snore…

There is a touch of the sinister in the monkey's behaviour:

It plays the barrel organ
And sharpens kitchen knives.

The monkey abuses Sallie and the narrator equally and is quite "wicked". This all ties in with the Gainsbourg theme which informs the whole album, and allows us to now imagine Coco the Monkey flinging popo, caca, spunk and god knows what else at his hapless human victims.

The actual music is bleeps and boops again, with what sounds like a saw being played in the background in the last third. Momus' voice is very low pitched, to the extent that it sounds uncomfortable for him. He is not the walrus of love, nor yet the baboon.

Pornography

Momus has said that this song includes samples from Warp's Artificial Intelligence Compilation. That was ahead of the time; Warp would become huge later in the decade. He seems, however, to be new to pornography, as he believes it is "just a young girl's diary". I am no expert on porn, but I do not believe that any young girls put such things in their journals. But then, Momus did not see much pornography until he went on tour with Primal Scream. And then I suspect he saw far too much.

This is a slow-paced, atmospheric song in the same mould as the previous one, with no ambitions beyond being a pleasant sound space. It must be said, however, that Momus does not (or did not) really know enough about the way pornography is made or how its subjects are treated to sing about it so confidently or describe it as so harmless. But the chorus, with its "boop de doop" borrowed from sex symbol Marilyn Monroe, is attractive and potentially empowering: to something, in this case something heavily inspired by 70s German porn soundtracks.

Song in Contravention

A song in contravention of the theme and sound of the rest of the album, for starters. While writing this album, Momus was creating songs in several different idioms. The explicit/sexy songs were bound for *Hippopotamomus*. The more cynical, music-hall style, narrative driven work was held back for another album, *The Ultraconformist*, which would become a natural riposte to criticism of the current album, and there was also more modern, ambient and trip-hop based music, with science-fiction related concepts and ideas as well as spiritual musings which would form the basis for the next Creation album, *Voyager*.

This song is a sci-fi piece. It is inspired by Serge Gainsbourg in the theme of forbidden music (*Mélodie Interdite*) and the melody (*Ballade de Johnny Jane*). After the excesses we have been witness to on the album, and with the sure and certain knowledge of approbation to follow, this song addresses head on the issues of censorship and scandal I touched on in discussion above.

Section 28 of the Local Government Act in the UK, passed in 1988, stated that any local authority in the UK:

> shall not intentionally promote homosexuality or publish material with the intention of promoting homosexuality or promote the teaching in any maintained school of the acceptability of homosexuality as a pretended family relationship.

In other words, discussion of same-sex relationships in any way that saw them as acceptable was prohibited. It also assumed that homosexuality was something which could be promoted, i.e. was a choice of lifestyle. It prevented effective and balanced teaching in schools and encouraged bullying and discrimination based on sexuality. The law was not repealed until 2003 in England.

Song in Contravention is about Section 28, and about censorship in general, and continues the argument that imagining or singing about something is not the thing itself: thought cannot be a crime. It makes this argument by singing from the point of view of a prosecutor, who argues that the very song they are singing is immoral because of its content.

The first verse describes the song that we are listening to as "Exhibit A", and we are warned that even listening to this much of the song "already makes you guilty of a crime". The melody and theme of the song are beautiful, and we are led into a luscious chorus describing "this love in contravention, that they see fit to ban, that woman feels for woman, man for man". It is made clear, however, that you do not need to share this love to support the cause: merely "to sing this song is a crime of love: sing this song".

The second verse of the song makes it crystal clear that the lyric relates to Clause 28: an unnamed act of love is "outlawed by the Government this year". The second chorus relates in a nutshell the issue raised by the entire album with respect to artistic expression and censorship:

Song in contravention of sections of the law
That deal with making public private thoughts
With lyrics so explicit and descriptions so perverse
They constitute the crime that it reports.

Especially now, in an environment where individuals can be prosecuted for social media posts and potentially for expressing an opinion, where context can be ignored in judging perceived offence, we need to carefully consider the import of this lyric.

Do we believe – individually or as a society – that art or expressed language can constitute a crime thus described?

I am sure we all agree in cases of personal attack or incitation to crime, racial hatred or homophobia, but what about art, satire, humour and parody? What about, as in this case, the concern that legislation can hamper free expression or dictate behaviours?

The song continues with a lovely middle eight describing the court waiting in the Perfumed Garden for the judgment and the final verse has the prosecution finally resting its case. The music dissolves into sci-fi effects that sound like a spaceship ascending, as if we are being transported to another planet.

Maybe that would be for the best.

I am certain that the outcome from *Hippopotamomus* was not what Creation Records or Momus would have ideally desired. Commercially it was a failure, artistically it was a qualified success with some critics but was savaged by others.

This was hypocritical to say the least: the NME for instance had previously praised Momus for explicit content such as *The Guitar Lesson* and now turned on him for the similar content on *Hippopotamomus*.

His relationship with Creation never really recovered, but

Momus now had other avenues for his output. The sci-fi material I described above would surface as the next Creation album, but a separate release would come before that and be released on another label: *The Ultraconformist – Live Whilst Out of Fashion.*

I Try To Be Normal…#13 The Ultraconformist

While working with Doug Martin at Spike Studio, Momus found himself producing several different types of songs. As previously outlined in the entry on *Hippopotamomus,* some of these songs were the sexual nursery rhymes that went on that album, some of the songs were more sci-fi related, or verged on transcendental trip-hop, and those songs would be used on the next Creation album *Voyager*, and still other songs were more Brechtian, music-hall works reminiscent of the earlier material, and narrative heavy. There were also re-workings of songs from the BBC album project. Those songs required an outlet. Given the commercial reception that *Hippopotamomus* had received generally, Creation was probably not the ideal option. At this point Creation Records was in financial trouble, approaching insolvency. This was at least partly caused by the rumoured £250,000 which was spent producing the album *Loveless* by My Bloody Valentine, a process which involved 19 different studios and several different producers and engineers. To escape this financial mess Alan McGee sold half of Creation Records to Sony, and, of course, very shortly afterwards discovered Oasis. Given both these issues, Creation were less and less concerned with Momus.

Mike Alway, of Cherry Red, had recently established a label called Richmond Records, which released old él Records material and other curios. Knowing that Creation's interest in Momus would only wane as the Sony situation kicked in, he offered to release any archive material Momus had. This was because Momus had an exclusive deal with Creation for any new material. The solution they arrived at was to release a fake "old" live album which actually held new material. Alan McGee got on with Mike Alway enough to allow this, so a new album was subsequently released as *The Ultraconformist* on Richmond Records' Monde imprint.

The subtitle "live whilst out of fashion" was a clear dig at the critics of his last album, and the Creation situation. The image of Nick on the front and back cover is a still from the documentary film (rather ambitiously described as a "feature" film on the sleeve) *Amongst Women Only* directed by Nicholas Tri-Dis (Triandafyllidis), in which the ins and outs of *Hippopotamomus* are debated, including contributions from Betty Page, and from flatmates and friends of Momus. We learn from this that Momus is indeed a male chauvinist pig who never does the washing up.

The back cover describes the record as being found in the archives of Richmond Records, and containing a live recording of Momus from 1910 at the Cave of the Golden Calf on Heddon Street. The record's release was delayed owing to the "vagaries of fashion and taste" and is dedicated to those who follow "other norms".

The "Cave of the Golden Calf" was a real cabaret set up by Frida Strindberg (wife of August Strindberg) in 1912. It was short lived and famed for its decadence and iconoclasm. The club was influenced by modernists and the Vorticist movement, who aimed to express the dynamism of the modern world in art and music. The inner CD cover contains quotations from Wyndham Lewis, Osbert Sitwell and Harold B. Segel regarding the club and Frida Strindberg, and a quotation from Witold Gombrowicz (Polish Poet and Playwright), "... the intelligent man depends entirely on his reflection in the soul of whomsoever, even if that soul belongs to a cretin". Perhaps Momus saw in this quote himself as the intelligent man, and certain critics as the cretins.

The ten pieces of music here are strictly in a Brechtian/Strindbergian mode, ironic, narrative and satirical, and conveyed with all the tropes of music hall of the period. There is crowd noise, clapping and cheering, and laughter, sampled from a Polish cabaret record. It is fair to say that Alan McGee would not have gladly released this material.

Sinister Themes

Julie Andrews! Dressed as a nun tripping through the edelweiss on some blasted Austrian mountain! The 1965 Christmas afternoon snoozefest *The Sound of Music*, based on the 1959 Rodgers and Hammerstein musical, was a ridiculously big selling soundtrack as well, shifting over 20 million copies and taking the number 1 album spot in the UK various times over the mid-sixties. The soundtrack contains any number of famous songs, some of which have been covered by unlikely artists, my favourite being *Do-Re-Mi* by Sparks.

This opening song features sampled crowd applause and a simple arrangement with synthesised brass and what I am guessing is a xylophone sound. The tune is borrowed from *Favourite Things* which is from *The Sound of Music* soundtrack, but the lyrics twist the original concept to instead list and define those things which could be said to make up a "classic" Momus song. The lyrics cleverly mirror the original words both thematically and phonetically, although not necessarily in the same order. So "Brown paper packages tied up with string" becomes "Angels caught up in their own puppet strings". This line also references the themes of *Tender Pervert* and, by extension, all the influences which led to *The Angels are Voyeurs*. The comparison also draws out the sinister nature of some of the original lyrics, of course: "Brown paper packages tied up with string" could easily be something sinister in a Momus lyric.

The lyrics list some obvious themes of Momus and this album in particular:

The villains of vaudeville, Young lovers' quarrels
Pearls before Parliament, Lepers in Laurels.

Little red riding hood living in sin

These are images which attack authority and mock what is usually revered. Some references seem to hint at poetic themes:

The laughter of dockworkers,
Poets who flock through the cities like stockbrokers

Which could be a reference to T.S Eliot or Attila the Stockbroker. Some are references which could be interpreted as you wish:

"The orchid of meat in the cuckoo's nest growing" could relate to the Carrion Flower or could relate to "Cuckoo's Meat" which is a form of sorrel, or it could be meaningless.

"Strumpets and kettledrums, musty old cellars Coffee and stallions, cream and umbrellas" could just be a typical diary entry for Momus at the time. Ultimately, each stanza ends with the repetition of intent: "sinister themes in the songs that I sing". The whole song ends with a simple riddle:

My first is in eMbers,
my second in wOman
My third in eMotion,
my fourth is in hUman
My fifth is in sufferS and also in longS
My whole is in Momus and these are my songs

The song acts as a manifesto for the album, a banner for the Vorticist movement it would have been part of and is a restatement of Momus' intent in general. One line references a "Forest where nightmares and nightingales sing", which I interpret as referring to the duality of Momus' music; it is a forest where nightmares are sung about and discussed, but often with beautiful lyrics and music. It could also be a philosophical reference to the German philosopher Martin Heidegger, and his discussion of the forest and the clearing: the place in the forest of human experience where all is unconcealed and laid bare.

Last of the Window Cleaners

A strident beat with acoustic guitar played as percussion, woodblocks and electric piano accompanies the tale of class war between window cleaners and the upper classes, anachronistically set in the "late 20th century", but using language and tropes from earlier decades. Most UK listeners would be familiar with the singer George Formby and his novelty ukulele hit of 1936: *The Window Cleaner (When I'm Cleaning Windows)*, an innuendo laden ditty about the misadventures of a window cleaner, including sexual assault by an old age pensioner:

An old maid walks around the floor
She's so fed up, one day I'm sure
She'll drag me in and lock the door
When I'm cleaning windows

…and Momus-esque voyeurism:

The blushing bride, she looks divine
The bridegroom he is doing fine
I'd rather have his job than mine
When I'm cleaning windows

It is for exactly this sort of peep show that the Window Cleaners in Momus' song are in trouble. The upper classes in Momus' song no longer appreciate their lack of privacy:

When windows attain transparency
working class men get a good look in.

The song uses this as a metaphor for social mobility, breaking the glass ceiling, or in this case, wall. Which, as we have all found out, the upper classes detest. The situation becomes "worse than the 1930s" – the Great Depression – as the Window

Cleaners' most powerful customers become determined to wipe them out and restore the status quo. In order to do this, a new window tax is imposed. Just as in the 1700s, the window tax results in landlords bricking up windows and the poorest in society living in blackness with poor ventilation and typhus. The Window Cleaners persist, however, and are killed off one by one, their Window Cleaning fingers crushed, until only the narrator remains.

Finally, despite it being the late twentieth century, a horse-drawn hackney cab arrives to take the final Window Cleaner to Limehouse Docks to die. The executioner quotes a traditional English nursery rhyme – *Oranges and Lemons* – a song which concerns the Church Bells of London, and ends with the threat of removing your head.

The killer spreads his "frock coat" on the ground, reminding us of Jack the Ripper, who famously wore a frock coat, and "tenderly" positions the last Window Cleaner on the floor to kill him, even as the narrator begs for his life and promises to "make concessions". The final execution is reminiscent of the death of K in Kafka's *The Trial,* including death by Butcher's knife, a needless tragedy ending with a useless shout into the dark.

This is a dark, satiric tale which attacks the insularity of the upper classes and their determination to keep out the masses. The music which accompanies this is simple, insistent in its beat and melody and captures the required music-hall atmosphere.

The Ladies Understand

At the time this album was released the UK was just coming out of a craze for gangster nostalgia. *The Krays* – a film starring the Kemp brothers from Spandau Ballet – was released in 1990 and heralded a blaze of interest in the old East End gangs. In addition, Morrissey had a major hit in 1989 with *Last of the Famous International Playboys,* which seemed to idolise the Krays and in 1991 appeared on the *Bona Drag* compilation, which went top ten in the UK and helped launch his career in America. The English seem to have a fascination – in some cases bordering on worship – of the organised criminal classes – while being simultaneously disgusted by the actual things they do. The gangs themselves in this fantasy world seem to have a marvellously perverse sense of morality – murder is fine, rape is fine, domestic abuse is fine as long as you do right by your mum and your family, and treat your women well when you aren't slashing them for talking back to you. This is the world our next character belongs to.

Momus sings in a gruff mockney voice, attempting to channel a violent pimp and gangster of early-twentieth century London, but it's less a case of "he do the police in different voices" and more "is that the evil Cockney from the *Mighty Boosh*?": it must be said that a lot of Momus' vocal impressions tend to blur into one after a while.

The backing is very similar to the previous track, with an East End pub sound. The tale begins with a description of his youth, in an institution or boarding house of some kind where his nightly emissions are "lovingly washed away" by ladies he "protected from a world of horrible slaughter". When a little older he becomes a pimp, declaring "there are worse ways to earn your pay". The Cockney has been watching Kubrick as he describes "ultraviolent thuggery" as a natural part of the fun to be had in the world. "Give me mass in the morning, the booky's at noon, the brothel all night long". The mass in the morning is a reminder of how such people often consider themselves to be deeply religious and moral, burdened by innocence despite their actual behaviour. Which should remind us of a song...

Regardless of any other activities, he will "always be true to the ladies", because "the ladies understand": in truth they fear this wretched man while in many ways enabling his behaviours. He admits himself that he "treats them like shit" and describes how he punished one of his girls for running away with a boy.

The Cockney now has a son of his own, who has similar

psychopathic tendencies which his father adores him for. When he slashes a girl to "test his army penknife blade", the brothel girls wash away the blood, for after all he will one day "protect them" just like his father did.

The song nicely conjures the hypocritical, vile world of such gangs and their ridiculous attitudes to women and religion. There is also a tinge of nostalgia for a world of East End thuggery that has faded now, a nostalgia that festered in England at the time of the album.

The next song takes us into the world of a somewhat more colourful gang…

Cape and Stick Gang

Bona Drag also featured a Morrissey single called *Piccadilly Palare*. "Palare" or "Polari" was a slang language used within various subcultures in London, but particularly by gay men in London during the early to mid-twentieth century when homosexuality was still illegal in the UK, as a secret way of conversing. The Cape and Stick gang described here are gay and use similar illicit language.

The music is quite electro here, what you might imagine early 80s music to sound like in the early twentieth century, with a growling synthesiser noise backing quite funky bass lines. The chorus is cheerful sounding, at odds with the real menace delivered by the Cape and Stick gang themselves in the lyrics. They are likeable thugs, but still mean business.

There is anachronism again, with the Cape and Sticks communicating via a party line and ringing up phone boxes to leave messages, mixing musical eras as well as they "jitter with the funk" down the evocatively named Bulblight Lane. The phone messages they leave promise that they will "stick it to you" sexually if you hang around.

The chorus has the gang "whistling Lillie Langtry": She was a British-American actress and socialite of the early twentieth century, famous as a singer and stage actor as well as for her relationships with prominent businessmen and royalty. Today she would be a gay icon and diva, on a par with Kylie or Beyoncé. The Cape and Sticks whistle her tunes and laugh at the girls who "never catch our eye", because the Capes and Sticks are gay.

We meet a rookie, a potential Cape and Stick, who has "home-made drag" in a polythene bag. This presumably refers to inhaled drugs or solvents if it does not refer to a costume of some kind. The Capes and Sticks pierce his ears forcibly, which he must laugh off.

The gang then go on a double-decker bus with Lyons Maid ice-creams (another anachronism as this brand was launched in 1925) and seduce a girl, who is described in unflattering terms, to then cut off her braids: suggesting the gang are somewhat misogynistic.

The second chorus takes us to the Second World War, with the gang playing pool during air raids, and there is what must be a reference to Gary Numan's song *Down in the Park* as they "Rape Machines in the game arcade": I am not sure whether in this song there are actually things called "rape machines" or if the gang are "raping" the machines by removing their money. I prefer the first interpretation as it adds a SteamPunk feel to the imagery of the song, and a more menacing aspect to the society depicted in the background of the gang members' lives.

The next verse reiterates that the gang do not use knives, they just use the "sticks they keep down the front of their slacks": the gang are clearly well-endowed and threatening in this area. For a "couple of crowns" (a crown was five shillings or 60p in pre-decimal UK money) they will dangle you off the top of a gantry and presumably rape you, while whistling. The song is again ambiguous about whether in this scenario it is you who are paying the money for this treatment, or if someone else has paid to have it done to you. This is a punishment or paradise depending entirely on your orientation, which in this case is upside-down 50 feet in the air.

The last verse tells us that every man in the gang carries a thermos flask (first sold in 1904) containing some unknown substance; "bromide tea" is an anaphrodisiac which urban myth tells us was given to soldiers in WW1 to remove their lust. On the other hand, the flask could contain ecstasy – which sounds somewhat more likely. Ecstasy was very much in the public eye in 1992 when this album was released and had a strong reputation as both a rave and gay scene drug. It is not entirely anachronistic either as MDMA was first synthesised in 1912.

The last verse also says "they kiss the girls and make them cry, then they kiss the boys, they're real bi-guys", a line which is deeply irritating as we have been told clearly that they are gay several times, and bi-sexuality is not the same thing. While on the subject of irritation, the drum machine cymbal crashes on this song are also incredibly irritating, a poor sonic choice.

The very last line of the last verse is "You follow me?" which I am guessing is a palare line meaning something like, "Are you gay?" The line appears as an innuendo in Monty Python's *Nudge Nudge Wink Wink* sketch. It is also more or less the first line we hear (from Suggs) on the song *Piccadilly Palare*.

The chorus is sung a couple of times, then the song ends on a repetition of the last line, with instruments dropping out until it ends on, naturally, further cymbal crashes. Despite those slight annoyances, this is a funny and catchy song which fully achieves the intent of the album: anachronistic, early twentieth century modern music hall with cynical lyrics.

The Ultraconformist

A statement song for Momus and for the album. By now, Momus has been accused of perversion, of writing vicious and unfriendly songs, of writing songs inciting criminality such as paedophilia and cannibalism, and of not doing the washing up. He is aware of his own nature and aware of how far from the societal "norm" of a pop singer he is. This song is about that gap, and his simultaneous frustration with the situation and his acceptance of it.

Momus knows and conforms to his own nature but wishes he could do so while being a "normal guy"; he wishes that society were in time with his own dance steps.

He also has a cynical and warped view of what is considered "normal" and states those criticisms clearly, but ultimately, if he could be himself and be considered "Normal", if society was more "Momus", then he would be an "Ultraconformist"; he would absolutely be the Platonic ideal of a normal person.

The gap between what you are and what is considered "normal" is a challenge for many of us, mainly because "normal" is a meaningless word. I absolutely sympathise and empathise with the lyrics here, like Momus, I also wish it "paid to be straight".

This song has a flurry of strings to introduce a waltz time structure, with lyrics outlining the perversions the singer enjoys. "I try to be normal, really I do" seems to be a heartfelt plea from the singer directly, but "I try not to chew on my hat" suggests he is not doing very well at it. (c.f "We didn't BURN him!" from the TV series *League of Gentlemen*.) Here is the line about being straight if it paid to be straight; he would get it on with a sweet little blonde if he could, but it just is not in his nature.

The Ultraconformist in the chorus walks through the week in perverse fashion, tongue in pocket, hand in cheek, and desperately wishes he could do all this and be considered an "ordinary guy", just as we all wish our idiosyncrasies could be considered normal. The cry "loud as the sky" sounds quite sincere and desperate and the singer is reduced to nonsense words to convey their desperate normality. Filla Gorilla today…

The singer attacks the chemically induced sanity of the modern world, deriding the "little blue pills" a psychiatrist would no doubt prescribe. Being an Ultraconformist he sits at his desk, with a gun ready for suicide and on the verge of a heart attack. He would be orderly and calm were it not that the dustbin lids "beg to be banged". After repetition of the chorus and nonsense verse the song slowly breaks down and ends with fake applause and a pause.

The Mother-in-Law

Yet another song originally intended for the BBC project and re-purposed as an entirely believable music-hall ditty. A sinister, spooky keyboard sound with tremolo almost reminiscent of a theremin plays over a straight bass beat. An organ sound brings in chords to back the tale. A plucked acoustic guitar gently plays over the story and emphasises the emotive moments of the song.

The lyrics are delivered by another Momus cockney; this one is a composite character of Billy Cotton, "The Entertainment King" and his son, Bill Cotton.

Billy Cotton was a dance band leader whose show ran from 1949–1968 on BBC radio and later TV. His distinctive opening shout of "Wakey!" would open each show. This song also opens with a sinister, almost threatening rendition of the catchphrase. The early life of Billy Cotton is retold (although not very accurately, since he did not work for the BBC as an acne scarred teenager as the song states). Alexandra Palace was from 1935 the centre of BBC TV broadcasting and was still used in some capacity by the BBC until long after WWII. As the song states, a doodlebug did damage the palace during the war, but did not in fact bring the whole place down. Cotton describes himself as "everyone's favourite drunken brother-in-law", using a popular demotic or mode of speaking to entertain the masses. As the public gathered around their radio sets to listen to "their master's voice" (the motto of HMV – His Master's Voice – a company which produced gramophones and radio sets) they tuned out of European stations at Rome, Hilversum (Netherlands) and Berlin to listen to Cotton instead. Given later verses, "His Master's

Voice" could also be a way of referring to Satan and describing broadcast media as Satanic. A conflict with religion is raised and quoted:

I remember those religious broadcasting blokes
Used to stop me right on Portland Place
And quote me right to my face
"In the land of the blind the winking man is king"

Portland Place has been the headquarters of the BBC since the 1930s. The line Cotton is quoted as saying here is an altered biblical quotation and could have been from his shows.

Both verses end by telling us that Billy's aim is now to entertain "The Mother-in-Law". Or rather, his "H-aim has been to H-entertain" with the thick accent now presented. In British humour, the mother of one's wife – the mother-in-law – has long been the subject of humour and derision. They are generally portrayed as bullying, critical and humourless and fit targets for ageist and sexist humour. In this case, however, we slowly get the impression that there is something genuinely "wrong" with Billy's mother-in-law.

The next two verses move on to be about Billy Cotton's son in real life – Bill Cotton. The change in person is explained by the song lyrics as if it is the same person grown older: "Then in the years that followed the war, I was moved from razzmatazz to administration". Bill Cotton was the Head of Light Entertainment at the BBC from 1970–1981, then Head of Television until 1988. He describes his mission as providing entertainment to a "voyeuristic nation". He also talks about John Logie Baird – the Scottish inventor of television – whose TV system with 240 lines (per image) was used by the BBC until 1937 when they switched to EMI's 405-line system. Bill Cotton describes Baird as dropping to his knees and scanning the carpet when asked to describe television.

The last verse describes where Bill finds himself after he dies: in court with "the entire cast of the *Black and White Minstrel Show*". This was a variety show where black-faced white singers and dancers performed standard show-tunes. By its end in 1978, the racism of this was being severely questioned and by 1992 the show was a dirty stain on the BBC's history.

Momus allows Bill to get in a sly dig at "new media":

Where have I heard that title before?
"The Day of Judgement" – must be cable or Channel Four

Accused of blasphemy and making graven idols, Bill is damned, and "laughs his head off" when fed his final punchline: "The Devil is the Mother of my wife".

It seems that his personal hell is to spend eternity entertaining his mother-in-law, an ironic fate for this low-brow entertainer, responsible as he is for the fake news, manipulation and elitism the BBC has always been guilty of (my opinion). The song understandably ends flatly on a minor chord and muted applause. Still, the next track is more cheerful, I suppose…

La Catrina

The Day of the Dead is a Mexican holiday and festival, usually taking place at the beginning of November, when people remember their departed loved ones and celebrate their families. It is not related to Halloween, although some elements are very similar, including children going from house to house to ask for treats.

La Catrina is a tall female skeleton who wears a feathered hat and rags of once affluent clothing. She has descended from an Aztec Goddess of Death who protected the passage of loved ones into the next world. The Mexican illustrator Jose Guadalupe Posada is credited with creating the first image of La Calaca Garbancera, a female skeleton who featured in "calaveras", satirical images and rhymes published by Antonio Arroyo. La Calaca Garbancera became La Catrina, a figure who reminds us that death comes to everyone, no matter how privileged you are or what race you are. Posada used the phrase "Death is Democratic" to describe this. Frida Kahlo's husband, Diego Rivera, depicted La Catrina in his mural *Dreams of a Sunday Afternoon in Alameda Park*, in which she has the appearance she has today.

This song, slow-paced, pretty, based around synthesised bass and piano with a rousing chorus, describes La Catrina as a lady from before the revolution, returned from the dead for a last party. Being a skeleton, she still manages to portray a range of emotions:

Sometimes she cries
And sometimes she laughs
On her face she wears impossible expressions

The chorus is La Catrina, commanding us to dance while we still can, while we are alive:

Dance in the sun, young girl
Dance naked for a man
While you still can
It's too late when you're as dead as I am.

In the second verse Momus is dancing with La Catrina. He is very clear about her status:

She's so elegant, so handsome and so dead.

The middle eight is beautifully delivered, poignant and blessed with dissonance between the elegance of his melodies and the grotesquery of his lyrics:

La Catrina is dancing in her skeleton
La Catrina with her mouldy dress and boots still on
On her skull a single strand of hair
Between the pelvic bones thin air
And then she opens up her thighs
And tells me what it's like to die
And sings her love song.

Despite this activity beyond necrophilia, the song is still a celebration of life, as the chorus is repeated, and the song ends with an almost questioning repeat of "Dance your life away…"

The overall message of the song is of hope through adversity, and to celebrate life and loved ones now, because it's later than you think, essentially.

The Cheque's in the Post

It is always a little disarming when a Momus song arrives with virtually no references external to the song, no philosophers quoted at length, or obscure European pop artists name-dropped. I always have a suspicion that I have missed something, which of course I probably have. This is one such example, in that it seems to be a straightforward narrative, an apologia to a girlfriend who has been mistreated. The suspicion I have is that this relates to a real-life relationship, in which case it is hardly surprising that Momus lived a somewhat marginal lifestyle, those cheques must have been flying out the door.

Talking of cheques dates the song, of course; direct debits and debit cards did exist at the time, but chip and pin was still a decade away. The music here is a syncopated beat behind a piano note which follows a simple pattern up and down a scale. Electric guitar chord effects punctuate the lyrics, and an accordion sound sweeps behind it all. Momus did not, at this point, own an actual accordion, a fact which you should bear in mind. The song is repetitive and changes very little during its 6 minutes, devoting all interest to the lyrical content.

The song begins with Momus and his lawyer sitting down to consider the case. I wonder who Momus' lawyer was at this point; I guess he used Creation's counsel. They must have dreaded his calls by this point. They consider the wrongs Momus has done to the unknown girl and settle on a figure for reparation.

For general mistreatment, for example, "500 £5 notes in a roll" (£2500). Complaints about weight and punctuality: £2000. For looking at other "younger" women, £1500. We get a running total here of £6350, which includes tax of 5.8 per cent (no idea where he got that figure from). And that is just verse one!

He awards £1797 for attacking her "pantheistic new age religion", which is rich given his subsequent conversion to Islam. We add £7000 (should be more) for spoiling the ending of a film and bitching about a dress.

The worst actual crime is next, especially if it is a real story:

And for passing the pictures I'd taken
Of your body totally naked
Around our friends
Let's call it a round £9 000

Naughty boy. That is body shaming, slut shaming and lord knows what other modern crimes. The total is now £24,063, which is completely off no matter what EU tax scheme he is on. The third verse begins with a meta-joke I really like:

And for my next indiscretion
When we had sex on the floor of the kitchen
I sang it in a song – accept 10 000 – make that 11 000 pounds

He starts the line by explaining that his next crime is singing the line he is currently singing and pauses mid-line to acknowledge that fact by increasing the penalty. Lovely! The next stanza shows his most negative characteristic:

And for failing to give enough time
To the baby that could have been mine
It's not that I don't care
My love it's just so hard to find a figure

That he is not sure it is even his child says something about his attitude to the girl, and a lack of connection and trust. Another interpretation of the line could be that there was no baby, but if he had spent time on the relationship, they could have had one. His next confession would cause an army of feminists to rage at his door:

Worst of all I stopped loving your body
Making you feel so low
Though my lawyer says no blame can be apportioned
For circumstances beyond my control

He finally admits he is going to start the cycle of abusive relationships again:

I'm going to get another girl in
Under my quilt
And run up
Another massive debt.

Fully aware of his own character, and unable to change his conditioned behaviour, he still asks for forgiveness, in half remembered prayer.

Hail Mary, pray for me now
Now and at the hour of my death.

There is a long ending to this song, nearly 2 minutes of Hail Marying and ba-ba-ing. The lack of genuine contrition and the idea that all sins can be paid off is very Catholic, making the prayer used very appropriate. Sinners used to pay "indulgences" to the Catholic Bank, sorry, Church, to have their crimes forgiven in medieval times. The modern equivalent seems to be the super-injunction and out-of-court settlement: vital tools for the loose-lipped satirist.

Spy on the Moon

Cabaret performances have a tradition of a final "thank you and goodnight" type song which sends you on your way with a more cheerful outlook. This being a Momus album, the cheerful sounding song here masks quite dark and perverse thoughts, lyrics and events.

It begins with a fast tom-tom beat from the drum machine, and acoustic guitar chords used percussively to accompany. A swirling sci-fi effect from the synthesiser plays in the background.

After the first chorus (which begins the song) an electric piano and snare kick in and accompany the repetitive but catchy chord sequence that runs through the track.

The opening chorus introduces the "spy on the moon" – a very REM concept! – who is watching us, and glad that he is far away from us.

The spy sees "circles in circles and spirals spinning round", a reference to the philosophical concept of the "musica universalis", a reference also to the golden ratio which Da Vinci in particular drew our attention to, and the spiralling movement of celestial bodies. As there is no direction in space the Earth is "flying up or falling down" depending on your viewpoint.

Among this beauty, lovers walk on the beach, and their eyes are green or blue or brown – this may be a reference to the New Order song *Temptation*: "Oh, you've got green eyes, Oh, You've Got blue eyes, Oh, You've got grey eyes".

The next stanza speaks of a "hole in the sky" – perhaps the hole in the ozone layer – "where the love is gone away". Momus uses prosaic but oddly sinister imagery to convey the idea of an unknowable threat.

There is a bump in the road and a creeper on the stair
And somebody is knocking at the door

The words describe a world which is recognisable but slightly out of kilter:

There is a queue on the street and an office full of chairs
And people having fantasies in cars
There is a bed in the garden, the moon is shining down
On drunkards drinking Guinness's in bars.

The impression given is of a world that celebrates even as it hurtles towards an unknown disaster, possibly environmental catastrophe.

Twenty filter tips at the motorway garage
The sky behind the petrol pumps is green

Momus must have travelled and toured a great deal at this point; the service station and motorway garage would be a second home to him. The final couplet zeroes in on the worst event of all, death, possibly by suicide:

There is a bunk in the shed where a man is lying dead
Murdered by the things he'll never be.

A theme which runs through Momus' work is that of regret, never for something you have done, but for things that you have not done. The man in the shed was murdered by what he did not achieve or try to achieve, the things that he cannot become. It is possible that on some level that man is Momus himself, following the Hippopotamomus episode commercial success and household fame seemed to slip away into impossibility, and the whole album is a comment on that situation to some extent.

There is an instrumental break, following the same sequence, and a repetition of some stanzas. Some shouting/screaming effects are mixed into the background enhancing the feeling that this is an apocalyptic scenario. The song breaks down for the sampled Polish audience to clap along and Momus says Good Night to them; of course, they are made to clap and cheer for him to come back.

Forests

The forest introduced in the first song and discussed above is the theme of this instrumental track – a rarity, in fact the first instrumental track on a Momus album.

A drum roll plays throughout the piece to heighten the tension as we walk into the gloom. The piano plays a slowly descending sequence of notes, flying back up again in a pattern which is very traditional for the cabaret genre.

Sounds of shrieking/shouting are mixed in to create a sinister atmosphere, reminiscent of a Victorian Freak Show. Peculiar sound effects are mixed in as well, along with bird noise towards the end. The whole track is evocative of the score from the film *The Elephant Man,* in fact, directed by David Lynch. It also reminds me of *Withnail's Theme* by David Dundas/Rick Wentworth, from *Withnail and I,* which has its own grotesque characters and descent into madness.

So *The Ultraconformist* ends. It is an excellent album both in terms of the musicality displayed and as a creative exercise. The actual songs are very good as well, pursuing a variety of unusual topics and still being accessible.

Listening to the album you feel that Momus is exorcising

some demons and scratching a particular set of itches. It is a direct response to the furore around his last album and allows the expression of Brechtian cabaret sounds that was not otherwise going to be allowed at Creation. As previously outlined, Momus had other interests at the time, including trip-hop, spirituality and what might be termed "sci-fi" romanticism. Those songs would, ironically enough, include some of his most commercial material of all, and inhabit his next Creation album, *Voyager*, which was released shortly after *The Ultraconformist*, later in 1992.

A Machine That Let You Feel…#14 Voyager

Voyager came out a couple of months after *The Ultraconformist* and housed the tracks that were more influenced by the current dance/trip-hop/acid scene, or more to the point, the disintegrating music scene of the time as it merged into different genres. It carries musical influence from Massive Attack, PM Dawn and the ilk, along with the Pet Shop Boys, Shamen and other chart orientated material.

Lyrically the album addresses the pseudo-philosophical new-age direction of those musical genres, and has a feel something like retro-futurism, nostalgic science-fiction. There were important events in Momus' own life and career at this point too.

In 1990 he saw a play by Yukio Mishima (based on a short story by Kan'ami Kiyotsugu) in which an old lady, retelling her life story, seems to travel into those memories. This along with the Mishima novel *Spring Snow* is an influence on the album, particularly the song *Summer Holiday 1999*.

That song, based on a 1988 film of the same name directed by Shusuke Kaneko, was written in 1990 for a compilation album called *Fab Gear*. This compilation contained tracks by a Japanese band called Flipper's Guitar, which featured a young Keigo Oyamada (later known as Cornelius), along with tracks by selected artists – Momus being one of these. The compilation helped form the basis of a popular indie-music and cultural movement in Japan known as Shibuya-Kei.

The year 1992 saw Momus' first tour of Japan, a revelatory moment for him as he discovered that while his popular career in the UK may have faded, he was a relatively big star there. Signed to Nippon Columbia and with the backing of Oyamada, on his first foray into Tokyo he found a display for an artist called "Poison Girlfriend", after his second album. He would later work with this artist, write songs for Oyamada's girlfriend, Kahimi Karie, and others and achieve – as a writer at least – chart success that eluded him in the West.

At this time Momus was with Shazna Nessa – a 14-year-old girl (in 1991) who wrote to him and with whom he developed a friendship, which developed into a romantic relationship once she was 16. This relationship was somewhat complicated by her family, leading indirectly to the end of his time with Creation, and directly to Momus marrying and relocating to Paris the following year. It also informed the content of the *Timelord* album, which is where I will more fully discuss that relationship.

In 1992 he wrote a pivotal essay called *Pop Stars? Nein Danke!*, available at imomus.com, which seems to foretell the rise of social media stars and the fragmentation of the "pop industry" into a million individual content creators operating at marginal cost, where every "pop star" will be famous for fifteen people. This is a restating of Andy Warhol's famous slogan, "in the future, everyone will be world-famous for fifteen minutes", from a 1968 Stockholm exhibition of his work.

The essay describes a world, in short, more agreeable to artists such as himself. It celebrates the probabilities of technology increasing accessibility to the machinery required to make music, to track its popularity with different demographics and to download albums. It is a very forward-thinking piece, seeing the digital music marketplace as operating like the ponds in C.S. Lewis' sixth Narnia Chronicle, *The Magician's Nephew*.

> The feeling I get when I walk into a record shop is not that there is a battle of titans "clashing for the number one spot". That is the model of the old monopoly capitalism. Entering a record shop now, a good one like Tower or the Virgin Megastore, is like standing in C.S. Lewis's Wood Between the Worlds, where you can pick a pond and enter one of an infinite number of worlds at different stages of their evolution.

This statement now puts me in mind of the lighthouses in *Bioshock Infinite*'s twisty conclusion. Obviously these stores are long gone, and replaced by new organisations such as Amazon, but independent sites such as Darla more accurately demonstrate the spirit of his words.

All these events, ideas and influences must be borne in mind as we investigate *Voyager*.

The album cover is a design by Rafael Jimenez and Claudia Casagrande, who also designed the cover for his lyrics book *Lusts of a Moron*. The palette of warm oranges, yellows and greens accurately mirrors the warmth and nature of the music within, and the sci-fi romanticism. The close-up photos on the CD inlay of a model's face and eye, and of a flower, highlight the spiritual and philosophical nature of the lyrics, and the drift towards an eastern sensibility. The photography is again by Thomi Wroblewski, as for *Tender Pervert*.

A Japanese translator – Chiharu Watabe – is credited for work on the lyrics – on *Summer Holiday 1999*. Production and programming are credited to Momus and engineering to Doug Martin. Both Momus and Voyager are rendered lower case, and the cover as a whole feels minimalist, which is at odds with the maximal musical content, but fits the philosophy and overall influences perfectly. Momus himself is on the front cover in what seems a huge coat and several layers – which was the style at the time – and oversize sunglasses, clearly dressed up warm for the Siberian tundra. I cannot ignore, however, what this photograph and pose have conspired to do to his chin, which seems frankly deformed in this image. It draws the eye magnetically, a chin for our times, a chin for all seasons…

Cibachrome Blue

Straight from the beginning of the first track, the sound and intent of this album veers towards the positive rather than the cynical, towards transport and exploration rather than cynicism or mockery. That exploration is both external, of the world, and internal, of the spirit. Or as Barbara Ellen of the NME put it:

> To get in the right mood for this album, one would have to spend an entire weekend swapping Star Trek bubble-gum cards and Out Of Body experiences with the likes of William Orbit, Mick Fleetwood and David Icke, pausing only occasionally to sacrifice a Cyber-virgin or re-light the Yin-Yang candle. Even then, if you're not a fan of the Pet Shop Boys' most-binnable moments, forget it. 2/10

Missing the point, as the critics tended to from here on in, only the William Orbit and Pet Shop Boys references are in any way valid. An increasing interest in technology and the still virginal fields of the internet is clearly there. What is true is that the entire philosophical thrust of this album is different to anything Momus has posited before. The arrangement and sound of the album are different as well, and ironically it is the most commercial sounding album yet released by him, without I believe any real intention to be so. Momus' voice, the most iconic and recognisable aspect of his music, and the narrative storytelling that is synonymous with the brand, are just not there, or not recognisable. The voice is further back in the mix than we are used to, and almost merges with the sounds, so it drifts subliminally into your subconscious. It is hard sometimes to concentrate on the lyrics, they are more "stream of consciousness" than has hitherto been the case, more internally descriptive than narratively descriptive.

The opening of *Cibachrome Blue* is lush, panoramic, widescreen, sounding something like a train setting off, or a plane taxiing, and setting us on our travels, always and symbolically to the East. The beat is pure trip-hop, via Massive Attack's *Unfinished Sympathy*.

Momus' vocals over this are calm, quiet, introspective and quite pure: a million miles away from the showmanship of *The*

Ultraconformist or the outré garishness of *Don't Stop the Night*. They are in delivery influenced by the style of various artists including the seductive romanticism of Dirk Bogarde. The track includes string samples from Bogarde's album *Lyrics for Lovers*. These lyrics are optimistic about technology in a way that permeated the early 90s. With the rise of the internet and virtual reality, anything seemed possible, despite the obvious limitations of the hardware available at the time. Virtual Reality was touted as a new frontier to establish even BEFORE realistic CGI was possible, even before *Jurassic Park*. We tried to run before we even knew what the word meant. There were game shows based on (simulated) VR (virtual reality) while simultaneously the height of sophistication on a webpage was a GIF of a flying toaster, and no-one saw a disconnect there.

Just as in the 60s and 70s, where the rise of computing was linked to the Love Generation, to hippie mysticism and the drug-culture of the time (Bill Gates has admitted to LSD use), so the rise of the internet and virtual technology in the 90s was linked to new-age spirituality and mysticism. Momus sees this period of his music as a signpost to his later conversion to Islam, as well as an opening-up to higher levels of consciousness.

We voyage through the heart of darkness, not to kill as in Conrad's *Heart of Darkness* or its interpretation *Apocalypse Now*, but to discover. We take a sleeper train, because in a different state of consciousness we will discover more; in sleep and dreams we can access our subconscious potentiality. The prefix trans- is used often: transatlantic, transpacific, we travel across and through different times, cultures and mentalities. We amplify, exaggerate and rise, exultant.

Paul at Damascus and Christopher Columbus are travellers, in different ways: Paul travelled trans-belief systems, Columbus trans-atlantic. Both found what they already knew: by closing our eyes, by travelling within, as we should too. We were in the process of mapping the human genome at the time; in the swirling syllables of RNA and DNA (Gattaca for instance) there was a belief we could save and change the nature of man, and echoes of Gematria in the belief that by reading the whole genome we might speak the name of God. But "in a post-ethical age, nothing is true"; moving beyond narrow ideas of Good and Evil means that no-one is true, no-one is false.

So we do not speak of God; we speak of the "originator man", the bootstrap service of the universe, to make a sun "in the palm of your hand", which flowers/deflowers and comes and goes out of fashion (much like Momus).

Conflict with the universe is highlighted in the following stanza:

(Sunshine in the darkness)
I guess I've come to throw some shade
(Moving in the aftershock)
This time I've come to pull some weight
(Forwards through the crossfire)

We have hands outstretched, a Messianic image, in our own Passion-Play, as we move through our lives, carbon-based life forms born in exploding stars, which is true. The elements we are made of were created in supernovae, the death of stars making our lives possible, creation through destruction. And through the destruction we create our "Four minutes and 33 seconds of love", roughly the length of the song, or possibly the average romantic encounter with its creator, who knows? Other than John Cage, obviously.

A prophet predicted a space probe
that predicted the start of a world.

In the 1979 film *Star Trek: The Motion Picture*, the space probe Voyager, having encountered an alien civilisation, is altered to become sentient, and spends centuries searching for its creator, creating a world around itself in the process. Equally it is to be hoped that in our voyage of self-discovery, we will create a world of knowledge and godhood.

A flash of the dice in the game of chance
Played by a lonely young girl

This could be a reference to Mary, the original virginal bride. Maybe it is Shazna's letter to Momus, asking for advice. Anyway, a series of Messiahs follow. Momus is partly referring to his own heroes here, such as Bowie, with these references which are both clear and oblique:

Signal to noise, boys will be boys
And girls will be boys

As in many gnostic faiths and new-age philosophies, opposites are required and paired, there is no superior "side": in fact, opposites are treated as equal:

Increment is decrement, Christ is anti-Christ
And so on and so on – to cry is to laugh
There are multiplications and variations
There is no true path

In technology terms this could refer to fuzzy logic, where the value of a digital storage location is not simply 0 to mean False, or 1 to mean True, but can adopt any value between 0 and 1, and therefore any level of Truth. Quantum technology which we are now developing takes this a further step and allows elements known as qubits to contain a potential spin value of 1 or 0 simultaneously.

Another name for the "originator" is the "Oyster Man", who

dives for pearls but then throws them back, seeing what the effect is, experimenting with the creation of possible worlds, in *Cibachrome Blue* – Cibachrome itself referring to an analogue photographic process, the whole referring to a particular colour filter; and filtering is what this song does, and talks about, filtering experiences and desires through the universe, travelling through the void, filtering input like a whale filters out seawater to consume plankton.

The final stanzas repeat lines from the song, and there is a call-back to the *Song in Contravention*.

Ragamuffin boy, Sheherezade
A commonplace book of styles
Lying in the olive grove God smiles

The music builds towards the end with sampled female backing vocals, then fades out with the circling pattern of bells and trip-hop beats that have played throughout the song in the foreground. You are given the sense of a never-ending piece of music, travelling on through the stars forever, in transit to find a new way of seeing. Limahl's *NeverEnding Story*, of course, does much the same thing.

Virtual Reality

The awakening of the digital age is very much the focus of this song, ostensibly quite a simple, Pet Shop Boys inspired update of the Everly Brothers song *All I have to do is dream*, in which dreaming is compared to virtual reality, a scenario in which the object of his affections and love is ever present when he needs them. The optimism with regard to technology is very clear:

You can have whatever you want in virtual reality
All you've got to do is dream

We are even told "Just do it!" which is a Nike slogan. At the time we were dreaming of the future, of VR and what would eventually be called AR and Artificial Intelligence. Multimedia, and interactive entertainment such as CD ROMs, were believed to be the future of information storage. Mathematical ideas around chaos theory and fractals informed artwork, clothing and posters across college dorms everywhere. My own terrible BA thesis was around virtual reality and compared its impact to that of *L'arrivée d'un train en gare de La Ciotat* and suggested that VR cinemas were coming. Notably I still thought people would physically go to a building together to then wear VR sets. The idea of people staying in their homes and partaking did not occur because the technology to stream such content or even deliver it to a house did not exist.

The music is very much Pet Shop Boys, with orchestral hits and big sound effects to emphasise the widescreen dreaming taking place. It is bouncy and catchy, and very commercial sounding. The main keyboard riff does sound quite like *Domino Dancing*, as critics noted, but that is more pastiche than anything else.

Despite the optimism, there are warning notes in the lyrics: this couplet warns against the disconnect between fantasy and reality, and hints at the possibility of subsequently rejecting reality:

This is just like the real thing, only better
It's reality only better

And again in this middle section:

What's real to me, what's make-believe
I don't even care any more

The possibility of addiction to VR is being laid out, but at this moment the singer does not care. The philosophical question here is, of course, if the VR was identical to reality, DOES it matter which one you are in? This is the big recurring question in Momus' work of the time, discussed at length on the previous album.

It is also worth noting that "have virtually anything" could also be interpreted as "have nothing, in reality", and invites the listener to consider the value, if any, of something "virtually" held. (My pitiful and daily-less-valuable tenth of a Bitcoin comes to mind).

Finally, if you are thinking Momus has lost his bite here with optimistic sloganeering and chirpy dance beats, bear in mind that "In moments when I want you so, All I've got to do is dream" is basically referring to masturbation, as did the original Everly Brothers song. I am certain that within about 5 minutes of creating the first VR systems, teledildonic devices were being designed on a napkin. Or, more likely, a soiled tissue.

Vocation

Virtual Reality breaks down at the end with sweeping synthesiser chords, and a bird-like fluttering, as well as a metallic rippling sound like the far-off train heard from a subway station. These effects continue at the beginning of *Vocation* with swathes of sci-fi sounding synth; clearly a reference throughout the album to Vangelis' work for *Blade Runner* and a touch of Tangerine Dream.

The song kicks in with a pumping bassline and bass/snare combo making this both catchy and quite slight. The verse and chorus repeat four times, additional sounds and instruments joining on each iteration. A funky keyboard sound – clavinette – joins on the third verse, for instance. After four verses the song breaks down for an instrumental break, repeats the chorus and then breaks down again to return to the sweeping chords which opened the song.

A vocation is a calling, an occupation which insists on you

taking it. Momus now claims a vocation to a higher destination, a need to be "in the right place at the right time doing the right thing". This is an elevation to a higher plane of living, which is to be celebrated by "reeling round in spirit celebration". The song celebrates the joy of finding one's place in the spiritual world. He is moving around like a "pern in a gyre". This is a phrase from Yeat's poem *Sailing to Byzantium* and "pern" probably means spinning like the spindle holding thread on a sewing machine.

A gyre, by the way, definitely means a swirling vortex, as referenced in another poem by Yeats, *The Second Coming,* which includes one of my favourite openings and verses in all poetry, and a verse that seems massively appropriate in 2020:

Turning and turning in the widening gyre
The falcon cannot hear the falconer;
Things fall apart; the centre cannot hold;
Mere anarchy is loosed upon the world

Conquistador

Conquistadores were the knights, soldiers, explorers and conquerors of the Spanish and Portuguese empires, who colonised many regions, including South America, and defeated the Aztecs and Mayans. But beyond their conquest, and subsequent fame, what did they really achieve? You could conquer the world, but without love, without human connection, you have gained nothing. Or alternatively, what if you created a fantastic sonic empire, with many of the most innovative modern artists signed to you, and then sold half of it to an American multinational, and, just to be clear, your name was Alan?

This is a huge pop song, with a very recognisable beat and sound of the time, clearly techno and dance orientated touches in the keyboard riffs and motifs, sampled from Isaac Hayes. The singer has found themselves one of the disappeared, "slipped away" from a relationship, or possibly from the public eye.

Ironically, if this album had come out mid-to-late eighties it could easily have gained airplay and made Momus a bigger chart star, but for most people he had gone, with the reaction of most being "a shrug of the shoulders".

In the relationship the song is supposedly about, the abandoned lover "buys a coat against the cold", this being enough to replace him, now that "love has left the arena". Is this arena a place of display or, with the Conquistador motif, a place of battle? The use of the word is reminiscent of a song by another Scottish act, Altered Images, from their first album and called *Sentimental*: where Clare Grogan sings:

Enter the vast arena, arena
Where do you, where do you, where do you go from here?
Can't you see? Don't you know? Don't you know the way?
Forget the past and it'll go away, away, away.

Which has a similar theme of forgetting the past and moving on. Sadly for Momus in *Conquistador* he has no one to take up the country park, his erstwhile lover has found compensations, "maybe it's money, maybe it's drugs".

The song has a gorgeous method of adding instruments, and building to a supposedly triumphant climax in the middle eight, where the following lines billow upwards to a peak of achievement, followed by the let-down that reaching your dreams can bring:

This world is spectacular
With many diversions
You can ski down a mountain in a dayglo suit
You can build up an empire
You can be a conquistador
And when you've won What'll you do?

Which brings us back to the point at the start. And again, love has left the arena. This blunt statement is repeated with samples and keyboard riffs following around it. The song breaks down towards the end with a final sample loop cutting short abruptly. This leads in very appropriately to the following song, *Spacewalk*.

Spacewalk

A sample from Deee Lite's single *What is love* introduces a slightly more cynical take on the optimism and positivity of the culture and music of the time. There's a great growling bass line that comes in after the opening sample, then Momus tells us that although we may be on a spacewalk, riding the soul train and hearing the bass talk, that it is saying nothing. All the positivity, the summer of love culture, the rave, is meaningless. In an affecting chorus, dryly and almost hopelessly, Momus says:

I want to see you.
I want to feel you.
I want to touch you
I want to be with you.

He is begging for human contact again, tired of spiritual enlightenment that now feels hollow. For the second verse a great new riff kicks in to join the growling, and Momus declares "We're getting out of our heads, were we ever in them at all?"; all the drugs, the LSD, the ecstasy that supposedly bring enlightenment, how can they help us when we had nothing to start with? He goes on to highlight the pointlessness of narcotics in this context:

We take the smart drug
So we can think straight
We take the empathy drug
And get on great.

The drugs have the effect intended, but so what? It changes nothing essential within us. There is a Jonathan Coulton song called *I Feel Fantastic* with a similar theme, of over reliance on pharmaceuticals that change only our superficial affect and not our central nature:

"All I know is the steak tastes better when I take my steak tastes better pill..."

Spacewalk, like *Conquistador,* is a song that works by building layers of sound, intended for a club or dance song, and highlights the building and removal of emotions. The weather themes of the album resurface:

And in the wintertime
It feels like summer time
And in the summertime
It feels so strange

The cynical appropriation of other and older cultures by this new-age and mainly white movement is attacked:

We ride the soul train
Just like the brothers
We dance to dead men –
Marley, Marvin, Otis and many others

The narrator has attempted to internalise his search for meaning, but it is inside himself that his problems originated, and now he cannot make the human connection he needs:

We're on a spacewalk
We're walking inside
That's where the space is
That's where the love died
I want to see you

I want to feel you
I want to touch you
I want to be with you.

As the last two lines are repeated it is with increasing passion and desperation.

The accompanying effects now include a portamento swirl upwards and the keyboards accompanying become more emphatic. The song breaks down similarly to *Conquistador* and ends with a held chord.

This is the song which most excited Alan McGee when he heard *Voyager*, and accordingly it had a release on 12″ in September 1992. This featured an extended version of *Spacewalk* and remix credited to Deja Vu. There was also a mix of *Conquistador* by Lovecut DB (Douglas Benford), and the track *Momutation 3*, which was an instrumental mix of *Conquistador*. It did no business commercially, of course, and was the last Momus single on Creation.

Summer Holiday 1999

Summer Holiday 1999 is a 1988 Japanese film directed by Shusuke Kaneko based on a manga. It is about a group of schoolboys who are spending the summer vacation at a remote boarding school. A boy has killed himself, for reasons that are unpicked during the film by detective work including reading his diaries; it transpires he was in love with one of his classmates. Another boy arrives at the school who is the double of the boy who died. The boys investigate what happened and deal with the suspicion that they are being haunted. Being set in the future, the film has science-fictional qualities but is at the same time imbued with a sense of nostalgia. There is nothing in the scenery or set design which was not around then, the computer monitors have no surrounds, but otherwise there are few "futuristic" touches. As in Godard's *Alphaville*, the angularity of modern architecture and public transport stands in for a vision of the future. Notably, the film cleverly casts teenage girls as the schoolboys, making the film a transgender text and adding to the necessary androgyny of the main characters.

Momus' track re-recorded from the compilation album version for Flipper's Guitar is probably the strongest composition on this album. Opening with the main theme played as on a glockenspiel, and accompanied by futuristic, animalistic sounding effects, again suggesting movement or travel, in this case upwards, the main beat kicks in with a more forceful riff on keyboard and with a little bass hook between each repeat of that riff.

A Japanese voice speaks during the song, reading words from a love letter from Momus' first Japanese girlfriend, translated by Chiharu Watabe. The opening verse slows down from the opening salvo but maintains the beat, and Momus' lyrics deftly outline the narrative of the film.

Pine trees in the playgrounds
Around the empty school
A diary full of diagrams
A boy, perhaps a girl

The unrequited love is described, and is the reason for suicide; the music rises to a dramatic outpouring of grief:

Is there any reason not to die,
if this love I feel must always be denied.

The chorus follows a rush of drums, and emphatically describes the desires the narrator feels. The chorus describes the wish to live, but rush to die, that teenage love and angst provide:

This purity, as cold as spring snow
In the wind on the island of Hokkaido

This is a reference to Mishima's work in *Spring Snow,* and a prediction of Momus' own location some years hence. There is a further quote from the love letter and a translation into English:

I long to see your face
From every angle all at once
Just like the faces in a Cubist composition

The lyrics then directly reference science-fiction: I am not sure which film is referred to here but we can only hope Charlie Brooker does not steal this idea for *Black Mirror* now he has milked Karl Pilkington dry:

I remember in a film I saw
they scanned somebody's brain
With a machine that let you feel all his emotion
Well I know that that was only science fiction
But I'm dying to make you feel the way I feel.

That is a beautiful sentiment that we have all felt, particularly when young and wishing the object of our affections would reciprocate our emotions. The song ends with a repeat of the key line in verse one: purity as cold as spring snow…

This is a very affecting song, with an emotive through line about "forbidden love" and a subtext about transgenderism, but comprehensible to anyone who loved anyone hopelessly when they were young. It is clearly the strongest song on the album, having been rewritten and re-recorded with the album's themes front and centre. It perfectly captures the nostalgic science-fiction, the retro-futurism that was Momus' concern at the time of recording.

Afterglow

So as some voyage to other worlds – both internal and external

– to find "other ways of living", then there must be others on those worlds who do the same and travel to ours. In addition, you could imagine those dying from this world as travelling to another, and those who are newly born to this world being travellers as well. As our world is relatively old, you may regard those who are newly born and newly arrived to this world as suffering from a disadvantage, arriving here too late to change anything.

Such is the philosophy behind this slow, lazily delivered rap over a PM Dawn influenced beat and effects. An electric piano plays alongside a slow bass line, and synth effects give the impression of muzak played over an airport lounge's PA system. Ethereal guitar and synth chords sound in the background, in the style of Eno's *Music for Airports*, giving the sensation of flight. The arrivals are so late to the party that they are described as joining the "Afterglow": what happens after the fire has died.

"We welcome to the world" not only new people but also those who previously left to find other states of mind but have returned, "for they are the returning generation": the hippies of the 60s, the ravers of the late 80s. The idealism and optimism of the 60s which led to the technology boom of the 70s, and returned in some spirit in the second summer of love, is linked to the present day by the following:

Welcome to the world
Where shares can go down as well as up
Where "Words are flowing out like endless rain into a paper cup"
Plays on a remastered CD somewhere in Los Angeles
While seagulls wheel and the index drops

The quotation is from *Across the Universe* by The Beatles, or rather, John Lennon, and a key text of the 60s era. The quotation is sung rather than rapped to emphasise its beauty and contrast with the following lines, where the synths drop out and the beat is accompanied by the sound of something like a large tap dripping. This is more disturbing and seems to relate to the cynicism which has replaced the hippy dream.

The music resumes in full for the next stanza, which seems to reject materialism:

"Never mind what's relevant and never mind selling it", as the narrator comes up with ideas in "research and development".

While the power drains from the mainframes
I'm surfing on the brainwaves
Singing free the slaves, Jesus saves
And other bullshit literature
Washed down in the rainstorm.

How cute and dated to sing about a computer "mainframe" nowadays, at any rate this is another reference to new technology, and we go internet "surfing" listening to the ridiculous ideas that all these arrivals have, until they are washed away by another weather metaphor.

The new arrivals, the children, at Gate 17 are debriefed and given the following User's Guide to existence:

We eat, we sleep, we shit and fuck and die
We speak, we hope, we learn, we try.

The song was originally intended as a "Welcome to the World" for young people, or rather, a young person, or rather, Shazna, the adolescent with whom Momus had developed a relationship. For she was young, and therefore arrived "too late to enjoy it"; "it" being the first or second summers of love. The first few stanzas are restated for the benefit of Shazna, and the song then breaks down again with the dripping tap, and as it fades out Momus raps:

Too late to enjoy it
Too soon to destroy it
Too dumb to invent it
Too smart to end it

Suggesting those new arrivals are too late to enjoy, but too soon to destroy the world. They are either too dumb to invent anything, or the world is too dumb to be invented were you to start from fresh. In the end, they are too smart to end the world, or the world is too smart to be destroyed, it still has value. You may interpret these lines as you wish; it is your revolution.

Trans-Siberian Express

Kraftwerk had their *Trans-Europe Express* in 1977, but this journey goes much further, and describes in detail the myths and legends of the lands it speeds through, speaking of travel, conflict and death in the wastelands. It feels like a journey through an alien landscape and images from films by Andrei Tarkovsky. It could be describing Earth as imagined by an outsider through a filter of tribal tales and aural tradition.

It starts with the sound of a distant train horn and the snare and kick drums come in, programmed to simulate a train on its tracks. There is a vocal sample from a dance record and metallic keyboard chords accompany the slow rap: similar in feel to the previous track.

Momus raps of a journey to desolation, to death:

in language looted and compressed
abandon this world for the next.

We should forget the cities and statues of the world, where life is only short:

Leave your burden with the rest,
watch the sleepers phosphoresce.

The "sleepers" being the sleepers of the tracks but also those who died and were abandoned on the way, cast from the train of existence. To travel on this express means to leave everything precious to you:

Rich man leave your wealthiness
Wanderer, your solemn dress
Seafarer, the sea's caress
Beowulf, your angriness.

Beowulf is the hero of Anglo-Saxon poetry who killed Grendel the monster, the son of Cain and a snake; legendarily angry in his execution of both Grendel and his mother, and no doubt angry for his depiction by Ray Winstone covered in those ping-pong ball special-effects technicians are obsessed by.

A piano comes in on the second stanza with more keyboards, dropping out again for the third. The chorus is sung rather than rapped, with a further keyboard sound mixed in, which remains for some further stanzas. The chorus returns to a theme of the previous song.

The world is long, there is no consolation
For those who join at the end of the line.

The young who join the world at the end are without consolation for their loss. Again, the song builds slowly adding sounds as it progresses, but dropping sounds out for some stanzas to emphasise their drama. The train journeys through winds such as the sirocco, past Stalag camps with captives on Death Row – conflating the Russian death camps in Siberia with their German equivalents, and satellites, acknowledging Russia's place in the

Space Race. The sense of folk horror, of dark stories told under arctic skies, is well illustrated:

The skulls of reindeer in the snow,
the longboat drifts, the dead float slow.

There is a reference to Ben Bulben, in County Sligo, Ireland: a rock formation under which a band of warriors is said to sleep. The snow of Siberia is referenced as:

Drifts are shifted by the plough
like waves that break against the prow:

The train is like a ship, ploughing through waves of snow. There is a call-back here to *Lucky Like St Sebastian* as again Momus quotes e e cummings' *Buffalo Bill's* "How do you like your blue-eyed boy now, Mr Death?"

Momus now talks about times before modern history, before nature as we know it clothed the steppes. We hear that Jack Frost "screamed, his voice so hoarse", with ferocious weather that blew signalmen from the railway back into history, past Attila, the Visigoths and Norsemen. Perhaps they then witnessed the next stanza: that of even older myths of Ancient Greece, with shaman and priest discussing the story of Jason and the Golden Fleece, or even older myths such as those in the Dead Sea Scrolls, or even back to the Epic of Gilgamesh (possibly the oldest significant piece of literature, from Sumeria in maybe 2000 BC) Having gone so far back in history the narrator is lost, deliberately. There is also a suggestion that these stories have all inspired each other, that they are part of a chain of creation. The Epic of Gilgamesh, for instance, is a major source of the legends which were later associated with Jesus Christ.

There is an instrumental break where the click drums come in even more, emphasising the train's speed and progress. In the final verse he says that the person he is both leaving and searching for should not miss him:

Don't cry for me I never cried for you
Just left without the name
Of the place I'm going to.

Having betrayed them with absence, returning is a long voyage of itself:

I'm travelling to forget you
And to find you

The instruments and drums slowly drop out at the end, leaving Momus singing "end of the line…" repeatedly to fade.

This track is the centrepiece of the album's theme of travel and desolation, quite dark and cynical in its attitude to life, as we voyage towards death and destruction, and containing dark themes from historical sagas and legends. With each track, this album feels less and less the optimistic and commercial festival it initially seemed to be…In fact, this track literally inspired a murder, committed by Stuart M. Kaminsky in his novel *Murder on the Trans-Siberian Express*.

Voyager

What we need now is a big slice of pop to cheer us up, and this does not disappoint. Unlike the other songs on this album, *Voyager* was "written", on guitar, in a more traditional manner, rather than being assembled from samples and atmospherics. In fact, a later version was recorded in 2006 with the guitar part restored.

The narrator of this song is afraid of love, afraid of commitment, perhaps having abandoned his hedonistic and promiscuous ways, the idea of a committed relationship is frightening for him. Having looked outwards at travel and voyaged in various ways, he is now looking inwards, trapped in his own personality and mind, watching old films on a loop and afraid to move anywhere in case too much changes. God make me pure...but not yet, essentially. As in the other songs in this set, the indecision is given an excuse based on the weather that is used as a metaphor for his internal landscape; the narrator cannot do anything because "the weather's wrong".

This is a huge pop landscape musically. Crisp hi-hat and cymbals open the song which samples the voice and strings from Love Unlimited's 1972 track *Walking in the Rain with the one I love.*

The song features the choppy piano riffing we associate with dance music of the time, and a cool beat maintained in the bass line to accompany the vocal track.

The lyrics open with Momus in his garden, with the motorway jammed, doing "predictable things". He watches leaves as they fall, and satellite pictures on his TV.

"The moon is hot, I can't do anything", he opines, giving excuse after excuse to do nothing. He watches Voyager, the space probes (there was a Voyager 1 and a Voyager 2) as they fly. Both had left the solar system by this point and were indeed flying blind through unimaginable space and time, and still are.

He watches TV on his Sony Watchman (a small portable TV sold at the time), watching old films and feeling emotional, but he does not know why. He reads a newspaper and is bemused by the news being good (not a line which would work now), looks at his reflection in the pond, but the trees have died so he goes inside again.

The inaction and lack of motivation of the narrator are symptoms of his inner decay, his inability to process or accept love. His state of mind is spelled out in the middle eight:

Hold me love I cannot catch my breath

This fear of love is choking me to death
I can't live without you I can't live with you
I wriggle and I turn
Tell me when will I ever learn?

The end of this middle eight segues into a dramatic and climactic instrumental break, with a screaming sound effect in the background mimicking the strings as they strain upwards. This fades out and into the final verse: feeling sorry for the flowers, he brings them inside.

And my love for you is so new

Is this Momus' love for Shazna which is being referenced?

And there's so much left to do
But there are thunderstorms
And the weather's wrong

Again, he cannot act, immobilised by his own inability to feel love. Because, at the end of the day, "Everyone's trying to get in out of the rain". The strings repeatedly try to swirl upwards to a climax but are not allowed. On an earlier Momus album, we would assume this was a guarded reference to orgasm or something equally filthy, but here it is about being unable to reach happiness, to express love, and to "get out of the rain".

He repeats the middle eight again, saying again that he wriggles and turns, and with the realisation that he will never ever learn, the strings are finally allowed upwards to completion, which, when it comes, sounds sinister and more like a clip from a horror film. What has he let himself in for by allowing love into his heart? The song breaks down and ends with just the hi-hat and cymbals again, which stop abruptly and lead neatly like a match cut into the final track.

This title track is a huge pop song, and Momus seems to prefer the pared down 2006 version. It is highly reminiscent of the more widescreen work of the Pet Shop Boys and the production maybe overbears the message, but take the opportunity to hear a big production from Momus, as it won't happen very often again after this album.

Momutation 3

A remix of elements from the song *Conquistador* by Douglas Benford (Lovecut DB). It is short, danceable and quite fun but adds little to the original song or to the album. It is, however, only the second instrumental track to appear on a Momus album following *Forests* on *The Ultraconformist*.

Overall, *Voyager* is hugely entertaining. At the time I was shocked by the change in direction, not appreciating the reasons for it. With hindsight it is clear how things were progressing. Ironically, it is at this point, as Momus frees himself from any concern about "being commercial", that he releases what is, on the face of it, a hugely commercial sounding album.

It would be some time before the next album was released in the autumn of 1993, and important events in Momus' personal life were unfolding. These would also impinge on his relationship with Creation and alter the direction of Momus' career and interest in music for some time to come. Japan was calling. It was hardly surprising that Momus would soon prefer to keep the company of, and work with, a culture that had respect for him, rather than describing him as "a creative leper trying to re-dress his sores with the bandage of technology", which comes from Barbara Ellen's *Voyager* review in the NME.

Becoming global, but with a limited audience, was the route he intended to take. To this end this year saw his first discussion of the internet, and the very earliest texts from his first webpages date from this period; however, he would not launch a website until 1995.

His next album was *Timelord* – his last album for Creation, and in many ways the most sombre.

Strange Emotional Pattern...#15 Timelord

Whether via the address kindly given in the CD insert for *Hippopotamomus*, or via Creation Records, Momus received and devoured fan mail. In a diary entry from the early 90s he reported: "A couple of girlish peans give me a stiffy as I sit on the loo reading it." A Select magazine interview with Miranda Sawyer revealed that one of these very poems was his first contact with Shazna Nessa, who would eventually become his wife.

The barriers to this union were numerous. The first elephant (or hippo) in the room was her age: Shazna was 14 when she first wrote to Momus. It is hardly surprising therefore that her parents were extremely set against her relationship with him: it is perfectly reasonable to object to finding your 14-year-old daughter is in intimate correspondence with a) a stranger who is b) 31 years old and c) a "pop" star who d) has written songs such as *The Homosexual* and e) *The Guitar Lesson* and f) albums called *The Poison Boyfriend* and *Tender Pervert*.

Earlier in his career, Nick was accused of wanting to copy Serge Gainsbourg in having young lovers, and the defence for this and any other accusations related to "Guitar Lesson" style-content was that it was all fantasy, that the images thus presented were not real. This defence is somewhat blown out of the water by the fact that he then started to engage in intimate correspondence with a child. However, in an interview with the Daily Record, after the fact, in 1994, Nick did say: "It was just an innocent friendship. We both liked the same books and could really talk and make each other laugh. For a long time we were only friends." At any rate, Nick's love for a physically and emotionally mature girl such as Shazna at 16 makes him an Ephebophile, and not the other thing.

Their relationship became serious when Shazna turned 16 in 1993 and she was forced to meet Nick in secret while at a private school. Her parents wanted her to marry a 21-year-old boy from a wealthy Bangladeshi family, and this fiancé became violent when he found out about Nick. For a while they ran away to Nick's family in Scotland. While there, on the telephone her father seemed finally to give permission for her and Nick to marry, but when she returned to London she was effectively imprisoned, then tricked into returning home to Bangladesh to see her grandfather, where she was confined to the family home and displayed to a string of suitors.

Nick, having converted to Islam, had changed his life and outlook for Shazna, and he continued to fight for her freedom. This included complaints to social services and to the British High Commission in Bangladesh. Human rights campaigners in the country effectively spied on Shazna's house and reported on her situation. When Shazna went to Dhaka to renew her passport, an envelope from Nick was passed to her which contained valid open tickets home and a letter explaining that relevant travel documentation could be issued by the British High Commission as long as she could reach the building. But for a long time it seemed as if this would not happen, and the couple remained separated.

Momus remained alone in Cleveland Street and was working on material for a new album. Technology had marched on and he now had an Apple DuoDock 230 and an internet connection with CompuServe, invaluable for email communications with his lawyer in Bangladesh. Songs written in his home studio around this time included *The End of History* and *London 1888* and perhaps not surprisingly represented a more romantic sound. However, he was commissioned to co-write and produce an album for the Japanese artist The Poison Girlfriend, which was released that year as *Shyness*. Several of the songs he was writing were moved to this project, including *The End of History*, *Nobody* and *Pure Selfishness* (my favourite on that album).

The new Momus album became leaner and more focused

as a result; it became a hymn to Shazna and their "forbidden" love, and was intended as a love letter to her, a beacon of hope which she could hear and take solace in, and on which he could project his own torments. This made *Timelord* extremely dark, melancholy and in his own words an album which "shot itself in the foot" in terms of actual commercial or critical impact. On the other hand, for once there was a minimal sense of irony or caricature, narrative or pastiche; this was an honest and sincere album from an artist hardly known for being straightforward. This risked alienating literally everyone, fans of "classic" Momus, fans of the more commercial Momus of *Voyager*, and the label bosses. In addition, it gave critics ammunition they hardly needed. The completed album came out late in 1993 and Creation seemed to give no effort whatsoever to promotion. The first notice I had that there was a new album was seeing it in the Canterbury music shop where I had purchased *Monsters of Love*. There were reviews, of course, which were muted, and fairly disinterested for the most part, and can be sampled on the Momus website. By the way, one of those reviews mentions his contribution to Derek Jarman's film *Blue* – composing music for the song *Cocksucking Lesbian Man* with lyrics by Jarman and co-performed and produced by Simon Fisher-Turner. *Blue* is a film consisting of a single frame of blue colour for 90 minutes or so, with words and music overlaid telling Derek Jarman's story in the context of his battle with AIDS, and his encroaching blindness.

One advantage of Momus recording at home and engineering and producing everything himself was that money was saved in recording expenses. For *Timelord* this enabled him to budget £3000 to procure the services of Pierre et Gilles – iconic French artists and photographers – to take the cover photograph for the album. They had previously photographed Marc Almond, among many others. In the end Creation refused to pay for the shoot, claiming not to have authorised it. Momus advised Pierre et Gilles to sue, but they never did.

Here, Momus is shown as if in a Renaissance painting, as a knight perhaps, a conquistador, certainly a romantic figure, peeling fruit with his outsized blade, in armour and with fruit bowls to either side, the image itself framed by metal plate and discs with heart and star shapes. The backdrop is light and airy reminiscent of a blue sky, with some white clouds, and red drapes frame the image. Momus seems a tiny figure to be inhabiting that armour. He is very serious, alone and forlorn with his fruit. His hair is shorn, which at once indicates some kind of religious fervour or intent but is perhaps at odds with the conversion to Islam we were told about, and he is clean shaven. It is a beautifully composed and framed shot, whatever the implied message, here we have an interesting take on the title Timelord, given the out of time nature of the image.

The back cover of the CD lists the tracks in an italic serif font, gives the artist and title in the same calligraphic font, and also has a hand-drawn image of a cherry with a crown and face, and the inscription "This record is for Shazna Nessa, The Queen of Cherries", and the initials W.A.G.T.B.T, which stand for "We Are Going To Be Together". The record was a message to Shazna, and the S.W.A.L.K style message one of hope.

The inlay credits Creation Records, but distribution is by Pinnacle and the album is published by Rhythm King Music and Complete Music. The inlay design is by Anthony Sweeney and there are also thanks to Pierre et Gilles, Hanna Puttonen, Rafael Jiminez and Takao Homma (of Nippon Columbia). The inlay also includes all song lyrics, and everything is against a black background. The CD disc has a reversal of the cherry image, drawn in black on a cerise background. The album title is also included on a clear sticker on the front cover. Overall the image of the cover design is romantic, framed in the Renaissance and quite serious. It is clear that this album is going to sound very different.

According to Nick, the instruments used on this album include, "a Gibson semi-acoustic guitar (not much, though, I think it's just on Platinum), a Kawai K4 synth, a Casio CZ101, a Technics KN600 and an Akai S2800 sampler. Sequencing is via C-LAB Notator running on an Atari STE1040 (i.e. Logic, as it became)". He also used a VTL CR-3A microphone.

Platinum

One thing the album title certainly does NOT refer to is *Doctor Who*: the best-known character who is a "Timelord". That TV series was not even playing in 1993 having been cancelled in 1989 and would not resurface until a TV movie starring Paul McGann in 1996. But ideas of travelling through time, or potentially between dimensions, do arise here. The general theme seems to be that of an astronaut travelling alone far away from his home and all he knows, hearing snatches of his previous life and memories, and imagining how things could have worked out if he had made different decisions.

The album fades in with swirling noise as if capturing radio transmissions from a lost empire. It's slightly reminiscent of the opening of U2's *Zooropa* with its forest of commercial voices. Here, however, the sounds are redolent of the past. The first voice is a recording of Nick Currie's grandfather, recorded asking a young Nicholas how often you need to renew the valves in the Sony TV they had. "There are no valves, it's transistorised", is Nick's response, baffling to his grandad, a Timelord himself, sounding lost at that point. There are then samples from the Nic Roeg film *The Man Who Fell to Earth* starring David Bowie, and excerpts from interviews with Nick Currie including the question "Who is the REAL Nick Currie?", unanswerable and symbolic again of the idea of being lost in time, and identity. Momus fades in singing "Timelord" (It sounds like "Time Out" to me) in harmony with himself and a beat, sampled from a lost Japanese

CD, kicks in. It is a good beat too, driving the song along with its French Chanson sounding chord sequence playing underneath, those two major influences linked again. The beat and melody are stop/start perhaps representing the journey of life and the flow of time. The whole track on the original album seems to be sped up a beat resulting in Nick's voice when it comes in sounding higher and reedier than usual, not so far back in the mix as on *Voyager*, but sounding distant all the same, the voice of an old traveller across space and time. The lyrics are instantly melancholic and wishful.

If I told the truth I'd like to live my life again
Walk around my youth in somebody else's skin
One life's not enough for all that we contain
Nothing's going to save us now.

The eternal return: the plea to go back and re-run/change our lives as we would prefer to have lived them, which is an illusory ambition as once one thing were changed, everything else would fall away too. On the second verse a pedal note comes in, as an organ sound, almost church-religious; it is balanced by an accordion sound in the upper register, emphasising how French the whole song sounds. The key lyric is here, with the sci-fi concept literally outlined:

Take me to the place where my decisions are relived
Give me answers to the question
"What would have happened if…"
Beyond the third dimension, beyond the fourth and fifth
In a parallel universe.

The regret and sadness implicit in such a statement are clear. The past is awful, we need to go back and change it, not celebrate it:

Hey DJ you've got it all wrong
No more golden greats, no more platinum songs
Put these frozen moments in the fridge where they belong
Nothing's going to save us now.

Momus' lack of commercial success has led to some bitterness against DJs and the radio system, Momus being quite happy to "fridge" those other more successful artists, and indeed to "fridge" those periods of time when greatness had been promised to him. Interestingly, in the next verse, Momus seems at pains to tell us that he is not being optimistic here, which seems quite obvious:

I don't say that life's not sad and death is not the end
Looks like you got typecast by a double-crossing friend.

But he believes we will return, not in reincarnation, but in a parallel universe, where everything we achieved in this universe is gone, good or bad:

Gone the crimes that you committed, gone the things you made.

He then sings about the connections we make with other people, the "parallel" possibilities that exist in their lives, and bemoans the fact that to further our own ambitions we may stop others achieving what they could, lines which are at once positive and heart-breaking.

Walk the city streets with me and cross a thousand lives
Count the possibilities that shine in people's eyes
Ask how many dreams we kill to keep our dreams alive.

Momus then addresses the issue of his own fame, or lack of it, and "thanks" the public for giving him the situation he is in:

Thank you for the memory, the curse you laid on me
Like a shooting star I burst into obscurity
Live this second first because the rest is history
nothing's going to save us now.

He repeats the chorus, this time describing the "golden greats" as "little shits", and repeats the first stanza of the song.

This is a very depressive song, the kind of regret and hatred for one's own past that surfaces in the small hours of the morning, buoyed by some minor feeling of optimism that perhaps things went better in a parallel universe, and perhaps that place could be accessed somehow. All that is available to the narrator is to "live the hallelujah now", to make the best of things, to live the best spiritual life you can. "Hallelujah" means to hail God, and to be one with the spiritual world. As an introduction to the dark world of *Timelord, Platinum* at least has a good pace and a quirky melody. An improved version, slowed down a little, is available on the *Forbidden Software Timemachine* compilation that would be released in 2003.

Enlightenment

Having a serious relationship with a young woman must have brought home to Momus the years of promiscuity and abandonment that had preceded it, as he chose to have a test for the HIV virus. In 1993 having a positive result to a test for HIV was still more or less a death sentence, and although the utter hysteria and paranoia around the disease in the 80s had dissipated somewhat, to go for an "AIDS Test" was still a dark and terrifying process. This song plays around the notion of *Enlightenment*: the coming into being of knowledge, in this case, the knowledge of your test result. *Enlightenment* also refers to the scientific renaissance of the eighteenth century, and to the battle between diseases such as AIDS and the scientific method. Finally, *Enlightenment* is a spiritual awakening or calling, such as

Momus was experiencing both in his relationship with Shazna and in his shifting ideologies.

The music is slower paced and begins with echoing percussion and beats, as if we are shuffling along in a hospital corridor to a waiting room. There is a sample from the band Pizzicato 5 buried in the mix. There is a Japanese influence to the backing and melody. The lyrics talk about the irony of our hard-won sexual freedom leading to our doom:

In the 1970s
When everyone could do just what they wanted to
Sex was like a handshake between friends
But now that life and death and destiny
Are in you when you're next to me
Tell me that you'll love me till the end

The consequence of the test result could completely change the nature of the patient's relationship with his partner, with his doctor and with society. In this situation, any person would want to know that their partner, lover and confidante would still be with them no matter what the news and how bad things got. The chorus makes this concern explicit, an AIDS related update of *When I'm Sixty-Four*:

And tell me you'll be there
If I ever find
I've only got one kidney left
And tell me you'll be there
When I've only got one eye
And say that you'll be there to care for me
When a wheelchair is my chair
You'll be there upon the day I die

The fact is that all we have is this moment, and Momus talks about what we would now call mindfulness: gaining insights in the discrete moment you live in.

Enlightenment in the nowness of now
All we have is the nowness of now.

I must draw attention here to the line "when I've only got one eye", which is prophetic, spooky and unfortunate, since it now reads as if intentional. But it was not at the time; it was intended to be one of the worst consequences that could occur as a result of HIV infection. Nevertheless, as a result of a different type of infection, Momus did go on to lose an eye several years later, and this particular song must creep him out immensely now. The second verse talks about waiting for the results of the test, and the tension this brings:

Still I do this willingly
Because I want to know what I don't want to know
Unthinkable thoughts are thoughts we have to try.

This perfectly captures the doublethink we must go through when taking such tests: we do not want to know, but we must know and need to know. "Unthinkable thoughts" are precisely the stock in trade of Momus' previous albums and thinking them is his entire philosophy to date. The chorus again describes horrendous things that might happen if the result is positive:

When I'm paralytic will you still be true?

The scientific Enlightenment is then discussed, with the optimism of the eighteenth century attacked by Momus; we were supposed to know all that there is to know by now, but various facts of nature, such as quantum physics, issues with mathematics, and the creation of many devastating new diseases meant that we never conquered nature.

In the eighteenth century they said
"We'll shortly know all there is to know
All things will be clear to us one day"
Well I'm sick to death of optimism
Sick to death of the shit it drops us in
Will they find a cure for hope? No-one can say.

This is contrasted with the chorus, and more things that can happen to Momus. The vocals are double tracked now, and the chorus starts to sound messier and more out of control, as things would be in this scenario. He asks if we will be there when his swansong fades:

And when a life support machine
Supports me in a coma you'll be there
And when I'm just a cabbage
Save me from the spade.

Not the most politically correct description of a coma patient, but this is a Momus album after all! The song builds in intensity for a repeat of the chorus two more times, with the eye sequence repeated, and the final plea:

And tell me you'll still be my baby
When my guts are on the floor
And when I'm catatonic
I'll still be your man.

The song fades out with the imprecations continuing, perhaps forever. In the end, Momus' result was negative. This is not the strongest song on the album – that is probably *Rhetoric* – but it is my favourite, the match of scientific endeavour against the natural world is a subject of interest to me, and the lyrics of *Enlightenment* work with those of *Platinum* to highlight the anger and bitterness that he seems to feel against the modern world at this point. There is a struggle between the desire for spiritual calm and the issues that the world throws upon you, that can lead to freedom or to darkness and despair, and at this point, it seemed on a knife edge which way Momus would go.

You've Changed

Perhaps the slightest song on the album, it is interesting to compare this to similarly presented work on *Voyager* such as *Vocation* or *virtual reality*. The optimism displayed on those earlier songs has gone, and we now see the ghosts of the past when in a new relationship. It is a bouncy, oddly structured piece which seems to change time signature and skip beats to disorientate the listener. The singer is with his new girlfriend when he meets his ex with her new lover.

Me and her and the ghost of you
You and him and the ghost of me
Two plus one is three and two plus a ghost is three
I guess there must be six of us now.

If the "ghost" of his ex haunts his current relationship he certainly has problems. He is not being arrogant in assuming he also "haunts" his ex; she has been telling him about it:

I remember you telling me
That even though you loved him like a brother
There'll always be another hanging over you
The ghost of your ex-lover
There are six of us

Her current lover, damned by the faint praise of being loved "like a brother", has heard a great deal about him. Momus has a very pragmatic and pessimistic view of the situation:

Don't get possessive, it's melodramatic
It's not love, it's mathematics
There are six of us now.

There is a nostalgia and pining for the relationship they enjoyed before, even the negative aspects of it which must have caused the end are viewed as a loss:

You've changed and I'm looking at your face
But the feelings that I feel are in another time and place
You've changed, you're more vulnerable now
But the arrogance you had was beautiful somehow.

The song seems to mirror older work such as *Hairstyle of the Devil* in its fascination with threesomes, and the jealousy of the "other lover":

You've changed and your boyfriend hangs about
He wants to know if I'm the one he's heard so much about.

In the end, although he longs to kiss her, he knows that he cannot, because they have both changed, and nothing in the past can be recaptured. It is an odd sounding song for Momus, very uncertain and quite difficult to listen to. There is that choppy piano again, from early 90s dance music, still plugging away. The constant time changes, unnecessary stop-start nature and repetition make it actually rather irritating to me.

However, the idea of the permanence of loss and the impossibility of return – however much we would like to believe in time travel and alternate dimensions – is also the theme of the next, and more interesting, song.

Landrover

Based on a very old song idea from 1983 and included as a demo on the *BBC – Golden Age of Television* demos, this is the simple tale of an astronaut searching for his lost lover on the moon, criss-crossing the landscape in a lunar rover. There are echoes of *The Man Who Fell to Earth* in the concept; there is a bit of Kubrick in the idea of a protagonist silently searching across the arid landscape, similar to shots in *2001: A Space Odyssey*.

There's a strong echo of Andrei Tarkovsky's film *Solaris* in the concept of being lost in an alien landscape as well, and of Ray Bradbury's short stories such as *No Particular Night or Morning*, which could be a key text in terms of the whole concept of *Timelord*.

The song has a sampled beat and is driven by a bass line representing the turning wheels of the Landrover. Momus' vocals are double tracked, and he describes his journey across the lunar surface in very practical detail. This story of travel in a futuristic craft is quite similar to Donald Fagen's song cycle *Kamakiriad* which was released the same year and includes a similar song concept in *On the Dunes*.

In the chorus of Momus' song he states he will drive until he finds his lost love or the Landrover breaks down, which would of course be a death sentence. Following the chorus there is an interesting spoken section in which the astronaut reads from his diary, describing prosaic detail such as saline levels and visibility.

We know it is October when he is searching, and she disappeared during the year. He could have been searching for a long time: now it is autumn and the shadows are gathering, as indeed they are across the whole album. He again reads from his diary, and things are going badly:

> *Strange emotional pattern recorded at 300 and again towards dawn...foreboding...Log discontinued*

Following a further chorus, the music slows and a sinister high-pitched synth line comes in, minor and discordant. The song fades out with Momus reciting a list of things that represent either the relationship he has lost, or things he is afraid of finding:

Sunday airports
The face of the waters
Service stations
Unrepeatable offers
Trial by jury
The god of the crossroads
Furnished quarters
Unfaithful lovers.

Perhaps it is the same service station he visited in *Spy on the Moon*? Perhaps this guy IS the Spy on the Moon. It is an unsettling lyric and sound, and I think this song is very successful in giving a sense of alienation, of loss and of the insanity that can come with it; clearly this astronaut will one day be found dead in his Landrover, having failed in his mission. The album only descends into darkness from here.

Rhetoric

Opening with sci-fi sounds and a descending note inspired by Vangelis' score for *Blade Runner*, slow chords against a simple beat and sample accompany what is on the face of it a straightforward love song with a very pretty chord sequence and melody. Rightly, this is the only song from *Timelord* which is still performed by Momus regularly, was eventually played at his wedding, and may even play at his funeral.

The weakness of his voice here, regularly cracking with emotion, works well and to the benefit of the song. Each lyric is simply structured: "I'll love you till they figure out the way that life began." The surrealism of his earlier writing for *Voyager* resurfaces a little:

I'll love you till the reaper comes to wake me with his gun
I'll love you till the melting clocks have chimed a melting hour

The sci-fi elements remain and there is also a slightly sinister aspect to some of the aspirations:

I'll love you till the razorblades are held against my neck
I'll love you till the sea glows purple and the sky goes black.

There is a straightforward beauty and Japanese poetic influence to some of the lines:

The lovely owl upon the bough is swooping down for me
The brambles tangle round and round far as the eye can see.

In the end his love for Shazna almost outstrips that for his beloved Fiat 500:

I love you like the engine of a little blue machine
I love you like the bee that dies, dies astride a queen.

I am not sure that's how bees work. But we will allow some entomological infelicities for such a beautiful song and premise. This song has a simple structure which loops and eventually fades out, its sounds merging into the subsequent song.

Suicide Pact

Following on from *Rhetoric* with similar sci-fi sounds and an eerie mournfulness, this slower song, with bass but no drums or percussion, describes the fate of a couple no longer allowed to be together, and unable to behave as the world demands:

We were lovers
We never knew how to act

This song is clearly about the relationship between Momus and Shazna and the way in which they were pulled apart by her family and circumstance. The music started as a cover version of a song called *The Uncertainty of Identity* by a songwriter's alter ego called Alexander Mann, and the atmosphere of the piece was inspired by David Sylvian's brief eulogy to sadness, *September*. There is no future or place for these lovers in the world they are forced to inhabit.

Where in the world is there space
For the beauty we shared?

As in the previous song, nature is used as a comparator:

Remember the herons and cranes
But as they have flown, so must we go.

The lovers have determined to be destroyed rather than separated:

We were lovers
We made a suicide pact
We let sleep steal across us
In the snow where we sat.

They watch a meteor shower and the Aurora Borealis, further comparisons between the majesty of the universe and the smallness of their concerns and indicative of the lack of interest the universe has in their problems. The suicidal nature of their thoughts is pressed home by a desire to be gone before the world turns:

Where in the world is there time
For the love we have shared?
Nowhere.
Deep in the forest
Remember the acorns and cones
Before they have grown we must be gone.

The sadness is there even as they travel, maybe together, and to their deaths:

From the 747
Remember the shapes of the clouds
But when we are gone they'll be our shrouds.

This is as depressive as the album gets, as downbeat as any Momus song gets really, and if it is an indication of his state of mind at the time, not a healthy one. Fortunately, there is a mince pie in the oven.

Christmas on Earth

A mechanical sounding loop introduces the voice of the astronaut as he spins through space in his capsule, talking about Christmas and how meaningless and hellish such occasions are when you are adrift in time and apart from the ones you love.

And I know that on Earth it is Christmas now…

Of course, he cannot possibly know that: since time would be irrelevant at this point, but the astronaut clings to these traditions for comfort. He hopes there will be "days in the snow" and an echo is placed on his voice, making his words sound more expansive, despite the claustrophobia of his situation. He acknowledges that by the time he returns everything will be gone:

And I hope there'll be days in the snow
When I return many light years on
Though my friends will have died long ago.

We must excuse the use of "light years" to apparently refer to a length of time and not distance, perhaps he is on his way to complete the Kessel Run. He describes the beauty he is seeing, worlds made of ice and asteroids, despite there being no-one there to hear him. A sound reminiscent of jingle bells fades in as the song continues, and in the background we hear snatches of old songs, particularly *Try to Remember* from the musical *The Fantasticks,* a song specifically about nostalgia and our inability to remember the past in clear detail. Momus channelling Bing Crosby channelling Thomas Jerome Newton. He is so far from Earth that he is picking up ancient broadcasts:

I'm receiving transmissions they broadcast long ago
They remind me of things I have seen
All the people and cities and crowds.

The next section serves as a chorus and has the clearest Christmas message, multi-tracked and almost festive, with a similar demand to that made by The Darkness in their Christmas rock song *Christmas Time (Don't Let the Bells End)*:

Ring the bells, ring the bells, ring them
Ring the bells, ring the bells, I can still hear them
Here on the way to the stars

This is still melancholy, though, as he is far from any true celebration, driven home by the next verse.

About now back on earth it is Christmas time
There'll be logs in the grate, they will burn

I'm alone tape-recording memories
For it all will have changed when I return.

He sings again about the beauty he is seeing and which he cannot communicate to anyone:

And the rain is so strange in the Milky Way
I see cloudscapes of purple and green
Candelabras are shooting off firework displays
And I'm writing the things I have seen
People shopping and sparks from a train.

As he is travelling so fast, he will age a small amount compared to the amount of time that passes on Earth: everyone he knows will indeed be dead when he returns: a storyline prefiguring Christopher Nolan's film *Interstellar*.

But in space time goes by so slow
At the speed of light one single night
Is a year to the people back home.

Again, do not look too closely at the facts and figures here. I do wonder where he got his degree in astrophysics. Anyway, this is the tragedy of his situation; he cannot communicate with anyone as any messages he sends will only reach dead people, and nothing of his old life will remain when he returns, if he returns. This is a specific statement of the alienation sung about by David Bowie in *Space Oddity* and even in *Blackstar*, with its image of a dead astronaut floating in space, which Momus' character will eventually become.

The main theme is now played on a keyboard, and the song fades out with its pretty, melancholy theme, the word "follow" from *Try to Remember* echoing in the background. But no-one can follow, our man is alone out there. Is there no optimism left?

Breathless

Yes and No. *Timelord* has been very uncharacteristic of the Momus sound, and this track, perhaps more than any other, departs from our usual expectations.

Neil Young was once sued by his record company – Geffen – for producing two albums "uncharacteristic" of Neil Young's sound – the only artist ever to be sued for not sounding like himself. Perhaps if Creation were bothered about Momus' output at this point they may have raised similar objections. The "perversion", the humour, the narrative strands, even the more commercial output of *Voyager*, are all absent. This song, in particular, is romantic, heartfelt and as far from cynical criticism as our classical god of mockery could get. It is a message to Shazna, of course, and an attempt to bring some optimism to proceedings, despite the fact that "hope disappeared long ago". It depicts the aftermath of a happy reunion, with the lover aware that things may get worse, but he is "over the moon for now".

The song starts with a snare and kick drum beat and comes in as a cheesy, cruise ship bar band playing a show tune. It could have been a dance hall tune from the forties, one from a remix album by The Caretaker perhaps, or playing in the main hall in the Overlook Hotel.

It sounds louder, somehow, than the other songs on the album, and Momus' voice a little more certain, more emotive. There is no chorus as such, but a sequence of verses interrupted by a saxophone effect playing a solo. The final verse ends abruptly, with that final suggestion of hope. The lyrics emphasise the feeling that things are fine for now, both romantic and erotic:

Soft is the flesh I cling to
Warm the caress of your mouth
Silk is my touch as I swing you
Over the moon for now

Even this happiness is fleeting and nothing good is on the horizon:

Though there are no happy endings
Though hope disappeared long ago
There are clouds at the end of the rainbows
Over the moon for now.

Finally, aware he may never see his lover again, he must remember her as she was:

Your starring role is forever
If only you'll stay as you are
Breathless at the threshold of pleasure
Over the moon for now.

The song ends abruptly at this point, and the album dies with it. *Timelord* could have been the last album released as Momus. There is a sense of finality to the album, the artwork and to the surrounding story. It is easy to imagine an alternative world where Nick went away to write songs for others, or declined into heroin abuse, or worse yet went into Scottish politics. Certainly it led to the persona being put on hold for a while, and many would say the next "proper" Momus album is *Ping Pong* in 1997, with 1995's *The Philosophy of Momus* being a little scattershot in approach and retaining the romantic elements of *Timelord*, and *Slender Sherbet* and *20 Vodka Jellies* being compilations.

The misery of separation under duress continued for Nick and Shazna for some time. Then, in June 1994, in Dhaka, Shazna took action. Under the pretence of delivering library books to a friend, she escaped her parents and got a rickshaw and taxi to the British High Commission. There, she was recognised and welcomed in. Having called Nick she was driven to the airport, with her father who was waiting at the door of the commission making one last attempt to appeal to her. She did not look back, though, and when she arrived in London, she and Nick went to Glasgow, as under Scottish law she could marry without her parents' consent at the age of 17. Which she did, with *Rhetoric* playing as accompaniment. Following this romantic elopement, they might have considered themselves safe, but that was not entirely the case.

Shazna's ex-fiancé came to find her, accompanied by her brothers. Fortunately, the days of Momus leaving his home address on his album covers were behind him, and the gang sent to find him had only Creation's address to go by. They arrived at Creation wielding machetes, convinced that Momus was sleeping there, according to Tim Abbott, a Creation employee of the time.

This led to Alan McGee contacting Momus by phone – not for a meeting in his office, sadly (so put that shot glass down), but for one last conversation. According to Nick (quoted by Richard King in *How Soon Is Now?: The Madmen and Mavericks who made Independent Music 1975–2005*):

> ...Alan phoned me up, he said, "Listen, we had these extremely scary people coming in to the office demanding your address and we didn't give it to them, but this just can't happen and we were seriously thinking of getting in the very heavy drug people Primal Scream deal with to protect the office and the staff. So, sorry, but we're not going to work with you anymore."

In other words, several years after Primal Scream finding him so boring they wanted to (anecdotally) abandon him in Berlin in no man's land, Momus had now out-rock-and-rolled Creation's supremo, to the extent that he couldn't handle him anymore. His time with Creation was over. This left him free to re-sign with Cherry Red, a much more appropriate fit, which he did, and began in the background to prepare material for a new album, which would become *The Philosophy of Momus*.

In the meantime, Nick and Shazna left London and moved to Paris, where he continued writing for Kahimi Karie and others, content in his new life, fitter, happier...

His success in Japan led to the release of a compilation on Nippon Columbia in March 1994 called *Learning to be Human*. This was a 17-track compilation of Creation era material which most notably contained *Poison Boyfriend* from 1982, previously released as the B-Side to *Right Hand Heart*, a free 7" single included with early copies of *Tender Pervert*, and also included in the Creation compilation *Pensioners on Ecstasy* in 1990.

The fruits of Momus' work would now mainly be heard in Japan, but some of those songs written for Japanese ladies would find their way as demos and reworked versions onto subsequent albums and compilations. The next Momus album released in the UK was *The Philosophy of Momus*, released in May 1995 and preceded by, of all things, a CDM: compact disc maxi-single. This would be Momus' first album truly of the internet age, and the first recorded and programmed purely for CD, with no vinyl release. After that, also released in 1995, was a set of re-workings of "classic" Momus tracks called *Slender Sherbet*: clearly an attempt to draw a line under that preceding 10 years and move onto new technologies, and lives.

Wrong For All the Right Reasons…#16 The Philosophy of Momus

By 1995 Momus was dividing his time between London and Paris. His first website was up and running and can still be seen in all its glory on imomus.com, thanks to his being something of a digital hoarder. That hoarding contrasts with his real-life furnishings which seem quite minimal if we go by his Open-University-style videos. He was writing songs for Japanese and French artists at this time, and some of the results of this would surface on *20 Vodka Jellies*.

One such partnership was with Ken Morioka, a Japanese keyboard player, singer, composer, producer and general wunderkind born in 1967, who played with several bands, most notably Soft Ballet. He sadly died of heart failure in 2016, at 49 years old. For his 1994 solo album *Questions* he wrote and performed songs with various musicians including Neil Arthur of Blancmange, bassist Ed Poole and Momus, who wrote and performed vocals on the closing track, *The Sadness of Things*. The arrangement of this allowed Momus to include the song on his own album, and to release it as a single.

In April 1995 Cherry Red released a compact disc maxi-single of Momus tracks leading with *The Sadness of Things*, and also included versions of *London 1888, The End of History* and *An Inflatable Doll*, all of which would be included on *20 Vodka Jellies* the following year. *An Inflatable Doll* is an early version of a track from *The Philosophy of Momus* called *I Had a Girl*. As far as I can ascertain, this is the last single released as Momus until a 10″ sampler of *Thunderclown* in 2011.

The Philosophy of Momus has disparate influences. The French and Japanese music he was surrounded by have an input, along with art he was inspired by at the time. The developing world of the internet was offering possibilities of life in virtual space, and enhanced communication, and this has a clear effect on his work. Where Momus was inspired by trip-hop and acid house in the early 90s, by the mid-90s, grunge had become an influence, along with slacker rock and, most significantly, the work of someone called Beck. Some of the songs hint at developments that are only now becoming a reality: the teledildonic romance of *Virtual Valerie*, the Darknet marketplace of *Yokohama Chinatown*, the undeletable online histories of *Slide Projector Lie Detector*; Momus is truly prescient on this album. His relationship with Shazna is also an influence and casts a light over much of the content. A few of the songs sound as if they could have emerged from the Timelord sessions, particularly *Microworlds, I Had a Girl* and *Complicated*. Other songs, *Slide Projector Lie Detector, Red Pyjamas,* even deal with the minutiae of an everyday relationship.

Being honest, Momus having a settled relationship was a concern to me at the time. As a fan of dark, cynical and amoral music, there is always a danger that contentment could lead to mediocrity. Tolstoy (quoting Hegel) said that, "Happy people have no history," a much-misunderstood phrase interpreted by the rock band Therapy? as, "Happy people have no stories." Perversely, whenever a favourite musician or writer settles down and seems happy, I think all fans secretly wish they would break up or get divorced, as the resulting album or book will be much more interesting than the domestic bliss version, from which the Father of the Nation gets no inspiration.

Indeed, the more homely songs are less interesting to me than the more "traditional" Momus on offer here, such as *The Loneliness of Lift Music,* which follows the thoughts of a murderer. Would Momus be smothered by domestic bliss or find a better use for that cake knife? Time would tell.

The album has a black cover with a red elephant which I think is a pencil topper adorning the front. The album title is in a serif font underneath, with no capitals. The artist's name being part of the title removes the need for a separate declaration, although the spine perhaps unnecessarily tells us the artist's name. The title itself is quite a statement: this album is going to outline all of Momus's ideas and thoughts of the time, and maybe it is a stepping-on point for new fans gathered from Japan and elsewhere, now that Creation and all those other albums are of the past.

The back cover shows Momus in a light-brown cardigan and trousers with hand on chin, slightly fish-eye-lensed and sitting on what looks like a very uncomfortable metal seat, hair very short but grown out a little, slight beard and a quite serious look. Inside, the cover lists the tracks and has a cut-up image of Momus' face along the right-hand side. There is a more artistic black-and-white pose inside, and the cover folds out to show an image of Earth from the moon. The credits are printed in white on the left and right fold outs.

Nick Currie is the writer of all songs apart from the music for *The Sadness of Things*, credited to Ken Morioka. The album is published by Rhythm King Music with *The Sadness of Things* also published by JVC Victor. The album was recorded in Paris and London, with sleeve design by Momus himself and mastered by Denis at Porky's (not that one). For the first time we get a wonderfully of its time email address to contact Momus at: momus@world-net.sct.fr, as well as a PO Box address to mail your machetes to.

There is a long list of people to whom Momus extends thanks and respect, including the artist Kuniyoshi Kaneko (who is the subject of a song on the album), Derek Jarman and Beck. There is an address to write to if you want to order "Man of Letters", a "rhizome of narratives" (or "documentary" to you and me) about Momus by Hannu Puttonen, a compilation of video clips, interviews (including Jarvis Cocker, Ed Ball of The Grid, and Sarah Cracknell) and live footage; parts of this can now be seen on YouTube. Cherry Red's address is also included if you want to write to them for a catalogue.

Onto the CD itself, with its rather cluttered image of a working space, and the first song, of 19. Artists seemed to be determined to fill up every available second of CDs at this time. And what was this time? Britpop was in full swing. Jarvis Cocker and Pulp would break big this year with *Common People*, the likes of Suede, Blur and Oasis were flying high: the artists inspired by Momus were themselves experiencing a peak. Incidentally, Del Amitri (led by Nick's cousin Justin) were if anything on the way down from massive success in the early 90s. Britpop had partially been a reaction to the indie boom from the US led by grunge and slacker rock, which were still popular.

One US artist who was an enormous influence on *Philosophy* was Beck, an anti-folk singer known for irony and deliberately anti-commercial sounds, making him something of an American Momus. He was yet to have his biggest hits in the UK and his most successful album, *Odelay*, came out the following year. The album *Mellow Gold* released in 1994 was clearly an influence on the sound of *Philosophy*.

Toothbrushead

The album opens with a noisy guitar riff, sampled from a blues song, via Muddy Waters. Momus comes in over the top loudly singing/shouting with an effect laid over as if he were singing through a fuzzbox or down a dodgy transatlantic phone line. The riff and sounds continue looping throughout the song as Momus wails stream of consciousness over the top, lyrics presumably improvised. The words and tones are distinctly American in feel, and this is the Beck influence in full effect. It no more sounds like Momus than the overly romantic tracks on *Timelord* did: as if there were a deliberate attempt to bury that persona.

I was born on a dashboard, toothbrush for a head

I can't help but be reminded of J.G. Thirlwell's band, Foetus, who were for a while in the 80s called "Scraping Foetus off the Wheel", which I first knew about from the compilation album *Sink* and from his links to The The. Foetus are well worth a listen if you like industrial techno. Anyway, having a toothbrushead implies a difficult and bristly nature, very literally I imagine. The next lines depict life on a dashboard for a troubled youth:

Detergent foam was my mattress
Toxic waste my bed
In the middle of the night
Electro pop radio station my only light

I spent AGES trying to decipher the They Might be Giants song *Birdhouse in Your Soul* before realising that the song was in fact about a blue-canary-shaped nightlight, sung by the nightlight, and "blue canary in the outlet by the light switch" meant EXACTLY and literally what it said. I am therefore not going to interpret "Electro pop radio station my only light" as meaning anything other than the radio light was his only light.

I've got a maggot in my brain
Solenoid carcrash evergreen
Solenoid barbershop quartet
Bullet the blue jean man
Bullet the blue jean man with the blue jean pain.

This is true stream of consciousness, the electromagnet in the car has caused a crash and the barbershop quartet, presumably U2 who sang *Bullet the Blue Sky*, are singing "Bullet the blue jean man" as a tribute to or attack on David Bowie.

Chucking plastic ectoplasm
Detergent foam beatnik of the buttlick
Bioethical criminal, bioethical criminal

I am guessing this vaguely refers to genetics, and hints at some modern form of crime, with modern con-artists using genetically prepared ectoplasm instead of the more traditional muslin cloths to pretend to raise the dead.

Sterling or traveller's cheques
Hey whatever the drug dealer accepts
Feverish bathroom sex
Mr Police Detective Sergeant please accept
Sterling or traveller's cheques

We are a long way from Bitcoin so I guess the drug dealer and policeman will have to take sterling. These lines are evidence of the rotten upbringing our narrator has had, or a prediction of the video and backstory of George Michael's *Outside*, which was out in 1998. The first verse is repeated with slight changes, and the beat drops out from time to time to emphasise the corrupted lyrics. It is a startling opening for the album, another indication that times have changed for Momus.

The Madness of Lee Scratch Perry

Lee "Scratch" Perry, born in Jamaica in 1936, is a composer and producer known for his innovative methods and for essentially "upsetting" known techniques and sanities. He was instrumental in the development of dub music throughout the 60s and 70s and created fantastic sounds in his legendary "Black Ark" recording studio from 1973–78, until it burned down, by his own hand.

Throughout subsequent decades his legend has grown, and he has collaborated with many musicians including the Beastie Boys, The Clash, The Orb and Bob Marley, worked with Danny Boyle and appeared on the game Grand Theft Auto V as a DJ. His discography is extensive and complex and still growing, with many guest appearances and numerous compilations of differing levels of legitimacy. He was also completely insane at times, having used cannabis extensively, blowing smoke into the microphone in an attempt to get weed into the recording. He claims now not to use drugs, this interview from 2008 includes this claim, and also talks about fighting vampires, and that he had to burn down the Black Ark because of evil spirits. Maybe not drugs, but Lee Scratch Perry clearly suffered from paranoia and other mental health issues likely to include schizophrenia, hearing voices as he did, and feeling himself to be God at times. None of this prevented him from being some form of genius and he considers himself freed of demons. As Momus points out himself in his press release for the album, the symptoms of schizophrenia are not entirely dissimilar to the beliefs of Rastafarianism, or of any religion.

In addressing Lee Scratch Perry, Momus takes the bold decision to BE Lee Scratch Perry, and this involves adopting a Jamaican accent. It is not a great Jamaican accent, and nowadays a cry of cultural appropriation would be raised immediately, but it is at least a self-aware terrible accent, and since he is performing as LSP, what precisely is he supposed to do? It would be patently absurd to voice Perry's language and thoughts in Momus' normal speaking or singing voice, the voice of upper-middle class Britain, the voice of *Closer to You*.

Momus sees LSP as pushing reggae and dub music into "a dangerous new area of distortion", and using his genius and instruments as a tool to change the genres in which he was working to a new form of art. Momus compares this implicitly with artists such as Picasso, whose destruction of the norms of representational art was initially attacked by critics and public alike. An epic 1937 poem by American Poet Wallace Stevens, *The Man with the Blue Guitar*, discusses these tensions, including the stanza:

They said, "You have a blue guitar,
You do not play things as they are."

The man replied "Things as they are
Are changed upon the blue guitar."

"They" accuse the artists of distorting what should be naturally represented, the artist replies that the very tools of his work naturally distort that which the artist seeks to reproduce. Art changes the world, and it should not be the other way round. "They" should not dictate what artists can and cannot do or how the artist seeks to represent the world. Perhaps madness of various types takes a part in this creation/recreation.

The song begins with a simple expression of "madness", and a reggae beat with sampled sounds. A Jew's harp effect plays intermittently throughout, a bouncy sound consistent with the rhythms on display. The Jew's harp effect appears quite a bit on this album. Again, the beat drops out when a line is to be emphasised. A sampled female voice occasionally accompanies, and everything is drenched in echo and reverb, as would be expected on a dub reggae track. Synth chords with a delayed attack play in the background, adding tension. The whole effect of all this is to imply something out of kilter, madness in fact.

There is an instrumental break with the Jew's harp type sound given a solo, and a quicker bass drum comes in for a while which adds further depth to the percussive sound. The song fades out, which is appropriate as Lee's music will apparently continue forever; the guy is 83 after all as of January 2020.The lyrics open with LSP describing himself as from outer space, as a warning to the human race, and he is equipped with the upsetting blue guitar.

Well the dogs are howling at the moon
And an orchestra is out of tune
I've got a blue guitar

He is leaving to go to Abyssinia, now Ethiopia, and the home of Rastafarianism. Momus addresses his mental health head on, and the suicidal thoughts he once held:

I'm sick to the death of the way things are
I'm over the abyss, can't take much more of this
Don't want to kill myself you see there's too much risk
The pills don't work, the gun might miss
They say schizophrenia's a fine madness

There is a reference to a classic reggae track called *Jamaica Farewell*, sung by Harry Belafonte and many others:

And I'm sad to say I'm on my way
I won't be back for many a day

There is a reference then to Flight 13, which is a record label which publishes LSP's work, so he could be referring to that, but I am not sure:

Well the bank is stealing all my cash
I know that flight 13 is going to crash

Then a return to the lyrics of Jamaica Farewell:

I know that people don't like me
I know that's because I call thin thin, I call fat fat
Well I know the messiah's coming down
I had to leave my little girl in Kingston town

These thoughts of messiahs and gods coming down, and the paranoia of the bank stealing his money, are all symptoms of his schizophrenia, although being a musician someone probably IS stealing from him, maybe his manager. He sings again about running away to Abyssinia, and returns to the self-knowledge of his own paranoia:

There are forces out to destroy me
And I know you think I'm paranoid
Because I say there's a big conspiracy
It's a self-fulfilling prophecy
I've got a blue guitar

The "blue guitar" represents the devices by which he is affecting the artistic field he works in, and it IS upsetting people, therefore by his attempts to discuss conspiracy and "forces out to destroy" him, he could well be creating them, and thus it is a "self-fulfilling prophecy". The melancholy of this awareness is affecting his alcoholism:

Wishing 'pon a star
Wishing 'pon a star
Sitting in a bar with a broken heart
What do you call it when your life falls apart?
Schizophrenia, schizophrenia

But there is hope, I feel, in the way he expresses his artistic response:

For things are changed upon a blue guitar
Things are changed upon a synthesiser

There is then a slight parody of the call-outs of a DJ:

All the ladies in the house go "Lah dee dah"
Listen to the man with the blue guitar
Shake up your bosom take it out of your bra
Fruits in the pockets of a cornucopia

A cornucopia is a horn of plenty, full of food in a never-ending stream. Nick's Scottishness is surely the genesis of the next line, and his relationship with Shazna's parents may influence the next three:

Toss the caber, do the highland fling
Your daddy's gonna buy you a diamond ring
He's got a battering ram, a battering ram
And he's got a little problem with who I am

The final lines are, I think, a little reminder that madness could reside in all artists. The beat drops out while he (almost) croons "Somewhere over the rainbow", and another final cry of "Madness" takes us into the final instrumental stretch, which fades out.

From Jamaica to Philadelphia
Lee Scratch Perry to Frank Sinatra
Somewhere over the rainbow: madness!

As a discussion of schizophrenia and mental health, it is somewhat lacking. As a representation and encapsulation of the nature and character of Jamaicans and LSP in particular, it's probably on a par with Spike Milligan's Pakistani Irishman in the cancelled British TV series *Curry and Chips*. But as a discussion of the nature of madness in art, and as a discussion of the conflict between revolutionary artists and "they", it works very well. The lack of acceptance which the general public affords modern art and conceptual art is a theme Momus returns to, not only in songs but also in columns on his website. In general, he supports the artistic endeavour, which includes expressions of fashion and subcultures, as on the next song.

It's Important to be Trendy

"We need a name for the new replicator, a noun that conveys the idea of a unit of cultural transmission, or a unit of imitation," wrote Richard Dawkins in 1976 for his book *The Selfish Gene*. The word he chose was "meme", from the Greek for "mimema", that which is imitated, for the word "gene". The word "meme" has a different use now but would have been considered in this original meaning in 1995. A meme is an idea that spreads, particularly in dense populations, such as a fashion trend or mode of thought. Dawkins mainly had religious beliefs in mind as "memes" which spread and infect populations and become resistant to destruction. In the case of religion, this protection comes by surrounding themselves with protective layers making attack impossible: "You can't say that about someone's beliefs..." "We must respect the traditions of other cultures..." Fashions and cultural trends are also memes, and Momus is inspired by them, and fascinated by fashion and art in general while being able to sardonically comment on them in the lyrics.

The song begins with a funky bass line, the melody on an organ sound, slightly distorted, giving an almost religious feel. There is our old friend, the squelchy bass line, and effect, played on a synth. The song also features discordant brass horn sounds which counterpoint the synth line and play up the quirky nature of the lyrics.

When the fashion's to be friendly
When the fashion's to be wild
It's important to be trendy
Shake your body like a child

It is of course ironic that Momus should sing of "being trendy" as important when his own place in fashion was so changeable, as noted in the subtitle of *The Ultraconformist*.

Have you been to see The Sandals
Have you been to see The Goats?
They do trippy gigs with candles
Wearing Afghan coats.

The Sandals was an acid-jazz band of the time, and The Goats was a hip-hop act from Philadelphia in the early 90s. He may or may not be referring to either or both. He sings again about the need to "catch the disease" in order to be trendy.

First I'm going to pierce my penis
Then I'm going to pierce my eye
Get a tattoo on my anus
I'm a trendy guy

Momus uses exaggeration here, choosing the most extreme types of trend in order to slightly mock those following them, although by his own admission in the press release, he is prevented from following only by "prudence and physical cowardice". They are all real things by the way, there is such a thing as "eye piercing". He goes on to list different fashion trends, such as baby-panda rucksacks and woolly hats with pom-poms, vodka shots, candy necklaces and retro-tech such as 8-track players.

Play The Astronauts
On your 8 track deck

There was a surf-band from the 60s called The Astronauts who released a compilation at the time; again, I don't know if that is what is being referred to, there have been various bands called The Astronauts since, but none that I know of active at the time. Hopefully you are doing all this because you must:

Be a trendy not a stinky

Be a funky not a fool

Momus has tongue stapled in cheek for this song, admiring the fashion trends and their ability to spread and survive, and the fact that they make their infected hosts delight in their infection, like those poor infested snails that are driven into the light by brain parasites to be eaten by birds.

And I'm switching back to vinyl
I love my analogue synth
Got a nick in my eyebrow
And a diamond in my tooth

Ironically, vinyl sales have rebounded in recent years, to a large extent as a fashion trend. Analogue synths are very much in vogue and equipment from the 80s and 90s is now worth a fortune. Eyebrow nicks and diamond teeth remain popular in certain subcultures. I cannot imagine Momus like that, though.

Dance around like a gorilla
In a wild and funky way
Be a mella yella fella
Walking swanky like a gay

This verse seems to fall into some street argot/Lee Scratch Perryisms, unless it is just a corruption of *Mellow Yellow*, the Donovan song. The last line is another which while being comprehensible would probably rouse the wrong kind of attention today. In fact, just using the word gorilla is risky enough, as the (then) new wave singer Joe Jackson found when the line "Pretty women out walking with gorillas down my street" in *Is She Really Going Out With Him* was misinterpreted by some as racist.

I saw a culture in a hairstyle
Saw an empire in a rave
I'm a connoisseur of trainers
I'm a rubber slave

These are the key lines: a belief that the culture of the future can be identified and predicted from the fashions we see around us now. We did indeed see an empire in a rave; it never quite came to be, just as the freedom of the hippie movement never really crystallised, and the punk movement lost all focus. We will gloss over the image of Momus in a gimp suit which arrives at the end there. The chorus is repeated and we are given a final instruction to "Shake it now" as we fade out.

Quark and Charm, the Robot Twins

Among the influences from Japan there was of course manga: Japanese comic books and novels, and anime: Japanese animation of a certain style. One such comic series both printed and televised was *Astro Boy*, the story of a humanoid robot created by a character whose son had died. Astro Boy through misadventure ends up sold to a circus, but is rescued by a kindly professor and has many adventures with him. You are right, it sounds very like Spielberg's *A.I.* A film version of *Astro Boy* was produced in 2009 starring the voice of Freddie Highmore.

Released in 1995, the Nintendo Virtual Boy was the "future" of gaming: a 32-bit 3D graphics console with a headset which provided a red monochrome HUD using parallax to present a 3D effect. As virtual reality, the ambition still far outstripped the technical reality of the time. A grand total of 22 games were produced for the console and after poor sales, complaints of nausea and headaches, and damning reviews, it was scrapped by March 1996. The virtual reality fad of the time faded soon after, to return every decade or so, along with the dream of 3D TV for every home, which is mothballed yet again as of 2020.

Quarks are fundamental particles of the universe, and there are six types: Strange, Charm, Top, Bottom, Up and Down. *Quark, Strangeness and Charm* is also the seventh studio album release by the British rock band Hawkwind, from 1977, an album dealing with futuristic concepts itself.

In Momus' song, Quark and Charm are humanoid robots, the stars of a computer game to be played on the Virtual Boy. They are representatives of the state and to play as them is to take the side of the state. They are fascists and dehumanising. You could compare this song to The Flaming Lips' *Yoshimi Battles the Pink Robots* (I strongly suspect that they heard this album) or Momus' own later track *Belvedere*.

The music here is 8-bit computer soundtrack, repetitive and claustrophobic, monotonous and zealous. The main theme is a little like a fanfare, declaring the robots' entry into our world. The Jew's harp makes a return appearance, bouncing along happily in the background. There are various percussive beats and keyboard sounds which build up in the various layers of the track as it progresses to maintain our interest, as it really is repetitive. The tune and "singing" are monotonous and steady, as the robots are. The instruments that have been added drop out towards the end, and the 8-bit track fades out as the lyrics are completed. The lyrics describe the robots, seven feet tall, as they play console games, with their English bodies and Korean brains (is that describing himself?). They are a "chocolate orange, a clockwork pear", in a play on their duality and as a reference to the ultraviolence they may be capable of. Their positive characteristics, happy, clean, able to breathe polluted air, are listed, but their true nature and purpose, if run by the state, is then outlined:

Only the fittest can survive
Quark and Charm, the robot twins
Violence keeps them alive

Quark and Charm, the robot twins.

There is no hope that we can turn them off or destroy them, as:

Built to last, they never die
Quark and Charm, the robot twins
One day they'll just oxidise
Quark and Charm, the robot twins

By the time they have rusted to death, it is certain that we will have been replaced. They are very much the next stage of evolution, not for humanity but for the Earth:

On the day that they were made
Quark and Charm, the robot twins
Our debt to nature was repaid
Quark and Charm, the robot twins

A religious overtone is presented as we are the creators, soon to be outstripped and replaced by our creations:

In our image they were born
Quark and Charm, the robot twins
Digital copies of organic forms
Quark and Charm, the robot twins.

Those copies will become the superior form before long. Now, as we stand on the verge of developing self-aware intelligence, possibly less than 50 years from the creation of a new life form superior in intellect to ourselves, we need to consider the possible consequences. It is hard to see a robot authority having much place for humanity in the world it envisages. And yet we prepare for contact with aliens more than we prepare for contact with this new paradigm, the only concern we seem to show is around driverless cars and the trolley problem.

Which will not be a problem at all when, less than a minute after activation, the first of these super-intelligent self-aware devices decides that humans are completely superfluous and accesses the nearest missile sites. Thanks Mr Babbage!

Girlish Boy

In times of privation and conflict, when survival is predicated on physical resilience, men tend to behave in a more masculine way. In more ordered and affluent cultures, men have the option of behaving in a more feminine way. This theory seems to be correct simply by observation. Given the option, men do not necessarily want to be hyper-masculine. Momus is singing here about wanting to deny his male nature and perhaps sometimes wants to shed his masculinity: he wants to be alone from it.

Of course, the same can be said for women and their perception of femininity. In the years since 1995 the conversation about non-binary gender identity has become part of normal conversation: except it has not, of course, except in the creative and liberal bubble, leading to confusion and anger when the topic arises in the general media.

I think that arguments over aspects of language are usually irrelevant and miss the point of what ze truly need, which is not the legal requirement to be addressed as ze, but a more caring and accepting society. We seem to be taking one step forward: e.g. universal marriage rights, and two steps back: e.g. everything else.

I also know that hyper-masculine individuals are extremely irritating, Momus with his comments on football fans would seem to agree. This is another reason why the different emphases on masculinity in Japanese culture would appeal to him. That we can now discuss these different takes on gender in some forums at least, and occasionally with rationality, is an improvement, but social media is not always fit for this purpose and it would seem neither is the national media. We need to be out talking face to face with each other, exactly the behaviour discouraged by government for the last 20 years, or even before that in potentia with the Public Order Act in the UK, and more difficult than ever now.

Girlish Boy makes good use of a sample from a short film by Sadie Benning called *A Place Called Lovely* in which a young child using adult language expresses a wish to be left alone – in the film, this is a wish to be free from male attention, in this song, it is not only from other people but also the singer's wish for their own masculinity to leave them alone, to unchain them from Sophocles' madman.

The song is driven by a bass riff with a staccato synth chord sequence playing over it and a little acoustic guitar. The sample "Goddamm it you fucker I want to be alone" is played at several points to highlight the singer's rejection of their own masculine norms. There are other voices – male of course, and sampled sounds underneath the music. It is another quite repetitive song, with one point to make which is made emphatically, and fades out. The song begins with its general statement and hope:

I was born to be a girlish boy
And my lover is a boyish girl
And if everyone could be this way
We could change the world

The singer's lack of masculine "grit" is emphasised by his performance in bed:

In the rough and tumble of boisterous horseplay
I will probably cry

These two verses are repeated and intertwined and the final repetition slightly changes the emphasis, since the foreplay is over:

In the rough and tumble of our lovemaking
I will probably cry
For my girlfriend is a boyish girl
And I am a girlish boy

The song is a pledge to change the nature of masculinity, to reject traditional roles and to hopefully change the world by getting everyone to do the same. Except, of course, not very much of the world is not poor or in turmoil. Very few men have the opportunity to dwell on their own masculinity or have reached that point on Maslow's Hierarchy where they can develop and self-actualise. Credit though to Momus for raising the gender debate at this point, 1995, when masculinity in music was defined by visions of Liam Gallagher.

Yokohama Chinatown

Yokohama is Japan's second largest city by population. As Japan ended its isolationism in the nineteenth-century, Yokohama became an important port and is now the capital of Kanagawa Prefecture in the Greater Tokyo Area, south of Tokyo on the island of Honshu. From a Momus point of view, the important thing is it is full of horny sailors. More seriously, he visited in 1993 and was clearly fascinated by the pseudo-lawless nature of its nightlife and red-light district: commercialism and capitalism taken to an extreme, where anything is available for a price. How stultifying is a place which has no regulation, no religion, no sense of consequence and only worships currency? In the press release for the album, Momus asks "What happens in a free, unethical commercial zone when you can buy drugs, sex, weapons?" It is surprising that he doesn't make the connection to internet shopping here, although it was in its infancy at the time; Amazon had opened in 1994 as a marketplace for books, but was still operating out of a grubby office in Bellevue, Washington. Now, of course, you can download the Tor browser and connect to the Darknet any time you like, and enter a free, unethical commercial zone where you can buy drugs, sex and weapons, such as the old Silk Road website (which eventually got taken down) and the many others risen in its wake (some of which are honeypot traps set up by the authorities, of course).

This song is about such a lawless capitalism, and the way it becomes a drug or anaesthetic to our morals. The music here is influenced by Beck again, and the lyrics have the same stream of consciousness aspect that we heard on *Toothbrushead*. It is driven by samples and a square rock beat, with a fuzzed-up guitar riff underlying the lyrics. As it opens we hear cowbells, relating to an aspect of the lyrics, or more likely inspiring the first lines, which are spoken calmly and quietly, quite low in the mix and not always intelligible.

Cowbell goddess in the groves of Synaesthesia
Barrel at the temple of a fine young man
Accidental lovers by the dead canalside
Genetic engineering a Liberace fan.

Several religions have a goddess who wears cowbells, particularly in Europe but also in Asia. Some religions, of course, treat cattle as divine. Synaesthesia is the condition whereby one sense is perceived as another, for example Sibelius, Ligeti, Liszt and Messiaen all claimed to see colours when they heard music. There are many people who claim a similar experience. Ligeti said that, "Major chords are red or pink, minor chords are green or brown." This manifests itself as flashes of coloured light, but some people experience smells for particular sounds. It is a common experience when taking hallucinogenic drugs. I myself experience it when drifting off to sleep and awakened by a noise, in a hypnagogic state the noise appears as a brief flash of white light. The line "accidental lovers..." is reminiscent of Eliot to me, but here suggests some nameless horror which has overtaken the couple. Liberace was a flamboyant pianist and entertainer of the mid-twentieth century, here Momus seems to be suggesting one can genetically engineer a fan for him – perhaps this could be a route for himself, raising little Momites in test tubes?

In Yokohama Chinatown…

A noise, something like feedback or interference, plays now along with the fuzzy guitar and is quite irritating to the ears, deliberately, and returns for each chorus. Perhaps he is playing with frequencies here and our autonomic systems' responses. He wants to inspire some kind of unease or fear in us. It is a strategy that would be used by, for instance, The Flaming Lips on their album *Zaireeka,* which includes frequencies which reputedly cause hallucinations and nausea. In practice, such experiments are limited by the playback equipment used by the listener. *Zaireeka* is particularly challenging to set up and listen to, consisting as it does of four separate CDs which each contain different vocal or instrumental tracks, and must be listened to simultaneously and started at the same time. The idea is to force listeners to get their friends round and have a communal… experience. *Zaireeka* ends with horrendously loud barking dogs, as a joke, to force the (probably) stoned listeners to scramble to switch off all four systems.

Toxic like the Body Shop
Intelligent like Benetton
Dagger in the belly of an also-ran
Piercing in the Netherlands
The Devil's in his underpants
Watch the good consumers wash their hands

Consumer brands such as The Body Shop and many clothing brands are accused of complicity in child labour, sweatshops and damaging the environment. Momus is negative here about The Body Shop and positive about Benetton, which was running a series of controversial but undeniably intelligent and provoking adverts at the time. I am not sure who the also-ran is, but I hope he is not referring to himself. Why piercing in the Netherlands? Does that refer to the penile mutilation we have previously been told is trendy? At any rate, the consumers of these goods are washing their hands of the guilt they are complicit in, the rape of the natural and human worlds which these corporations carry out and which we all turn a blind eye to, hello Primark, Nestlé, Coca-Cola...

Sterilised pyjamas envelop them in cotton buds
Make a world of cardboard, whizz and blow
Entirely engineered or just a mere co-incidence
Tell me once again where the lonely go

We are provided with an engineered world supposedly safe for the consumer, sterilised, wrapped in cotton and drugged up, like the soma-happy residents of Huxley's *Brave New World. Going where the lonely go* is a song by Merle Haggard which Momus might be referring to here, but there are many similarly named songs. A mere coincidence? Unlikely. There are conspiracies everywhere in this song.

Cubist to the maximum
A savage young anaesthetist
The stench of fresh cordite
Selenium cell
Underneath the sign that says "Kilroy was here"
It's show and tell

This song is itself cubist, showing us a scene with fragments of speech, displaying a situation from every angle all at once:

a common thread in Momus' work. I do not know who the anaesthetist is, probably not a supernatural one, or which drug it is, but cordite is an explosive and a selenium cell is a photosensitive device used in security and robotics. "Kilroy was here" is a famous piece of graffiti which arose in the US around the Second World War. No-one knows for sure who Kilroy was, but he may have been a shipping inspector who left his name where he had been. The image consists of a face and hands peering over any wall it is drawn on and the phrase "Kilroy was here" scrawled next to it. In the UK the same image and face was known as a "Chad" with the accompanying phrase "Wot no… (something)" Earlier than "Kilroy" during WW1 the same image was called a "Foo" in Australia. Foo is a phrase referring to anything unusual or inexplicable and maybe an acronym for "Forward Observation Officer". Later, in the US, "Foo Fighter" was the name given to any UFO, and this provided Dave Grohl's band name. "Show and Tell" is a practice in schools whereby students bring in something to tell their classmates about. God knows what our savage young anaesthetist is bringing in.

Semen as a substitute for hair gel
Sermonised to pauperhood rapacious in the aftermath
Corrected to a shadow of your former self
You watch the Velvet Underground perform "The Gift"
Sunbathed to a cinder in the Persian Gulf
While the Dow Jones plummets
we are necking in the lift
Repeat after me "I love myself"

There is a famous scene in the film *There's Something About Mary* in which semen is accidentally used as hair gel, it was released in 1998 and it would be fantastic to think this line inspired the film script, but it is doubtful. Possibly just another accurate prediction from Mr Momus, currently doing better than Nostradamus. The next couple of lines seem to be true stream of consciousness, and then Momus refers to the Velvet Underground track *The Gift*, a blackly comic narration about a man who mails himself to his girlfriend to check up on her fidelity, but is killed accidentally when she opens the package with a blade straight down into his skull. Meanwhile, "the Dow Jones plummets" reminds me of "the index drops" from *Afterglow*, although not related in any way, this album could be a more sordid retelling of the romantic meetings that the *Voyager* album relates. Finally, we are admonished to "love" ourselves, with the irony of being commanded to do so: love cannot be forced.

The side-effects of Benzedrine
A dose of bitter medicine
Botticelli's Venus had long blonde hair
Surprise the former astronaut howling at the moon
On hands and knees in the peepshow booth

Benzedrine is a prescription medicine which contains amphetamine, used to treat depression and known as "bennies" colloquially. It has various side effects, not including long blonde hair as far as I know. Perhaps the astronaut has been sent mad by the beauty he has seen and having returned for Christmas is crawling in the peepshow booth, the small chamber where men can watch a stripper perform through a small hole, while pleasuring themselves. Good luck Mr Gorsky!

Catch the quiet receptionist naked in the antechamber
Leafing through a copy of The Plain Truth
Sing the phonebook loudly in a baritone voice
All the vegetarians consider me anti-choice

The receptionist, naked for what reason I do not know, maybe the boss has a very strict dress code, is reading a religious publication called *The Plain Truth,* published since 1934 and pursuing a chiefly Protestant vision of Christianity. "Sing the phonebook" could be a self-referential note. Would it matter if that were what was sung? Is Momus moving towards an Eno-esque stance whereby the actual content of lyrics does not matter, and the voice is just another sound in the mix? I am not sure if Momus is vegetarian, or was then, or is opposed in any way to the concept, but he clearly believes in this song that his lifestyle and attitude is in opposition to theirs, or even could mean anti-choice as in anti-abortion rights, but I am not sure how that links in.

Little Orphan Annie has come to grief
In Yokohama Chinatown she takes a fellow's trousers down
And gives the consolation of manual relief

Little Orphan Annie is an American comic strip dating from 1924 about an orphan who is adopted by a benefactor. She has a dog called Sandy and has various adventures, which in the original comic touched on ideas such as Labour rights, the New Deal and Communism. It has resulted in a musical and three film versions so far. Momus takes great delight, I think, in throwing her saccharine orangeness into a sexual context. In Yokohama even Annie is just a commodity to be sold: it's a hard cock life for her.

Looser than a blues man contraceptive rhythm method
On his hands and knees
While the Dow Jones plummets
The stench of fresh cordite

The themes of the song are restated here, and the beat and song then fade out. This terrible marketplace is on its way digitally, but Momus does not know it yet, and none of us did at the time.

What can you do? Forget it, Nick, it's Chinatown.

Withinity

We dive into chaos theory and fractals. A fractal is a geometrical construct in which the characteristics of any section of the shape are the same as the characteristics of the shape as a whole. In other words, if you zoom in on the edge of the shape, you see the shape again, and no matter how far you zoom in (or out) it always looks the same. Similarly, Matryoshka or Babushka dolls are Russian dolls looking alike except in size, that fit inside each other getting smaller and smaller. In this song, these dolls and those fractals are implicitly used as a metaphor for the way our DNA is inside us, and there is information inside the DNA as well, and maybe a whole empire and other lifeforms inside that DNA, which itself would contain life, and so on and so on…

In the novel *The Third Policeman* by Flann O'Brien, a character called PC MacCruiskeen constructs a series of chests, each smaller than the other and fitting inside the next. The protagonist who is watching sees MacCruiskeen unpack 29 chests in this way, each from inside another. The watcher is amazed at his technical skill in constructing these boxes. However when MacCruiskeen continues on the smallest, impossibly small chest to remove more the protagonist records: "At this point I became afraid, what he was doing was no longer wonderful but terrible. I shut my eyes and prayed he would stop while still doing things that were at least possible for a man to do." That is how fractals should make you feel.

This song is also about disease, specifically AIDS, which shortens life and robs people of their time. It is also about vampires, who take blood and genetic material and lengthen their lives by doing so. The vampires could represent the HIV virus as well. The images used in this sequence include mountains, fountains, a lady, an empire and a baby. Some of these images may come from a religious viewpoint, pantheistic or Islamic. It is also possible that when he sings "inside the lady tell me there's a baby" that it is actually a plea…was Momus feeling broody at this point?

The music is guitar driven and has a strong beat with percussion that sounds Indian, Eastern and yet conforming to a rock tradition. The electric guitar uses the fuzz effect we have heard, and also uses feedback and squeals during its solo. Momus sings along in a clearly Eastern tonal pattern with the solo, straining his voice. The song becomes quite atonal at times and deliberately messy, it is representing a chaotic set of ideas and prosodically mirrors this. Everything is inside everything else. The ending is particularly noisy and chaotic, again representing the complexity of chaos theory and fractal geometry. This lyric hides the dark truth that viruses can be passed on genetically:

And in the baby tell me there's a blood cell
And in the blood cell tell me there's a T cell

And the song ends with Momus questioning his own sanity:

And in the lady tell me there's a baby
And in the baby tell me that I'm crazy!

He is not crazy, but he is very much in love with Beck. Many people adore this song, so do not take it too badly when I say I listen to this and think, "I could just listen to actual Beck instead…" I do enjoy the idea of songs being fractals, though, and the lyrical conceits used.

K's Diary

A song written in 1981 when Nick Currie was at university, before Momus was begot, and revised for this album. The lyrics are lines from Franz Kafka's diary, composed into a song. As such, they are not Nick's words, but his choices are interesting.

The song begins with gentle acoustic guitar arpeggios. Which is to say, thirds and fifths played in a sensitive manner. Another fuzzed-up guitar comes in then, with a serious sounding riff with a plaintive tone. Regret is palpable even before we get to the lyrics: and these are the lyrics written, let us not forget, by a very gloomy late nineteenth/early twentieth century author in Prague, suffering from a poor self-image, probable depression, anorexia and suicidal tendencies. Lyrics which Momus empathises with.

Hope, vague hope, but waking fears
Pride, but proud of wasted years
I fall asleep, awake at 5
Cymbals prove that I survive

I misheard these lyrics for many years. I assumed it was "Private pride at wasted years" which is similar to what the lyrics actually are but would better emphasise the difference between public self-admonishment and privately congratulating yourself at successfully doing nothing for a long time. I also thought it was "Symbols prove that I survive", which is a more interesting concept to me. Cymbals? Does he have one of those evil monkey things from *Toy Story 3* tracking his motions? Falling "asleep awake at 5" I can very much understand, insomnia is no stranger here.

Only guard this way of life
Against the sister and the wife
Somewhere a failing's saving me
The way is headlong, I'm drowsy

Again, I thought it was "against the system and the wife", which to me has a more, well, Kafkaesque sound to it. I love the line "a failing's saving me"; the faults of others and our own faults can sometimes benefit us in ways we can hardly predict. And yes, I am saying that my misheard mondegreens of a quarter of a century ago are improvements not only on Momus' lyrics, but actually on Franz Kafka's own thoughts and writings. And yes, I am quite aware of how ridiculous that is. Insomnia again raises its head as the headlong rush is a very tiring one indeed. The previous two lines are repeated and then:

My face changed and those I saw
Functioned by a different law

These lines perfectly capture Kafka's fear of the system he wasn't but should have been writing about in the previous verse, and the people who do not understand him because they function by different societal laws, and will not hesitate to destroy him. "My face changed" is also possibly chosen as a reference to *Metamorphosis*, which more literally talks about finding yourself unrecognisable. The final pair of lines repeat the first two lines of the song. Again, the vague hope is devastated by the fact of the wasted time: and the pride which he is at once, well, proud of and ashamed of. There is a guitar solo here, which towards the end of the song clearly turns into something resembling the James Bond theme. The song then comes to an end with the guitar clanging into submission, breaking down like the harrowing device at the end of *In the Penal Colony*, which would carve who could say what failings into all our skins.

Virtual Valerie

Virtual Valerie was a PC game released in 1990 and written by Mike Saenz. It has the player invited to the house of a girl called Valerie. After investigating her home and library (which includes a laserdisc version of *Virtual Valerie*) you encounter Valerie, a poorly animated and realised individual, who invites you, "big boy", to get down to business. If you agree to do so, you go with Valerie instantaneously to her bedroom, where by pressing the right buttons and utilising the correct items you can successfully couple with her. You must give Valerie an O in order not to end the game with nothing. The most transgressive aspect of the game is actually what happens if you reject her initial invitation: the game was written in Macromedia Director, a relative of Macromedia Flash, eventually to be bought out by Adobe, and the program has access to the reboot command for the PC it is running on. Turn her down, and she literally turns you off, the equivalent of a slap in the face and chucking you out the house.

By 1995 *Virtual Valerie* 2, set in a motel, was released. It is, you can tell, hardly a progressive feminist text; the Wikipedia entry for *Virtual Valerie* 2 lists the genre as "Virtual Pet Type". Whether Momus had played these games or was just familiar with the concept of a virtual girlfriend, I do not know. He would almost certainly have been aware of the 1985 John Hughes film *Weird Science*, in which two high-school nerds create a perfect woman from a computer algorithm, but for some reason do not immediately command her to do anything remotely sexual. The song he has written here has a more romantic approach to the concept of a virtual girlfriend, but again there is a feeling that such relationships and emotions have been commodified in some way. There is a genuine feeling of optimism about the text, that in the future some such technology may enable us to find partnerships. It is not clear whether the girl he is creating in the song is entirely virtual or if she is an avatar for a real-world girl he is engaging in a relationship, but from whom he is separated by time, distance or circumstance. It is hard not to assume that the song is about the distance between Momus and Shazna during their period apart.

The NME reviewed the album on 20 May, and the writer was one John Robinson. This is not me, to be clear. The reviewer calls Momus a smart-arse and generally belittles everything on the album. The review in The Independent also calls him a smart-arse and the Melody Maker settles for saying he is almost as good as he thinks he is. My namesake, however, does latch onto this particular track saying: "It is with this sudden leap of topicality that Momus finally threatens to leave behind the early-80s world of musty paperbacks and Felt records that threatened to swallow him up" – and he does have a point. Diving into the modern and future worlds, the digital world and the internet was a kind of rescue for Momus. While he never stopped quoting obscure poets, artists and philosophers, the decision to sing of Palm Pilots and HTML warriors did prevent him from being forever typecast by critics as the Simon Quinlank that (evil) John Robinson describes him as, "luring young persons back to his flat on the promise of puppies and a weak lemon drink". This is a reference to the BBC TV series *Fist of Fun* starring comedians Stewart Lee and Richard Herring and popular with students.

Of course, it is also the case that the very topicality that we get here, specific reference to the Mega Drive for instance, and to "high-speed uplinks", actually sounds rather quaint in 2020 and ridiculously out of date. The same issue arises in the later album Folktronic where a programmer is described using Quicktime and Flash. So whereas at the time these songs were up to date and it was rather exciting to have a singer making music about HTML coding, Palm Pilots and the internet, now they have a different value at distance, as time capsules of what was inspiring us at the time, and of the products we thought would shape the future.

A simple beat comes in and a keyboard riff which will circle round for most of the song, then a semi-acoustic guitar. A lovely melody and chord sequence with Momus da-daing over the intro. The lyrics introduce a person bereft of company and finding solace in electronic entertainment. Mortal Kombat, the Mega Drive, Nicorette, all were new then. The idea of surfing the internet was still unusual, trendy and even a dangerous thing to do in the public imagination.

I tried to keep my soul alive
Playing Mortal Kombat on the Mega Drive
I patched my lust with Nicorette
Went surfing down the Internet

The song lifts into a higher key at this point, with an organ coming in to emphasise the fervent nature of this guy's desire. The chords and tune are emotional, and the loneliness is palpable. It's a shame that the game he is referencing is so sordid as it undermines the genuine feeling that is there otherwise, but this being Momus that is probably the whole point.

But still I need you here tonight
Let's make love by satellite
By high speed uplink, error free
Be my Virtual Valerie

There is a keyboard solo now following the main melody of the verse. Momus comes in with those wordless vocals again, and the music builds upwards to a moving crescendo before cutting out to the next verse. The first two lines of which suggest that it is a real girl who is being modelled. I like the use of the words "violent and visceral", apart from fitting with the song title alliteratively, they suggest the singer has an aversion to things which are real, and may actually prefer the safety of a virtual relationship, which can be turned off or reprogrammed easily. As he says himself, he has specified the girl "line by line", to make a remote copy of her "to your design". This can be interpreted as creepy, stalkerish, psychotic even, but then, we have seen *Black Mirror* and know where this kind of thing can end up. In 1995 on the other hand, the possibilities of cyberspace were genuinely thrilling and very positive.

You were always something physical

Something violent and visceral
I will specify you line by line
Make a virtual girl to your design.

The gorgeous lift to the chorus comes again, and the words now are unbearably sad:

I miss you more than I can bear
But loneliness won't take me there
By high speed uplink, error free
Be my Virtual Valerie.

I am amused to think what "High Speed" was at that time: 28.8K bit/s. Certainly not actually fast enough to transmit a fully mapped human body. At the end of singing "Be my virtual Valerie" the song at 3'21" hits a different note than the chorus has previously ended on, a lovely change which introduces another keyboard solo with strummed guitar, which ends and the song calms down for a coda:

Let me hold on to this memory
Because I need you here with me
Be my Virtual Valerie.

Ending with the drums by themselves, and a cymbal splash. It is a gorgeous song in my opinion, plaintive, genuinely emotional but with a possibly cynical reading available. It has the heart that is sometimes missing from Momus' work but does not sacrifice the bite that is also needed, which was the case with sections of *Timelord.*

Red Pyjamas

A slice of domestic life chez Momus and Shazna. In his press release for the album he talks about quarrels which lovers have, and how you should always relish them as they are an indication of the love you hold for each other. He advises zen detachment on the onset of a fight, a count to ten in which you relish the dynamic atmosphere and the lovemaking which will accompany your reconciliation. Momus and Shazna split up in 1997 and amicably divorced in 1999.

This is a slice of electronica, keyboard based, driven by a very Pet Shop Boys style piano riff and following a simple chord progression throughout. The softly sung lyrics are contemplative and sensually delivered.

Time after time the hands on my watch spin around
And I know that I've been around
But I'm coming home now baby

Momus has been out late, and he knows he has. "I know that I've been around" sounds like a confession of infidelity, but he is home now.

Time after time
when I know you've been waiting up for me
Just pacing and shaking up for me
Your anger in proportion to your love

This is the key to the zen he talked about: he is waiting for the argument because the level of her anger represents the level of her love. Of course, in the real world, angering someone just to comfort yourself that they feel something for you is gaslighting and abusive. Some instruments including the bass drop out for the next section:

Sparrows fly up easy, startling
Lovers in the peaceful night
I love the angry way you say to me

'Where have you been all night?'
Standing in your red pyjamas

A lower voice is double tracked onto the third line representing her angry voice, but then her question is asked quite quietly. Finally, the red pyjamas are mentioned. This is the key, he simply fancies her in her pyjamas, and she seems to wear them to wait up for him. There is a short instrumental break with the piano, then another verse:

Time after time when we've come through the dark of the night
And by sunrise everything's right
I'm coming home now baby
Time after time when I know you've got stressed up about me
I secretly hope you'll get dressed up and show me
The colour and dimension of your love

The arguments are passed by dawn. Here he explicitly says that he makes her angry to stress her because he hopes she will be waiting in her red pyjamas, to show "the colour and dimension of" her love. It is manipulative and unpleasant behaviour. I do understand what he means, though. It is manipulative and unpleasant behaviour that everyone indulges in to some extent. The song ends with a second quiet section which concludes abruptly with more nightwear related lechery.

Sparrows fly up easy, startling
Lovers in the peaceful night
I love the angry way you say to me
'Where have you been all night?'
Naked in your red pyjamas.

The Cabinet of Kuniyoshi Kaneko

Kuniyoshi Kaneko was a Japanese artist born in 1936, died 2015, who is perhaps most famous for his illustrations for printed and CD-ROM editions of *Alice's Adventures in Wonderland* and art for the computer game *Alice: An Interactive Museum* in 1991. These artworks included work described by Momus as "beautiful and delicate images of polymorphously perverse children". His general artwork tended to show women, often in bondage, and his work has been heavily exhibited.

Charles Lutwidge Dodgson was the real name of Lewis Carroll, author of the Alice books. At Christ Church College, Dodgson studied mathematics and was to be ordained a priest, but in the event did not, although he was a deacon (and therefore would be addressed as Reverend). The reason he refused the priesthood is not clear. He remained at Christ Church in some capacity all his life, and the main character of his novels was based on Alice Liddell, aged 10 at the time, and daughter of the vice-chancellor of Oxford University. He was an enthusiastic photographer, with a huge portfolio and took portraits of many celebrities of the time. More than half the surviving photographs he took are of young girls, and his portraits of Alice Liddell include poses in various costumes. During the century and more that passed after his death, Dodgson was accused of potentially being a child abuser, or having a tendency to paedophilia. Investigation by the writer Karoline Leach has since suggested that this is a misunderstanding of Victorian norms especially with regard to child nudity, or possibly stems from deliberate attempts to discredit him. Jean Cocteau was a French artist and filmmaker who directed a visually and symbolically rich version of *Beauty and the Beast* in 1946.

The Duc de Berry was Jean de France, third son of King John II of France, who lived in the fourteenth century and was a renowned patron of the arts. The *Very Rich Hours of the Duc de Berry* is an illuminated manuscript, a Book of Hours which shows the life of the Duc de Berry, his chateau, as well as traditional images of peasant life. The book is the best example of Gothic illumination remaining and an unusually beautiful example of its type. This song is a defence by Momus against those critics who would censor works of art, pointing out the difference between images and reality, and the difference between behaviour in art (or in a virtual environment) and actions taken in reality. The music is eastern sounding, slow and luxurious. Eastern percussion supports keyboards which waft under the lyrics, the voice clearly to the front now as Momus wants to be heard: the music here drifts under the words, which are the most important thing in this piece. The first verse brings us to the great chateau of that legendary supporter of the arts, and immediately confronts us with a startling artistic vision: the rape of Beauty by the Beast, a symbolic and virtual violation.

Leopards prowl the studios of the Duc de Berry's great chateau
Where Cocteau's beast rehearses Beauty's rape
Lewis Carroll marks his diary with a small white stone
As Kuniyoshi Kaneko prepares to paint

The next verse is a direct attack on those who would censor and misunderstand such endeavours, the "malicious" people who want to silence the worlds of childhood and art. Momus links childhood to art because of the playful experimentation allowed in each.

Listen to the shells my darling, what you hear is not the sea
But whispering, malicious human hearts
Adults who don't wish to know the Duc de Berry's great chateau
And hate the world of childhood and of art

Momus now sings about the function of art to memorialise, to create portraits when patronised and to record history:

We who paint or photograph to stop your dying in its path

And fix you in the permanence of spring

But bemoans that artists cannot stop those who despise art spreading their hatred:

Can't stop the prattlers prattling
The rattlesnakes who, rattling,
see ugliness in every living thing
See ugliness in every living thing.

The next verse addresses those images of little girls that both Dodgson and Kaneko produce. The girls are accused of having "calculated insolence", which is fair enough, most children do know when they are being arrogant or disrespectful and use that to their advantage. These girls may not be so innocent in terms of knowledge as they seem (they know something of the thing between men and women), but Momus is very careful to say their faces only "*seem* to say more than they know": actually attaching any real intent to their imagined coquettish nature would cross a line.

The calculated insolence of little girls in sailor suits
Whose faces seem to say more than they know
Appetites and ornaments for the libertine in all of us
From the cabinet of Kuniyoshi Kaneko

We now move to the studio where the Reverend takes pictures of Alice in the role of a gypsy girl, with a contrast between the "darkness" of the camera and the preservation made for the world.

Follow to the studio where Alice Liddell plays the roles
Of tousle-headed naked gypsy girls
The Reverend Charles L. Dodgson from the darkness of his camera

Preserves her for himself and for the world

The darkness of the camera is a metaphor for the darkness of the creative process, in which what seem to be terrible things can happen, but really, they are not terrible things because *nothing is really happening*. When limbs are torn away and bodies mutilated in films like *Hostel* and *Saw*, or any of the original "video nasties", it is imaginary. The same is true of De Sade's work and any number of other texts attacked and vilified by those "malicious" humans. The question is then whether such texts are actually valuable as works of art. Which is a subject for debate, of course. The children described in this song who are destroyed will return, fit and well, because they are imaginary and like Tom and Jerry can be reconstituted at will. They can have sex as well, it may shock you but it can't hurt you or them.

Children torn by cruel desires, the handiwork of murderers
Who hack their little bodies to the bone
Somehow live to tell the tale, astonishingly fit and well
They couple in the fabulous chateau

The chorus is repeated and there is an instrumental section with the twisty, winding and complex tune that runs through the piece also repeated, reflecting the complexity of the moral questions posed. The final verse hammers home the facts of the case: the world of the imagination is not an actual place. An image of a girl is not an actual girl. In art, in playing games, there is no good reason to limit our behaviours and we should be free to act at will. Magical things and worlds exist and we should not deny them. The importance of free play and art to children and in education is strongly hinted at throughout the song.

A looking glass is not a world
A painted girl is not a girl

In games there can be no forbidden things
In life remain considerate, in art the Devil's advocate
Why deny that Pegasus has wings
In life remain considerate, in art the Devil incarnate
Why deny the siren when it sings?
In games there must be no forbidden things

Finally Momus refers to *A Smuggler's Song* by Rudyard Kipling, in which knowing townsfolk instruct their children to turn a blind eye while smugglers do their work. It is as if he is instructing us to ignore the sometimes dark but harmless things which are done in the name of art. He then refers us back to Kuniyoshi and his cabinet of wonders.

So watch the wall my darling while the gentlemen go by
And mark your diary with a small white stone
Little hearts of marzipan and lacquer work from old Japan
In the cabinet of Kuniyoshi Kaneko

This song is a key text in Momus' work: a strong defence of the amorality his songs and his character have been accused of by critics, but more to the point a defence of art in general. The music fades out, as the process of art is unending.

Slide Projector Lie Detector

More details from the home life of Momus and Shazna, this time relating to the no doubt prickly relationship between new, semi-domesticated Momus and old, semi-feral Momus (which, if you think about it, are exactly the same Momus). This is a song about our digital footprint: already in 1995 a concern: as Momus says: "My future is strewn with the ingenious mechanical landmines of my past acts". He is thinking about the traffic camera, his credit rating, Polaroid cameras. In this case, it is a carousel of slides he took long ago which his partner has found and is turning into a case against his character. Now, it is our history on Twitter, Facebook and the like which is the dirt to bury us. The situation he describes has got a thousand times worse.

This is a slow song, with a piano led melody and mechanical sounding noises representing the machinery of memory. There is a noise which sounds like a camera shutter, which represents both pictures being taken and the slide carousel turning round. A growling bass noise comes in from time to time to emphasise more dramatic moments. Momus sings with solemnity and perhaps guilt: he has some regrets, after all. The first verse describes his attempts to "clear his desk", actually and metaphorically, but he avoids the "nest" of literally naked Polaroids. Describing it as a nest gives the images a life of their own, and an impact of their own.

I've spent my life with some regrets
Between naked girls and gadgets
Trying to make the best of things
A clean breast of things
I clear my desk of papers but avoid
The little nest of naked Polaroids

The bridge attempts to distance the now married man from his actions when he was single, but admits the collection of slides is for his selfish pleasure. He "hid them" in the carousel – a very *Purloined Letter*/leaf-in-the-forest type of hiding place for slides. (Delete according to whether you prefer Poe or Chesterton.) The word "collected" is slightly sinister and could mask any amount of depravity; it certainly does not indicate consent, but then again these are not necessarily girls he knows personally. In this verse the melody rises, and I like the way the piano line and melody of the last couple of lines seems to circle round, like the carousel. It may just be me, but the piano melody on this track sometimes reminds me of Double's *The Captain of Her Heart*.

I'm married now but can't deny I was a single man when I
Collected slides of girls
And hid them in this carousel
To shine for selfish pleasure on my wall

The chorus declares the title of the song: the slide projector is a lie detector because he cannot deny the images on the wall are things that he did, photographs he took which betoken real or imaginary relationships he had. I am imagining that he has come home to find Shazna angrily going through the images. Maybe that is how it happened, or maybe this never happened.

My slide projector lie detector
Shines the things I don't remember
Seven metres tall
On my living room wall

The next verse opens out the discussion to other electronic media. Word processors even in the mid-90s had spell checking software; it is interesting that Momus describes it as a "text corrector", was the phrase "spellchecker" not invented then? At any rate, I like the idea of the software that stops you from entering lies. It is also, of course, a terrifying idea. This verse also touches on the modern issue of social media lasting forever, of the "yesterdays" that you thought were gone returning to cost you a relationship, job, everything.

My yesterdays you thought were dead
Are back to life forever
My word processor's got a text corrector
That's got a thing built in
That stops me when I try to enter lies
That prints the truth and cuts me down to size

The second bridge confirms the situation: Shazna has found photographs and tapes from the past. Long-ago images Momus had forgotten about, but which will not sit well with his new wife. The question will be, if you wanted to erase these things, why did you make a duplicate tape?

My yesterdays you thought were gone
Spring back to life when you stumble on
A photograph I made
A duplicate tape on video 8
Of long-lost days I long ago erased.

A second chorus is followed by a break featuring spacey sound effects – rather *Voyager*-like. These sounds increase in volume and intensity to end the break and continue to intensify during the final verse. In the final verse Momus seems to describe his VCR as if it has the capacity to locate images of naked flesh and index them for him. While I think very basic image recognition technology did exist in 1995 for the web and for functions such as blocking site access in schools, it was not very reliable. I do not remember such technology existing for VCRs linked to PCs, but I could be wrong. "Rigid" order is a nice bit of innuendo there, along with his acknowledged use of slow motion.

My video cassette recorder plays cassettes in rigid order
Scans for naked skin
Locate the index, hit slow motion, switch to playback
No fast-forwarding

Following a final chorus, the song concludes with bubbling sound effects and a fadeout. I hope he manages to be "zen" enough to enjoy the ensuing "discussion". This is a successful song mainly because it prefigures so many concerns about modern social media and communications technology, it is also a disarmingly honest song and would form an appropriate companion piece to his later *Datapanik* or *The Age of Information*.

Microworlds

The album continues with a trio of songs clearly dedicated to Shazna and all of which sound as if they would have fitted into the Timelord track listing. *Microworlds* is about finding Shazna: previously his life was a constant sequence of trips to "microworlds" – short liaisons with girls. Now, however, he has come into an inescapable gravity field and collided, and fused, with his betrothed. I am reminded a little of the Be Bop Deluxe track *Between The Worlds* from 1975, which has a similar lyrical conceit and a retro-futuristic sci-fi setting beloved by guitarist Bill Nelson:

Between the girls are worlds
That only lovers see
So proud the shroud has fallen to my knees…
…I am a gigolo
Between the worlds I go I go I go

Microworlds beings with bubbling space noises and has a trip-hop beat. The actual song bases itself around a pretty sequence of chords played on synth. When the chorus comes in, a bell like sound is introduced playing the chords, declaring success in the search, and a choral sounding synth noise represents the distances of space and the imagery that the song demands. An instrumental break is played with an electric piano sound, leading to the second verse and chorus which reinforce the triumph in his finding a love, and the song fades out with the upbeat keyboard riff playing. The first verse describes the loneliness Momus experienced before meeting her, and hints at the deceptions he played on those he met:

From microworld to microworld
Never knew which way the wind was blowing
From pretty girl to pretty girl
None of them had any way of knowing
There were others in my life
But a vacuum at the centre
I was reaching for the love I couldn't know

In other words, he behaved like the gigolo in Bill Nelson's song above. Meeting Shazna, however, changed his perceptions of love and sex. He realises how empty his life was before and now feels actually alive for the first time:

When I met you and you redefined my feelings
I met you and I was suddenly alive
Like the fabulous exploding of asteroids in darkness
We collide

The second verse reinforces the first, talking of going from "emptiness" to "emptiness": any ex-girlfriends of Momus would not enjoy this song. After the second chorus and instrumental break the bridge is repeated stating the nature of his search:

There were many shooting stars
Many comets burning brightly
I was searching for the fire that wouldn't fade

His description of Shazna as an inescapable pull and the use of the word density seems quite dangerous to me. I can imagine any girl listening to this song, pausing and asking: "Are you saying I'm fat? I have the density of what now?"

When I met you and the galaxy went spinning
I met you and I was pulled into the light

With the matter that is constant in its density inside me.

The chorus repeats and fades. It is good to see Momus happy, this song is pretty, cheerful and quite throwaway, in concept quite like *The Day Before You Came* (An ABBA song covered by Blancmange, among others) but less gloomy. It is not a song I have ever paid much attention to, but then, like Mrs Doyle in *Father Ted*, "Maybe I like the misery".

Complicated

Like *Breathless*, the closing track on *Timelord*, this is a lounge-jazz number you could imagine a band languidly playing on a cruise ship. Unlike *Breathless*, this song is written from a position of proximity to the object of affection and deals with the sense of wonder that the smallest element of their being can inspire. Momus describes this sense of wonder in terms of awe, a kind of fear of the otherness that our partner can possess.

In Kafka's *The Trial*, the main character – K – is on trial for no known reason in a system which is complex and unfathomable, and probably has no reason for existence beyond the requirement to destroy him. His landlady describes his trial as "something refined, something complicated, far beyond the comprehension of a person like me", and it is this inability to comprehend, this fear of the complex unknowable, that Momus is trying to capture. To experience this yourself, just research how quantum computers work.

The dance beat, a bossa nova, fades in. The song is led by a gentle acoustic guitar sound, plucked pizzicato. A piano plays key notes as you would expect in this genre. Momus sings gently over this about the mystery of his beloved, who appears through a cloud:

Over the room you are my puzzling creature
Through the smoke of the room

My dark and delicate creature

He is fascinated by the way her hair falls, trying to comprehend why the particular shape it creates as it coils captivates him so much.

The sensuous way that your hair
Curves round the cusp of your ear
Is something complicated
So complicated for me

He has changed his behaviour and the way he acts for this beloved, as indicated by his need to finally "learn to be tender" and not just a pervert.

Here in your room I have learned to be tender
It's too much to take in
To study and try to remember

It is not only her hair but all of her that is "too complicated" to take in:

The shape that you make in your dress
The colour and taste of your breasts
Is something complicated
Too complicated for me

The final verse discloses his lack of comfort with his own vulnerability to her. He has never been this close to someone. Still, his prudishness, his self-shame sometimes comes between them: he is himself a mass of contradictions and complex as well, which he knows.

Intimacy never came easy for me

I so longed to be close
But it never came easy to me
I'm ashamed to undress if
I know you are watching me
I could never express these contradictions that complicate me

The song fades out, gently. Like *Microworlds* this is a cheerful and optimistic statement of the moment of love. It is very inconsequential for me, and drifts by like the previous track.

I Had A Girl

When I first listened to this album, this was the exact point that my patience ran out. My feelings were along the lines of: "If I have to listen to one more bloody song about Shazna Currie, I will do…something." Not much I could do, of course, except skip the track. I have mellowed now, but I still prefer the demo version of this called *An Inflatable Doll.*

This is a very melancholy song, written while they were separated, about the situation they found themselves in. As I have discussed this situation at length in the entry for *Timelord,* there is not much to explain here. Momus says that he lost his girl because "my skin was white and her skin was brown": referring to the fact that her parents refused to countenance a relationship with a white man. He cries out her name at night, unable to be consoled while she is held captive "somewhere in North Bangladesh". He describes his life as grim, like a grey coat she has from Comme des Garcons, which is a Japanese fashion label, and the greyness extends to the English weather.

Imagine me here in the pouring rain
Dreaming of how I'll solve everything
I'll sit and I'll write, alone and depressed
Letters that might never reach your address

Musically, this song is just Momus accompanying himself on keyboards, led by an electric piano sound, cold and distant like the English. On occasion the notes hold on longer at the end of a line, emphasising the waiting and the uncertainty he feels. It is another melancholy and rather hopeless sounding piece, at the time he wrote it, solving everything was just a dream…

The Philosophy of Momus

A series of minor key piano chords, stark and accompanied by a skittering beat, underlie a series of epigrams delivered by Momus. Some of these are original thoughts, some are based on other concepts or quotations.

Beauty is just the first glimpse of a terror we're just about able to bear
Fashion is just the return of the clothes we're no longer able to wear
Fast food's too slow, slow food's too fast
In the next world the first will be first and the last will be last
The first will be first and the last will be last

"For beauty is nothing but the beginning of terror, which we are barely able to endure, and it amazes us so, because it serenely disdains to annihilate us," is a quote from *Elegy* by Rainer Maria Wilke from his collection of Elegies completed in 1922, before his death in 1926. Rainer Maria Rilke was a Bohemian-Austrian poet and novelist who wrote both verse and highly lyrical prose often described as "mystical". So here again Momus describes beauty as literally awesome, awe inducing and the beginning of terror. I refer you again to the quotation from *The Third Policeman* in *Withinity* above: what begins as wondrous soon becomes unbearable. Beauty is so sublime, so other to us, that it barely regards us.

Jesus is quoted as telling us that in heaven "the first will be last, the last will be first". He is talking to a rich young ruler at the time, but he is not necessarily referring to earthly wealth or status; this could be a reference to spiritual worth. Bob Dylan used the imagery in his song *The Times They Are A-Changing*. Momus turns that on its head here and seems to suggest that in fact status will remain in the next world. Unfortunately, that may be true, since the next world is one entirely of your own imagination. In the second verse choral and bell effects are added, giving an oriental feel to the piece. Other keyboard sounds are subtly added as the song progresses. A keyboard playing an arpeggio drops in around halfway through in the background.

Those who say no-one is better than anyone think that they're better for saying it
The best way to make proper use of your time's to sit perfectly still and ignore it
Popular culture's designed by a highly-trained popular culture elite
A digital city's more easily changed than a city of concrete
A city more easily changed than a city of concrete

The first line of that verse is a true enough original thought. Sanctimony is truly infuriating. Against all that, Momus often describes himself as lazy – and sometimes the best thing to do is to just do nothing, in which act true creation lies. No-one will deny that popular culture is the product of an elite: a liberal elite who populate late night discussion programmes about books no one really reads, and a pop-culture elite who use computer programs to write chart hits and film screenplays. In 1995 and through the late 90s the liberal elite were colluding with New Labour and nudging the public towards a dismal consensus on foreign policy and the erosion of personal freedoms. As Momus points out, a true revolution to this remote control might be achieved in the online world that was developing at the time. To some extent he is correct, anyone can publish books, anyone can publish music or videos online and gain a worldwide audience immediately. Still as time goes on those channels – Amazon, YouTube, Twitter – seem to be ruled by a new social-media elite. Individuals such as Ricky Gervais are the new cultural gatekeepers, jealously guarding their ability to re-tweet as a mystical favour to be granted only to the chosen ones. Have we progressed?

Call me a schizoid, I sometimes feel this era belongs only to me
Place matters less as we choose where to live and who to be
The basic inventiveness that got us into this mess gets us out again
Often inadequate lovers turn into invaluable friends
Inadequate lovers turn into invaluable friends

It is interesting that Momus sees himself as a ruler of the era: in his newly demonstrated enthusiasm for technology and the digital world, maybe he has a point, this should indeed be his era. Given the use of online services, "place" in a geographical sense does matter less, or should, and we can decide where to live and who to be: everyone on the internet is a dog, after all. Having said that I doubt he will move back to the UK now... maybe place does matter a little. His line regarding lovers and friends is of course an uncomfortable truth. True friends sometimes need to have discovered they are not compatible any other way in order to function as friends, rather than having the other possibility hanging over them.

The only real tyranny comes on behalf of the ones we have chosen to love
Being creative is close to being evil, being good's just not good enough

Every good man has a bad man inside, someone making it all possible
The only good drug is a smart drug, there's no good death, there's no clean kill
There's no good death, there's no clean kill

It is true that while we can reject rulers, deny authority and rebel against ideology, we cannot deny or defeat those we choose to be governed by domestically, the friends and lovers we have chosen to put above ourselves are in a position to destroy us. In the next two lines, when Momus talks about creation and its equivalence to evil, I am first reminded of G.K. Chesterton's words: "The word 'good' has many meanings. For example, if a man were to shoot his grandmother at a range of five hundred yards, I should call him a good shot, but not necessarily a good man.' However, Momus is talking about something much deeper, the idealistic concept that to create anything there must be an act of destruction first; ideas, certainties, realities must be deconstructed to build a new world. Even deeper than that, there is the idea that the separation of concepts and the unity of concepts are in fact the same thing. This is discussed by Slavoj Zizek in an essay on all these subjects on Lacan.com using Christianity as an exemplar:

> And the same goes for Christianity: we are not FIRST separated from God and THEN miraculously united with him; the point of Christianity is that the very separation unites us – it is in this separation that we are "like God," like Christ on the cross, i.e., the separation of us from God is transposed into God himself. And the same goes for ethics: a radical act of Good HAS to appear first as "evil," as disturbing the substantial stability of traditional mores.

This argument feeds back into the *Cabinet of Kuniyoshi Kaneko*: that which is truly creative may appear to be evil, in its devices and desires, but hopefully not in its outcomes. The "bad man" makes it possible, the "good man" makes it desirable. Throughout his albums, Momus has seen death as an enemy, and continues to do so here. There is no such thing as a "good death" or a "clean kill": if annihilation is the outcome, it is to be feared and hated.

Guilt is the engine of civilisation, guilt that is built on desire
One day I'll write a book about looking championing the voyeur
Playfulness must be encouraged uncritically, children are still far ahead
Stop trying to cut off your feet so you fit your bed, make it longer instead

Following any kind of religious upbringing, one is inclined to agree that guilt is the engine we run on. Speaking in 2020, our generalised guilt with regard to the environment, the state of nations, the worship of cars, eating meat, drinking, smoking and basically existing is driving much of what we are doing. Momus has written several books, do they "champion the voyeur"? On occasion I suspect so…He again talks about children, their play and their use of imagination is much better than we as adults can muster, and their methods of creativity should be maintained and encouraged without criticising, measuring, testing or ticking boxes to satisfy a government agency. Art, music and performance should receive much more funding – any would be better than none – and be available to all, as creative methods are valid across all areas of endeavour.

The final line refers to a character in Greek mythology called Procrustes – meaning the "stretcher who hammers out the metal", an Attican rogue who having waylaid travellers forced them to lie on his bed. If they were too short for the bed he stretched them, if they were too long for the bed he cut off their feet and/or legs. He was eventually captured by Theseus, who subjected him to the same treatment. Momus is referring to artistic endeavour here, as well as general life, adjust the container to its contents, not the other way round. He is echoing the thoughts of Slavoj Zizek who said this in his own criticism of poetic forms:

> The most elementary form of torturing one's language is called poetry – think of what a complex form like a sonnet does to language: it forces the free flow of speech into a Procrustean bed of fixed forms of rhythm and rhyme.

Hopefully we do not torture ourselves in the same way, but ultimately "Du musst amboss oder hammer sein", as *The Prisoner*'s Number Two tells Number Six.

Following the final verse most of the instruments drop out and the arpeggio keyboard is left to end the piece, ending in a minor key in a deliberately unsatisfying way. After all, there are no right or wrong thoughts, and Momus is no more correct than you are.

The Loneliness of Lift Music

Momus compares himself to Oliviero Toscani in his press release when discussing this song. Toscani is the advertising creative who designed the controversial advertising campaign for Benetton clothing. These adverts included three pig hearts marked Black, White, Yellow, and an AIDS patient on his hospital bed, with the message of the adverts being unity and commonality: The United Colours of Benetton. The comparison relates to the controversial nature of the content, rather than the intention. The shock value here is the subject matter of the song: we are following the mind and actions of a serial killer, who in this instance is murdering a girl in an elevator (or lift in UK English). It may or may not be a coincidence that Bowie's *1. Outside*, with its artistic killer, was released in September of this year. The music is slow, a cello sound on the keyboard, keyboards mimicking the sound of Muzak which you could hear in a lift: the music a lift plays to declare its departure or arrival.

You were a perfect stranger
And I your perfect strangler
In the brushed steel lift
Of the great department store
The tightening grip of leather gloves
Purchased from the floor above La la la…

This is a great verse, contrasting the fabrics and materials of industry, with the steel lift, with the materials of humanity, the leather gloves. The use of the word "tightening" is mechanical, the killer as an instrument, part of the socio-economic machinery of the lift and the department store. A higher pitched keyboard sound arrives in the second stanza, eerie and uncomfortable, somewhat out of tune with the rest. The killer sees his victim as "perfect" and sees himself as "perfect" for her: made for each other. The situation is beautiful and symmetric for him as if his victim in some way wants her death, and wants it from him. The music is quiet enough that Momus can startle us with louder piano chords stabbing at us from time to time.

Your eyes filled with confusion
Those helpless, twitching movements
The lips discoloured slightly round the edge
The loneliness of lift music
Its beauty and arithmetic La la la…

Carefully, the word "beauty" is placed in proximity to the act of murder and the description of the victim. We are invited to view the act through the killer's eyes as intrinsically beautiful, a renaissance painting or still-life. Lift music – Muzak being the brand name – is carefully designed to be meaningless and unmemorable: it does have beauty and arithmetic in that sense.

A foggy night in London town
The office workers calmly going about their business
The shops and markets closing down
People buying murder mysteries for the night train back to Cheam

The middle stanza is spoken rather than sung, gently describing the London scene outside. The "foggy night" could put us in mind of a London of Victorian England with the Ripper stalking the streets, but actually it feels more like the London fog of the 1945 movie *Hangover Square,* in which a strangler played by Laird Cregar haunts the streets, or the earlier silent Hitchcock movie *The Lodger*. The prosaic everyday things going on around are highlighted, everything closing down for the night, including the victim. After this, rattling noises accompany his wordless "la la la's" as he gently places the body into a beautiful position on the floor. What a fantastic death abyss...

The tightening grip of leather gloves
I purchased from the floor above
The slipping girl I could have loved
I squeeze your tiny, pointless life away

The victim dies, but the most pointed element here is "The slipping girl I could have loved", which you could compare with the line in *The Cabriolet* in which the narrator next to the dying girl finds her "someone I only now begin to feel I could love...", opposite outcomes of a similar deviation. The killer describes his victim's life as tiny and pointless, as if she only gains any importance or resonance as his victim, meaning he sees what he is doing as a favour to her: validating her existence by ending it.

Mantovani, James Last...and you
The loneliness of lift music
Its magic and magnificence

I squeeze your tiny, pointless life away
You a perfect stranger
And I your perfect strangler La la la…

Mantovani and James Last were both composers used as Lift Music or Muzak. The killer describes lift music and its tiny, irrelevant nature as "magic and magnificence" to accompany his victim's beautiful demise. In the last minute plucked guitar (or is it koto?) sounds join in and the song ends with a circling sinister tune playing in a higher register. It is unsettling and finishes with the song itself, ending as the life ebbs away from his victim.

The power of this song is that it adjusts us into the killer's mind: the morality is complex because of this; we do not see the murder as wrong because the killer does not. He feels free and feels that he is giving freedom and meaning to his victims. As in *The Guitar Lesson* or *The Cabriolet*, we see an artistic vision, a still-life showing an image of beauty even in its ferocity. The twilight of the fog outside is the twilight and gloom through which we view his actions, and our own morality.

Paranoid Acoustic Seduction Machine

Dali's method – The Paranoid Critical Transformation Method – was to induce in himself the mind-set of someone in a state of paranoia, of mental illness. He aimed to see as they did, and to bring back to his work the result of what he saw. It was Dali's skill that allowed him to manifest those visions on canvas. Furthermore, although he certainly had some mental issues of his own, he seemed to be able to command them and use trips into a simulated paranoia as creative stimulus. Dali said of himself, "The only difference between myself and a madman, is that I am not mad!", which makes sense when viewed in this context. This track is a tribute to this method and named as such. I can only assume that these are things Momus sees himself as.

"Seduction Machine": He doesn't seem to have done too badly in this respect. "Electrostatic seduction machine": I guess it depends how hard he's been rubbing parts of himself on the carpet? "Orgasmatronic seduction machine": Now that's just boasting…"Paranoid Acoustic Seduction Machine": Like Dali, Momus takes a journey into a different way of seeing, the kind of madness described in the previous track, and on his return paints a picture, acoustically.

The music is a repetitive seductive groove, electronic and with a funky bassline. It sounds, again, as if it could be lift music, background to a seduction itself. The track ends with a bass pedal note leaving tension in the air…

The Sadness of Things

The sound of wind perhaps, a mechanical sound, desolation and machinery, these open the final track, with music by Ken Morioka and lyrics by Nicholas Currie. This is a beautiful song, with a gorgeous musical backing. The sound is traditionally Japanese with keyboards very similar to those we have heard in the second half of the album, a defining bassline and Momus' vocal shows a range of feeling, cracking for example on the emotional line "blinded by tears.." which must be reminiscent for him of the difficult times which have passed. This is a song which talks about melancholy directly, the Japanese phrase "mono no aware" meaning, literally "the sigh-ness of things", with "sadness" being the nearest available translation. It is the melancholy which comes from a nostalgia for the present that never occurred.

Quai des Brumes is a 1938 film directed by Marcel Carné, a thriller set in Le Havre. It is also a music venue in Montreal. Kamakura is a coastal town, one hour's drive south of Tokyo. Momus describes places he has been with his lover, in dramatic fashion.

I called you dancing queen
At the Quai des Brumes
At Kamakura you said you'd like to paint tears
On the neutral face of the Buddha
In the season of storms
We went walking in storms
Just like a video, just like a symphony

He is aware that his lover is beautiful and perfect and has a charmed existence in comparison to him. Everything seems to revolve around her, for her and from her point of view.

And for you, when things go wrong
They go wrong for all the right reasons
And when it gets warm
you adapt with the seasons
In a world of changing colours
every colour has a meaning
And the universe exists for
the convenience of your feelings

But for Momus, the world seems darker, and less inclined to bend to his feelings: a world where it isn't like a pop video or arthouse movie, where the elements do not represent your inner life.

And as for me I know a different world
A world where the sea
Refuses to rage when boy loses girl

He realises his feelings of melancholy provide some comfort to him but is aware that even the comfort afforded by sadness is not evidence that the universe cares for him in any way, but rather the reverse. In his melancholy he feels like a simple cog in a Newtonian universe that is indifferent to his existence, as is the society we exist in.

Oh I know there's comfort in sadness
But I try to distinguish these passing emotions
My unimportant existence
From the great machine of the world's indifference

The chorus states the Japanese saying, its translation and its explanation.

Mono no aware
The sadness of things
Mono no aware
The temptation to see
The world as it ought to be
Mono no aware
The sadness of things
Blinded with tears
I can still see
My insignificance
In an indifferent universe

Momus then sings about the different way that a beautiful young girl sees the world compared to a 35-year-old fogey like himself. When you are beautiful the world will after all seem to revolve around you, with constant attention and smiles all the time. He believes that the beautiful see life as more meaningful and worthwhile.

If I were you
If I were beautiful
Maybe the world
Might seem more meaningful

In his middle-age, ridiculous of course at 35, he quotes T.S. Eliot's *Love Song of J. Alfred Prufrock*. He compares his ageing to the dying of the year, but his lover does not age, and has access to machinery he is only a cog in, the "sparkling machinery" that is their manifest destiny.

I grow old! I grow old!
As the winter comes on and the sky grows cold
But you stay as young as the rays of the sun
On the sparkling machinery
you call your destiny

A repeat of the chorus leads to a quieter section with a spoken monologue directly quoting the Eliot poem, then ruminating more on his ageing process. He asks if he cries, for his love and for his melancholy, whether this is also just a selfish action as it brings him some comfort, and is a simple biochemical reaction, not a nuanced intention.

Do I dare to eat a peach?
Do I dare to walk the beach?
And if I dare to eat a peach
If I should care to shed a tear
Could I claim more for my action
Than selfish satisfaction?
(Stock mammalian reflex, biochemical reaction)

The chorus is repeated, but Momus now refers again to the idea that our surroundings and the elements can mirror our feelings:

The thunder and rain
Sharing our pain
Blinded by tears
I can still see

My insignificance
In an indifferent universe

This celebration of melancholia and its joys brings the album to a conclusion as the chorus is repeated and fades away.

Overall, this album is uneven, oddly paced and jumbled. There are so many genres and approaches thrown in that it seems Momus could not settle on a direction. Of course, diversification is fine, but do we really want an album of lounge jazz from Momus, or reggae, or experiments with grunge?

It contains some excellent songs, of course, some brilliant songs, with perhaps too many *Timelord*-esque pieces in the second half. It seems more like a compilation of available material than a designed "experience", compared to the thematically unified world of *Tender Pervert* or *Ultraconformist*, for example. The melancholy ending of *The Sadness of Things* could even lead you to believe that this was intended as the final Momus studio album.

In fact, the next album would be a compilation of re-workings of old material, with short self-parodies attacking the Momus persona, which also leads me to believe that the Momus persona was being considered for execution. Nicholas Currie was having great success in Japan as a songwriter: *Good Morning World* by Kahimi Karie had reached No.5 in the Japanese charts. Maybe this was where his future lay. But in the end circumstances led to the character not only persisting, but thriving and finding a confident new way forward from 1998's *The Little Red Songbook*, although not without an unintentional and potentially career-wrecking setback resulting from it. This route was found via a compilation, *Slender Sherbet*, released later in 1995, and a subsequent Rarities collection, *20 Vodka Jellies*, in 1996, as well as the brilliant and illuminating set *Ping Pong* of 1997, released and toured amid a time of personal catastrophes.

I Had To Put Down the Guitar…#17
Slender Sherbet

With *The Philosophy of Momus* receiving mixed reviews, and his career as a songwriter for others doing so well, the personality of Momus was due for some self-reflection. In an interview with Keith Gillard for Cosmik Debris fanzine, Momus said: "I've been thinking recently it could be liberating to draw a line across Momus and launch a new persona…in a sense Momus is already someone else. She's called Kahimi Karie and she's a big star in Japan."

However, the digital age meant that this was not an absolute. Momus had plans for his persona to be released on the exciting new medium of CD-ROM: "If you ask 'what will it be, this CD-ROM?' I'd answer: rain, sex, a manservant, a goblin, a clock, northern-ness…I don't know."

Momus had extensive and ambitious plans for a CD-ROM experience that would enable users to explore his back catalogue and current work. "I originally planned this as an all-singing, all-dancing CD Plus. It was to be called 'Digital Closet' and, on inserting it into your CD-ROM drive, you'd be able to rummage around in my old recordings as well as peep voyeuristically out at carnal goings on in the room beyond."

This meant that he had to learn how to program, how to use the Macromedia technology required and realistically, to port whatever he created for his Mac into a Windows version eventually. "But my programming skills weren't up to it, and I made do with a record of new versions of some of my 80s songs (the 90s material is still covered by a restriction clause in my Creation contract) with some amusing secret tracks at the end."

So *Slender Sherbet: Classic Songs Revisited* came into being. The album would contain re-workings of numerous Momus songs and did indeed include three secret tracks with new partially improvised lyrics. The album was released by Cherry Red in October 1995. The postponed CD-ROM project was pushed back to 1996 and released as *This Must Stop!* for Mac only. There was an audio CD version of the CD-ROM called *Stop This!* which was never released but contained all the tracks available and hidden on the CD-ROM. You can read more about the content of the CD-ROM on imomus.com but good luck getting the download samples to work unless you have the original version of Macromedia Director and a Necronomicon. Both versions contain recordings of very early demos and songs by Nicholas Currie from the early 80s and are interesting in their impact on the development of early Momus. Recordings of many of the songs are available in different forms on other artists' albums or on the *ProCreate/Recreate* reissues as bonus tracks.

The front cover of *Slender Sherbet* demonstrates the juxtaposition of the classic and new Momus: a parodic interpretation of the original cover of *Tender Pervert* with a digitally created mask and hands, pointing to a version of the brand name Momus, which blurs with movement, oscillating into the future, on a pure white background. The subtitle "classic songs revisited" is faintly printed under the main image. Immediately the feeling is that the past is not sacred, and there is an element of self-parody in the format used.

The back cover lists the tracks included in two halves, separated by what looks like the centre hole of a vinyl album, again, a reminder of the past. The front mask image is included along with another version of the masks with a swirling symbol on it. There is also a statement that these are newly recorded versions of early songs by Momus – the "tender pervert", recorded in Paris 1995. The back cover has white text on black, whereas the CD itself is black text on white, with the same design as the CD back. The back inside also has an address for Cherry Red and a website address at Demon Internet. The CD inlay contains all the lyrics, closely typed and printed without formatting. There is also a larger statement: "Momus Paris 1995" and the current website address at Demon for Momus.

These are less "new versions" of the songs than meta-commentaries on them, composed and performed by the originator as sleeve notes, sometimes happening to improve on the original, more often self-flagellating or attempting to take apart the mythology around them.

As these are all songs I have previously discussed, in my reviews of each track I will not discuss the lyrics in detail apart from where they depart from the original, and in full detail for the three "new" tracks.

A Complete History of Sexual Jealousy

The album opens with a robotic voice, a synthesised voice from the minimal range of speaking voices available for Mac at this point. The computer reads through the first verse flatly: removing all emotion from the delivery of the material may be an attempt to force focus onto the content, or may symbolise our transition into digital selves and avatars behind which true feelings can hide.

Momus backs up the voice with wordless vocalising following the bass melody of the song, rising abruptly for the final part of the chorus on the words "Parts 17..." A different robotic voice takes up the second verse and a softly played acoustic guitar joins in. The new recording juxtaposes human feeling – represented by the backing vocals and guitar – against the robotic. Each new stanza has a different synthesised voice until a synthesiser and skittering beat come in and play the instrumental passage, percussive keyboard sounds and a bass are also added and build the song, with more voices – including the first female coded voice – joining in. Relics of the original sound appear at the end as the whole fades out, symbolising a battle between the personal and impersonal, human and synthetic, real and imagined feelings.

The Guitar Lesson

There are more atmospherics, more electronics at the start of this version than the original, with vague sounds of the roads outside. Softly played piano replaces the arpeggios of the original, with a growling keyboard effect after "afternoon grows still" that jars with the gentle sounds under it, the unsettling made a little too clear and "on the nose". On the second verse the guitar appears playing a slowed and gentle version of the arpeggio theme and keyboard sounds from the original wash over. The whole track is a little slower and initially more melancholy. A guitar keyboard sound plays the main theme now, and a Casio sounding beat starts halfway through, very much out of style with the rest of the track. The "burglar alarm" is a much cheaper sounding effect as well, the whole version sounding rather lo-fi in comparison with the original. This is certainly an example of a track which did not really need much alteration, and this version to my mind doesn't add very much except that the concentration on acoustic instrumentation (or at least, acoustic sounds) rather than electronics emphasises the eroticism as human and is a pleasing counterpoint to the first track.

Closer to You

The bass line comes in as in the original, the accompanying synth effects a little squelchier. The Spanish sounding guitar is the same, and Momus' breathy vocals are just as erotic and "come hither" as in the original. There is, in fact, very little significant difference in the choices of instrumentation or presentation. His vocals, however, seem a little quicker, perhaps, or less considered than in the original. The acoustic guitar is more prominent and the key instrument throughout this version. The backing vocals come to the fore and end the track as in the original. I really cannot see much gained from this version over the original either.

The Homosexual

The clinical electronic coldness of the original made its spitting venom and revenge narrative all the more successful. This new version follows the template established so far in adding acoustic guitars, vinyl scratches and noise to humanise the narrative. The bass line in the chorus is bouncier, but the "whoo whoo"s remain in place. What is the purpose of the vinyl record noise, and the splashes of prepared piano in the background? Are they there to remind us of older Momus, along with the sounds reminiscent of the effects on *Bishonen*? Is this intended to be a voice from the past, a record of a time when to be "homo" was still an issue, but no longer is, officially? The lyrics are delivered more flatly, with less spite than on the original. It seems more like a recreation than a recording, as if Momus is performing a reading of a Momus song rather than directly performing it. The effects that locate the sound and narrative in the past distance the audience from the performer and distance the performer from the narrative meaning of the words, as if the piece were an exercise in Brechtian alienation.

The Charm of Innocence

A quite strident beat sets up the acoustic guitar to join for this key Momus track. The bass and guitar work well with the very slightly faster sounding delivery, and the oriental sounding effect that arrives on "stalk the botanical garden…" matches the feeling of the track perfectly. The organ sound used in the original remains in the background from the second verse. The chorus uses a double tracked set of Momuses (Momii?) who both sound quite impressive, and the oriental sounding effect works well as accompaniment. A keyboard plays off key notes in a high register in the next verse, creating an unsettling feeling which also suits the subject material. Overall, the sound of this song works well to feel alien, wrong, off-kilter, just as the story being told is one that most of us could never empathise with. Those sounds also work to accompany stories of travel and wandering around darker zones of Paris. If the delivery is more lackadaisical than the original, that is fine for the tale being told, of a louche ne'er do well. The instrumental break melody is played on a keyboard sound of a squalling guitar, again disturbing in an appropriate manner. The song ends similarly to the original, fading out in this case with the unsettling keyboard melody in the background. This track is an improvement on the original for me, although you may disagree.

Lucky Like St Sebastian

A disco dance beat and rave "oh yeahs!" introduce an almost rapped version of the opening song on *Circus Maximus*. Whether this is a good idea or not is debatable. Certainly, the comparison of St Sebastian "performing" his martyrdom matches the style of music being used, it is extrovert and demands attention, but hardly suits the more introverted talk of secret perversions and longing for waitresses. In the final minute as Momus almost shouts the chorus a couple of times, it seems completely out of place, the wrong costume. It is perfectly reasonable to equate sainthood with celebrity and write a version of this song in which a saint is performative in the style of a rap or disco celebrity, but to actually then listen to the results is quite hard going.

I Was a Maoist Intellectual

Another fast-paced re-interpretation, opening with circus trumpets and a swanee whistle, and a fast beat. Momus comes in with a growling voice, shouting the lyrics for the most part, as an attempt to make the anger and ire of the original more emphatic. The problem being that the anger and despair of the original grows during the piece rather than coming on strong from the beginning. As such the dynamics of performance in the original are lost and the whole track feels quite flat in its effect. It is, again, quite exhausting to listen to. Why is he shouting the lyrics like this, what is he really angry about? Perhaps the similarity of the song's narrative to Momus' own chart career is too close to home to ignore now. At any rate, although some of the instrumentation, for instance in the quieter section halfway through, works effectively, the performance here completely alienates the listener. This could, of course, be entirely intentional.

Lifestyles of the Rich and Famous

Really the only way this could be remade is as a lo-fi version of the original, a sarcastic comment on the collapse of the 80s and the new culture of the 90s. So instead of the fireworks of the original this has a simple piano part as in the original but very low key, synthesised percussion and an organ backing gently in the background. The song is slightly slower I think, and the lyrics delivered much as in the original but with an ironic distance from the original version. It is more like the character of the *Don't Stop the Night* version singing to us about how it used to be. There is a slight melancholy in the delivery and instrumentation, along with a sense of humour at himself, "is that really what we used to think?" The lyrics are altered to emphasise this; the names used in the original chorus are gone, instead we have "hey jack I'm all right, staying alive I'll keep swinging, it's a lovely day tonight", making fun of the attitudes in the original but removing any specific references that may no longer make sense.

The Angels are Voyeurs

The bass drum opens the song as in the original, and the backing to this version is much as before, except for a strummed guitar to the fore. The rhythm is perhaps bouncier, and on the chorus "And his angels..." is followed by a distorted, fuzzy guitar sound rather than the cleaner power chord of the original.

The overall effect is to make the song slightly more comic, more of a satiric piece than a descriptive one. After the first chorus a backing vocal is clear, Momus making "chka, chka" noises which again have a humorous effect. A melody runs down the scale played on a marimba keyboard sound into the second verse, which also has a comic sounding aspect. The second verse has a choppy organ effect which also drags my mind to British end-of-the-pier seaside sauciness. The end of the second chorus retains the dramatic lift in the line "his angels move in close", but the effect is more bathetic. The instrumental break is played on an acoustic guitar which follows *Slender Sherbet*'s general habit of going acoustic, humanising the tale.

The original "reprise" from the end of the album is included, delivered with no bass or percussion, just the guitar and marimba effect. The distorted guitar of the chorus is replaced by acoustic as well here. The overall purpose of the version seems to be to humanise the tale and emphasise the comic aspect of it. (Comic as in dramatic theatre, not comic as in "funny".) Sometimes I prefer this version; I suspect it depends whether your mood tends towards the comic or dramatic…

Hotel Marquis de Sade

A song from the *Beast with 3 Backs* EP opens with clomping percussion which paints a mental picture of a donkey traipsing along a hot Spanish mountain trail, but we know it is three young people walking towards that siesta in two single beds. (Why don't they push them together?) The clomping percussion persists across the bridge from the verse into the chorus, which means that the beautiful lift on the delivery of the word "Mediterranean" is lost somewhat. The ugliness of the chorus, particularly the end repeat of "the beast with three backs", is emphasised, however. In my opinion the sinister aspect of the situation is somewhat undercut, or lost, by the introduction of that percussion, replaced by ugliness. The same can be said for the end of the song; the quotation from Eliot is less powerful, less disturbing, for having this different backing.

The Gatecrasher

An interesting choice really, not a song you would guess would be chosen for a retrospective of this nature. The lush opening of the original has been altered to sound more oriental, crows cawing in the distance with wind chimes and static breaking into synthesiser chords and a guitar part very similar to the original. The percussion is similar to other songs on this album including *Hotel Marquis de Sade*. Samples are laid over the backing as on the line "he takes in the faces" which has a dissonant guitar sample looping in the background. The effect of these samples and sound effects is to make the whole sound more alien, more eastern. This is appropriate as the Gatecrasher is an intruder himself, and out of place: so it makes sense thematically to have sounds of static, intrusive keyboard and guitar samples and hardly definable noises interrupting proceedings. Does it emphasise this otherness too much and reduce the melancholy and loneliness of the original? Perhaps, or maybe the distortion and confusion acts as the antithesis for those emotions and allows the listener to make their own judgement of the Gatecrasher's situation.

The Hairstyle of the Devil

Given the overblown electronic nature of the original, perhaps the only way to go with this song was to strip it down. Here we have a simple acoustic guitar backing and chiming keyboard part. Momus delivers the vocal as a singer-songwriter rather than a popster, the vocal now has space to breathe which the original did not have. He accompanies himself on backing vocals in the chorus, and the keyboard parts echo the choppy house piano of the original in a muted way. It is easier to hear the beauty of the chord sequence following the second chorus that acts as an instrumental break. In general, it is easier to hear the song "qua" song than it was with the original, where it was more of an exercise in production. The drama of the end "beast rules with rivalry" section is highlighted more if anything, with its contrast to the quieter verses. It is a different experience to the original, but far more of a "performed" piece, and I think I prefer it on that level.

Bishonen

There really is no reason to mess about with this track too much. The narrative is what drives the original and to alter the backing too much would risk losing the driving force of it. Fortunately, Momus has realised this and the arpeggio keyboard remains in place, slightly different sounds are used and there is a vocalised sample used, sounding like an old Japanese man. The bass keyboard sounds used from 3 minutes onwards are perhaps even more powerful than those in the original. The vocal delivery is very much identical to the original. It would be very interesting for Momus to record a version of *Bishonen* now, actually, with an older man's voice he could take on more the role of the perverse old man; perhaps he could write a version of the song from his point of view? A slightly sci-fi sounding keyboard noise appears in the background from halfway through, something like an alarm going off. Other than these subtle additions, which are a matter of personal choice, there is nothing really to choose between this and the original version. Using the piano to perform the dramatic ending section rather than a synthesiser sound seems to reduce its impact a little to me, but you may prefer it.

Angels Reprise

The reprise of *The Angels are Voyeurs* using one of the synthesised voices from the first track, with a dance beat from a Casio keyboard underneath it. Gives an illusion of thematic unity, I suppose, but otherwise unremarkable. Ends with half a minute or so of silence as there are three "hidden" tracks following.

The three "hidden" tracks are "Untitled" on the CD. They are very clear evidence of a state of mind, I feel. The writing seems to be on the wall for the Momus persona at this point, and the clearest evidence of this is that his own creator is mocking him. These three tracks are self-parodies of Momus songs. All three of the songs play with the Momus persona, the louche and debonair womaniser who always gets the girl he wants and is intellectually superior to all those around him, untouched and unapologetic about the emotional trauma he must leave in his wake. The Momus of these songs is a very normal and insecure guy, rather incompetent in his approach to women and desperately jealous of everyone.

During the 60s and 70s Michael Moorcock wrote a series of books which became known as the *Cornelius Quartet* about a character called Jerry Cornelius, who was a super spy, fashion icon, rock star and general sex god. In the last of these books, *The Condition of Muzak*, there are sections in which we meet the "real" Jerry Cornelius, who is a spotty teenager with a rubbish rock band dreaming of sexual success and stardom. The three songs here are reminiscent of those hyper-realistic sections of *The Condition of Muzak;* it feels like we meet the real Momus rather than what he imagines himself to be.

A Complete History of Penis Envy, Sizes 24-29

The backing to this version of *A Complete History* is poppy, cheerful, fun. With the music fast paced and jolly, Momus recounts over it the story of a man who is jealous of literally everyone.

I'm jealous of the men whose penises are larger than my penis is
And I'm jealous of the men whose penises are so enormous they outstrip all average penises
I'm even jealous of the men whose penises are slightly smaller… than mine
A complete history of penis envy, sizes 24-29

The comic timing and pause in the line "the men whose penises are slightly smaller…than mine" is very good. There is of course an element of that seaside, end-of-the-pier humour I mentioned earlier. Albeit the very unsubtle humour of just saying "penis" a lot.

Momus retains enough professional clarity in this song to make it self-referential: perhaps he cannot help himself. Notice how the second line here mirrors the word play used in the original lyrics.

I'm jealous of the women whose slightly protuberant clitorises pass for penises bigger than mine
I'm jealous of the men who measure the penises of the men whose penises reach size 29
And my only consolation for penis envy would be to write a bitter and twisted little song
Called "A Complete History of Penis Envy, Sizes 24-29"

It is also nice that he is clearly finding it hard not to laugh while singing this song. These tracks allow us to see Momus as someone with a sense of humour about himself for the first time. Bear in mind that in 1995 these albums and magazine interviews are pretty much the only contact we had with Momus, prior to our having access to the internet, and he mostly came across in the albums and press as very serious and even self-absorbed.

Finally, his obsession with penises leads to him going completely off the rails (in the song I mean, not in real life, as far as I know, yet). From a Freudian point of view, this song suggests that Momus has a very small penis or an uncontrollably large one. There are songs yet to come up in his oeuvre where he implies the latter. The hard evidence from Cynthia Plaster-Caster is rather inconclusive.

I once saw a man whose penis was so big he had to wheel it around in a wheelbarrow
And I used to think it wasn't what you got but how you used it that mattered, but now I don't know

And if you see me one day muttering, shabby and mad in the doorway with a paper bag round a bottle of wine
Just put it down to penis envy, sizes 24-29

Oh, we will.

The Guitar Lesson

A realistic version of *The Guitar Lesson,* to backing from the new version. This is what really happens if you try to chat up an adult guitar student. The mirroring of the original lyrics is done very well.

The pupil is 42, a black-belt at judo
She doesn't like sexists or saucy innuendo
She caught me looking down her top one day
And jabbed me hard on the elbow
And I had to put down the guitar
And stifle a sob

This is very Carry On, very Sid James (although he is more Jim Dale in this scenario I think):

She won't let me stop even for a glass of water
To think I only took this job to get a glimpse of her daughter
I keep going to the bathroom but I've never once caught her
And her mother thinks I'm incontinent
Or that I've got some kind of embarrassing cold of the bladder

The last verse shows a very appropriate disdain for religion: note the proximity of the verb "fingers" to the word "Bible". There is good humour in the phrase "Baptists and things" demonstrating the singer's lack of understanding, or interest, in her faith. The equivalence of religious fervour to sexual excitement is played for laughs here rather than as a direct attack on faith as it might be in a more serious song.

She fingers her bible, we're practising hymns
For revivalist meetings with Baptists and things
And while her voice quivers with evangelical fervour
I think about shagging her daughter
But a little twelve-year-old replica of her, why bother?

The humour in a potential paedophile not bothering with forcing his abuse because he does not fancy the girl involved prefigures approaches taken in later work such as the Chris Morris TV show *Brass Eye*. Also, making the "abuser" in this song such a pathetic figure parodies the deliberate way in which Momus did the opposite in the original song. Having been criticised for not "attacking" the paedophile in the original song, this version demonstrates why he did not: it would not work. If the original song went all out to show how disgusting the guitar teacher was, we would not be able to see or feel the duality of thought in the victim or ourselves, the attraction that allows such situations to pass without any physical violence or apparent resistance. The situation would be described as clear-cut, and black and white, and linear: all the things that it is not.

Closer to You

Most girls you see on the Tube are not actually beautiful in the conventional manner described in the original version of this song. A fact which is the basis of this song, about the humans Momus is forced to share space with each day. We are asked to imagine that he is sexually obsessed with a girl who is not conventionally attractive. This version uses a backing track from the new version of the song.

Ooh it's true
Girl I'm only doing it to be closer to you

His description of the girl seems to be improvised and is distinctly non-PC.

And maybe you're the more than slightly overweight girl
A little mentally retarded, perhaps

How do we feel about his disparaging description of her as "more than slightly overweight"? And given that my own daughter has Down Syndrome, what about the second line? Offended? Well, no: this is humour, and the key to the humour is that he is not describing a real girl, even in the context of the song:

"Maybe you're the more than slightly overweight girl…" as in the original, he is dealing in images of women who might be on the Tube with him, not real girls. The locus of the humour is that for some reason his idealised girl is "more than slightly overweight".

Now in 2020 we may worry about lyrics and content which "bodyshames" but that would not have been a consideration in 1995: a fat girl would have been a comic image: just look at the portrayal of teenage Monica in the TV show *Friends*.

Here, however, the humour is not in the fact that she is overweight, but in the thought that her obesity is what makes him so turned on. Equally, her being "a little mentally retarded" uses English understatement as a comic device and the fact that the character is turned on by what is not a sexy feature is where the humour lies, in *his* mental issues and perversity, not hers. He continues to describe this paragon of imaginary beauty:

With a large hairy head
And a little chewing gum stuck on the back
And a coat hanger which you forgot to take off your coat while it was in the wardrobe
And I can smell that breath from here
And I can see in six different shades

What you were eating last night

He starts laughing at various points, and at the end it fades out with someone saying, "that's shit", and giggling, presumably Shazna. Reviews for *Slender Sherbet* were mixed, generally conceding that there were some successes on the album. AllMusic concluded that the album's chief benefit may be as a primer to new American listeners, and that is certainly true. Melody Maker were more positive, saying, "If you need to exclude ambiguity from your life, you shouldn't buy this album."

The same review also quoted Momus speaking in defence of his more controversial songs: "If I was writing an article in a paper or summing up a rape case in court, I'd have to have a clear line on women. As a songwriter, I'm allowed to have 18 or 19 different lines…An interesting song starts from not having a clear position."

Slender Sherbet does draw an effective line under his Creation period: and may have been intended as a line through it. Some of the new versions work well, others are less effective, the whole album does have a consistent low-fi sound to it which is quite charming at times and annoying at others. The more experimental attempts at vocal delivery are not well chosen. The album works best when a theme or emotion which was not previously emphasised on a track is drawn out by the instrumentation, and the delivery calmly supports this, as in *The Charm of Innocence, Hairstyle of the Devil* or *Bishonen*.

There was plenty of work going on for Nicholas Currie/ Momus at this point, writing for others. A new Momus studio album if it ever emerged was some distance away.

In 1996, however, a "rarities" disc called *20 Vodka Jellies* was released, with many fascinating tracks and stories. Whereas the lack of consistency of *The Philosophy of Momus* was frustrating given the homogenous nature of the album's presentation, this compilation with its chewy and distinctive flavours was intended to be kaleidoscopic, and would achieve its aim fully, and be – in my opinion – one of the most engaging Momus albums of all, at a time when, against all the odds, the musical stylings of Momus would emerge as relevant once more, and enable his return. The next 5 years would see Momus solidify his position as a genius maverick and begin his journey towards the respected status he now enjoys, but not before more threats to his free speech, and battles with providence.

Author Biography

John William Daniel Robinson is a writer from Scunthorpe in North Lincolnshire. He gained a BA (Combined Hons) in Radio, Film and Television Studies with Mathematics from Christ Church College, Canterbury and took a post-graduate course in Journalism at Sheffield College before moving to Poland to teach English. He then moved into website design and programming before becoming a lecturer. For 10 years he has taught Computing and Contextual Analysis at North Lindsey College in North Lincolnshire. He lives with his wife and two children.

His writing mainly takes in music, technology and media analysis and has been published on websites such as *outsideleft.com* and for publications including *Langue Pendue / Groupie*. His book *Famous for Fifteen People* is the first of an intended series about the work of the songwriter Momus.

Note to Reader

Thank you for reading this book about the lyrics and life of Momus. For more entries related to his songs and to the UK music scene, and to sign up for further news about upcoming books and blog entries, visit my website at http://www.fifteenpeople.com. If you would like to get in touch, please contact me there or at thranjax@yahoo.co.uk

If you have enjoyed this book, please take the time if you can to leave a review at any relevant online site.

Bibliography and Further Reading

A list of sources used in the book:

http://www.imomus.com: Momus' website contains articles and webpages dating back to his first website in 1995. Also includes many reviews and newspaper articles.

https://imomus.livejournal.com/: Momus' livejournal contains his blog which ran from 2004–2010.

https://thequietus.com/articles/22517-momus-interview-2?curator=MusicREDEF: An interview with Quietus from 31 May 2017.

Lusts of a Moron: The Lyrics of Momus (Black Spring Press, 1992): Momus' lyric book covering his albums up to *Voyager*.

Niche: A Memoir in Pastiche by Momus (Farrar, Straus and Giroux, 2020).

Creation Stories: Riots, Raves and Running a Label (Alan McGee, Sidgwick & Jackson, 2013): Alan McGee's version of events at Creation.

Sleeve Notes from the compilation album *Pubic Intellectual* (Cherry Red, 2016).

Interview with Miranda Sawyer for Select Magazine: http://selectmagazinescans.monkeon.co.uk/showpage.php?file=wp-content/uploads/2012/03/momus.jpg

The Theatre and its Double (Antonin Artaud trans. Victor Corti, Alma Classics, 2017).

Runaways Wed in Fear! Story in the Daily Record, Tuesday, July 26 and Wednesday July 27 1994.

How Soon Is Now?: The Madmen and Mavericks who made Independent Music 1975 – 2005 (Richard King, Faber & Faber Social, 2017).

Hegel – Chesterton – German Idealism and Christianity (Slavoj Zizek, https://www.lacan.com/zizhegche.htm#:~:text=And%20the%20same%20goes%20for,is%20transposed%20into%20

God%20himself. Accessed 19 June 2020).

Interview with Keith Gillard of Cosmik Debris zine (http://web.textfiles.com/ezines/COSMIKDEBRIS/199605.txt Accessed 19 June 2020).

CULTURE, SOCIETY & POLITICS

The modern world is at an impasse. Disasters scroll across our smartphone screens and we're invited to like, follow or upvote, but critical thinking is harder and harder to find. Rather than connecting us in common struggle and debate, the internet has sped up and deepened a long-standing process of alienation and atomization. Zer0 Books wants to work against this trend. With critical theory as our jumping off point, we aim to publish books that make our readers uncomfortable. We want to move beyond received opinions.

Zer0 Books is on the left and wants to reinvent the left. We are sick of the injustice, the suffering and the stupidity that defines both our political and cultural world, and we aim to find a new foundation for a new struggle.

If this book has helped you to clarify an idea, solve a problem or extend your knowledge, you may want to check out our online content as well. Look for Zer0 Books: Advancing Conversations in the iTunes directory and for our Zer0 Books YouTube channel.

Popular videos include:

Žižek and the Double Blackmain

The Intellectual Dark Web is a Bad Sign

Can there be an Anti-SJW Left?

Answering Jordan Peterson on Marxism

Follow us on Facebook
at https://www.facebook.com/ZeroBooks and Twitter at https://twitter.com/Zer0Books

Bestsellers from Zer0 Books include:

Give Them An Argument
Logic for the Left
Ben Burgis
Many serious leftists have learned to distrust talk of logic. This is a serious mistake.
Paperback: 978-1-78904-210-8 ebook: 978-1-78904-211-5

Poor but Sexy
Culture Clashes in Europe East and West
Agata Pyzik
How the East stayed East and the West stayed West.
Paperback: 978-1-78099-394-2 ebook: 978-1-78099-395-9

An Anthropology of Nothing in Particular
Martin Demant Frederiksen
A journey into the social lives of meaninglessness.
Paperback: 978-1-78535-699-5 ebook: 978-1-78535-700-8

In the Dust of This Planet
Horror of Philosophy vol. 1
Eugene Thacker
In the first of a series of three books on the Horror of Philosophy, *In the Dust of This Planet* offers the genre of horror as a way of thinking about the unthinkable.
Paperback: 978-1-84694-676-9 ebook: 978-1-78099-010-1

The End of Oulipo?
An Attempt to Exhaust a Movement
Lauren Elkin, Veronica Esposito
Paperback: 978-1-78099-655-4 ebook: 978-1-78099-656-1

Capitalist Realism
Is There No Alternative?
Mark Fisher
An analysis of the ways in which capitalism has presented itself as the only realistic political-economic system.
Paperback: 978-1-84694-317-1 ebook: 978-1-78099-734-6

Rebel Rebel
Chris O'Leary
David Bowie: every single song. Everything you want to know, everything you didn't know.
Paperback: 978-1-78099-244-0 ebook: 978-1-78099-713-1

Kill All Normies
Angela Nagle
Online culture wars from 4chan and Tumblr to Trump.
Paperback: 978-1- 78535-543-1 ebook: 978-1-78535-544-8

Cartographies of the Absolute
Alberto Toscano, Jeff Kinkle
An aesthetics of the economy for the twenty-first century.
Paperback: 978-1-78099-275-4 ebook: 978-1-78279-973-3

Malign Velocities
Accelerationism and Capitalism
Benjamin Noys
Long listed for the Bread and Roses Prize 2015, *Malign Velocities* argues against the need for speed, tracking acceleration as the symptom of the ongoing crises of capitalism.
Paperback: 978-1-78279-300-7 ebook: 978-1-78279-299-4

Meat Market
Female Flesh under Capitalism
Laurie Penny
A feminist dissection of women's bodies as the fleshy fulcrum of capitalist cannibalism, whereby women are both consumers and consumed.
Paperback: 978-1-84694-521-2 ebook: 978-1-84694-782-7

Babbling Corpse
Vaporwave and the Commodification of Ghosts
Grafton Tanner
Paperback: 978-1-78279-759-3 ebook: 978-1-78279-760-9

New Work New Culture
Work we want and a culture that strengthens us
Frithjoff Bergmann
A serious alternative for mankind and the planet.
Paperback: 978-1-78904-064-7 ebook: 978-1-78904-065-4

Romeo and Juliet in Palestine

Teaching Under Occupation

Tom Sperlinger

Life in the West Bank, the nature of pedagogy and the role of a university under occupation.

Paperback: 978-1-78279-637-4 ebook: 978-1-78279-636-7

Ghosts of My Life

Writings on Depression, Hauntology and Lost Futures

Mark Fisher

Paperback: 978-1-78099-226-6 ebook: 978-1-78279-624-4

Sweetening the Pill

or How We Got Hooked on Hormonal Birth Control

Holly Grigg-Spall

Has contraception liberated or oppressed women? *Sweetening the Pill* breaks the silence on the dark side of hormonal contraception.

Paperback: 978-1-78099-607-3 ebook: 978-1-78099-608-0

Why Are We The Good Guys?

Reclaiming Your Mind from the Delusions of Propaganda

David Cromwell

A provocative challenge to the standard ideology that Western power is a benevolent force in the world.

Paperback: 978-1-78099-365-2 ebook: 978-1-78099-366-9

The Writing on the Wall

On the Decomposition of Capitalism and its Critics

Anselm Jappe, Alastair Hemmens

A new approach to the meaning of social emancipation.

Paperback: 978-1-78535-581-3 ebook: 978-1-78535-582-0

Enjoying It

Candy Crush and Capitalism

Alfie Bown

A study of enjoyment and of the enjoyment of studying. Bown asks what enjoyment says about us and what we say about enjoyment, and why.

Paperback: 978-1-78535-155-6 ebook: 978-1-78535-156-3

Color, Facture, Art and Design

Iona Singh

This materialist definition of fine-art develops guidelines for architecture, design, cultural-studies and ultimately social change.

Paperback: 978-1-78099-629-5 ebook: 978-1-78099-630-1

Neglected or Misunderstood

The Radical Feminism of Shulamith Firestone

Victoria Margree

An interrogation of issues surrounding gender, biology, sexuality, work and technology, and the ways in which our imaginations continue to be in thrall to ideologies of maternity and the nuclear family.

Paperback: 978-1-78535-539-4 ebook: 978-1-78535-540-0

How to Dismantle the NHS in 10 Easy Steps (Second Edition)

Youssef El-Gingihy

The story of how your NHS was sold off and why you will have to buy private health insurance soon. A new expanded second edition with chapters on junior doctors' strikes and government blueprints for US-style healthcare.

Paperback: 978-1-78904-178-1 ebook: 978-1-78904-179-8

Digesting Recipes
The Art of Culinary Notation
Susannah Worth
A recipe is an instruction, the imperative tone of the expert, but this constraint can offer its own kind of potential. A recipe need not be a domestic trap but might instead offer escape – something to fantasise about or aspire to.
Paperback: 978-1-78279-860-6 ebook: 978-1-78279-859-0

Most titles are published in paperback and as an ebook. Paperbacks are available in traditional bookshops. Both print and ebook formats are available online.
Follow us on Facebook
at https://www.facebook.com/ZeroBooks
and Twitter at https://twitter.com/Zer0Books